Analyzing Multimodal Interaction

"This is an outstanding book, strikingly well focused to the point of view of readers new to its concepts. It will be essential, required reading on many courses and will be very useful in opening up a major cross-disciplinary literature and approach."

Ron Scollon, Georgetown University, USA

"The wide, varied range of materials discussed, matched with precise, detailed methods of analysis, demonstrated by carefully worked examples, will make this indispensable for anyone interested in getting at meaning in its rich variety."

Gunther Kress, Institute of Education, University of London, UK

Our perception of our everyday interactions is shaped by more than what is said. From coffee with friends, to interviews; and from meetings with colleagues, to conversations with strangers, we draw on both verbal and nonverbal behavior to judge and consider our experiences.

Analyzing Multimodal Interaction is a practical guide to understanding and investigating the multiple modes of communication, and provides an essential guide for those undertaking fieldwork in a range of disciplines, including linguistics, sociology, education, anthropology, and psychology. The book offers a clear methodology to help the reader carry out their own integrative analysis, equipping them with the tools that they need to analyze a situation from different points of view. Drawing on research into conversational analysis and nonverbal behavior such as body movement and gaze, it also considers the role of the material world in our interactions, exploring how we use space and objects – such as our furniture, cell phones, or TV. Considering a range of real examples, such as traffic-police officers at work, doctor–patient meetings, teachers with students, and friends reading magazines together, the book offers lively demonstrations of multimodal discourse at work.

Illustrated throughout and featuring a mini-glossary in each chapter, further reading, and advice on practical issues such as making transcriptions and video and audio recordings, this practical guide is an essential resource for anyone interested in the multiple modes of human interaction.

Sigrid Norris teaches in the Department of English, Linguistics, and Speech at Mary Washington College, Virginia, USA. Her research areas include multimodal identity construction and multimodal cross-cultural communication.

Analyzing Multimodal Interaction

A methodological framework

Sigrid Norris

Routledge
Taylor & Francis Group

NEW YORK AND LONDON

First published 2004 in the USA and Canada
by Routledge
711 Third Avenue, New York, NY 10017, USA

Simultaneously published in the UK
by Routledge
2 Park Square, Milton Park, Abingdon, Oxon OX14 4RN

Routledge is an imprint of the Taylor & Francis Group, an informa business

© 2004 Sigrid Norris

Typeset in Baskerville and Helvetica by
Florence Production Ltd, Stoodleigh, Devon

All rights reserved. No part of this book may be reprinted or reproduced or utilized in any form or by any electronic, mechanical, or other means, now known or hereafter invented, including photocopying and recording, or in any information storage or retrieval system, without permission in writing from the publishers.

Every effort has been made to ensure that the advice and information in this book is true and accurate at the time of going to press. However, neither the publisher nor the author can accept any legal responsibility or liability for any errors or omissions that may be made. In the case of drug administration, any medical procedure or the use of technical equipment mentioned within this book, you are strongly advised to consult the manufacturer's guidelines.

Library of Congress Cataloging in Publication Data
Analyzing multimodal interaction: a methodological framework/Sigrid Norris.
1. Interpersonal communication. 2. Oral communication.
3. Social interaction. I. Title.
P94.7.N67 2004
302.2′242–dc22   2003025307
p.cm.

British Library Cataloguing in Publication Data
A catalogue record for this book is available from the British Library

ISBN 0–415–32855–1
ISBN 0–415–32856-X

To
Alan, Kevin, and Luke

Contents

List of figures viii
List of plates ix
Preface x
Acknowledgments xii

1 Multimodal interaction 1

2 Communicative modes 11

3 Multimodal transcription 58

4 Modal density 79

5 Levels of attention/awareness 95

6 Semantic/pragmatic *means* 112

7 Modal density foreground–background continuum as a methodological framework: complex interactions 128

8 Analyzing multimodal interaction: a postscript 148

References 156
Index 174

Figures

5.1 Modal density foreground–background continuum 99
5.2 Modal density circles as heuristic tools to visualize the density employed for specific higher-level actions 108
5.3 Sandra's six simultaneously constructed higher-level actions placed on a modal density foreground–background continuum 110

Plates

1.1	A crossing guard communicating on different levels of attention/awareness	8
2.1	Proxemics	22
2.2	Posture	27
2.3	Gesture	31
2.4	Head movement	35
2.5	Gaze	39
2.6	Music	43
2.7	Print	47
2.8	Layout	50
2.9	Interconnection of modes	55
3.1	Transcript: proxemics and posture	70
3.2	Transcript: gesture	71
3.3	Transcript: head movement and gaze	73
3.4	Multimodal transcript	76
4.1	High modal density: layout and music	85
4.2	Modal density: high density	86
4.3	Modal density: modal complexity	89
4.4	Modal density: intensity plus complexity	90
5.1	Transcript: six simultaneous higher-level actions	102
6.1	Semantic/pragmatic *means*: deictic leaning towards an object/participant	119
6.2	Semantic/pragmatic *means*: eyebrow flash	123
6.3	Semantic/pragmatic *means*: hand/finger beat	125
7.1	Transcript: music instruction	130
7.2	Construction of social worlds	139
7.3	Transcript: multimedia and interaction	144

Preface

This book is an attempt to explicate a methodological framework for the analysis of human interaction in its vast complexity. With a foundation in discourse analysis, interactional sociolinguistics, mediated discourse analysis, and multimodality, I cross the boundaries between linguistics, nonverbal behavior, and the material world.

Language is of particular interest to the study of human interaction, as the mode has great informative as well as expressive value. This mode is probably the best understood mode so far. Yet people in interaction seldom communicate only through language. A person takes up a certain kind of distance to others, takes up a particular posture, gestures while speaking, and at times gazes at the interlocutor.

Modes like gesture, gaze, or posture have generally been termed nonverbal modes of communication. However, I will steer away from this expression, as *nonverbal* conveys that these are appendages to the verbal mode. If the so-called nonverbal modes were actually appendages to language, these modes would *always* have to be subordinate to language. However, this is *not* the case. Modes like gesture, gaze, or posture *can* play a *superordinate* or an *equal* role to the mode of language in interaction, and therefore, these modes are not merely embellishments to language. In this book, I only refer to these modes as nonverbal when I want to point out which generally accepted fields of study I am working in. But, exclusive of this, I use the term *embodied modes*: a term that refers to gesture as well as to language, showing that the modes are generally of an equal value, and allowing the analyst to decide which mode (if any) plays a superior role in a particular interaction.

All interactions take place in the material world, and the material world plays a role in every interaction. With material world I do not only mean the setting that the interaction takes place in, but also the material world that people in interaction utilize. People are dressed in a certain way, they eat, they listen to music, and they read magazines. All of this may be a part of an interaction. I call modes like music, print, or layout *disembodied modes*. These modes can also take on a superordinate role in interaction, and they can "overrule" embodied modes.

Thus, we have to consider all embodied modes (like language, gesture, and gaze), and all disembodied modes (like music, print, and layout) that people in interaction utilize. Additionally, we cannot think of human interaction without taking the human mind into consideration. A person always thinks, perceives, and/or feels something when interacting with others, and at least some of these thoughts, perceptions, and/or feelings are communicated through a person's actions. In turn, these actions trigger thoughts, perceptions, and/or feelings in the other person, who then also reacts by communicating at least some of their own thoughts, perceptions, and/or feelings through their own actions.

Although these considerations point to a theoretical basis, I actually devised the methodological framework for multimodal interactional analysis out of a practical need. A few years ago, I set out to ethnographically study the everyday identity construction of two women living in Germany. My findings were clear: the women constructed their everyday identity fragments on multiple levels in multiple modes. While I could talk about the findings, there was no applicable framework that allowed me to show scientifically how the women constructed several identity fragments simultaneously by employing different communicative modes. As a result, I developed the framework that I explicate in this book. Thus, this framework for multimodal interactional analysis is a practice-based methodology.

Acknowledgments

Many people have contributed to this book in various ways. I would like to particularly express my gratitude to Ron Scollon for the hours of discussion, his encouragement, and comments on the manuscript; Gunther Kress for his insightful comments; and Heidi Hamilton, Theo Van Leeuwen, and Ruth Wodak for their fruitful conversations. I spoke with numerous people at universities, conferences, and also via email about my framework, and all of these people had some impact on the development of my thoughts. Although I shall not attempt to name each person here, I would like to thank particularly Najma Al Zidjaly, Cecilia Castillo-Ayometzi, Ingrid de Saint-Georges, Doug Harper, Allison Jablonko, Andy Jocuns, Alex Johnston, Rodney Jones, Philip LeVine, David McNeill, Marilyn Merritt, Maurice Nevile, Jon Prosser, Suzie Scollon, and Jon Wagner. I am grateful to Tom Randolph for his detailed attention to wording.

A multimodal framework for the analysis of multimodal interaction can only be explicated multimodally. Images are as much a part of this book as the written words, and I would like to thank Maya Betts, Tracy Betts, Andrea Brandt, Annette Brandt, Gloria Buchanan, Shirley A. Hanson, Robert Le May, Marilyn McGonegle, Mary Lou Nale, Alan G. Norris, Kevin P. Norris, Luke Norris, Graziella Röntgen, John Schucker, Tammy L. Shapiro, and Suzanne S. Williams, DMD, who generously agreed to be videotaped and to have their pictures incorporated in the book to help me explicate the methodological framework.

My family has taken part in the book in countless ways, some visible and others not visible in the book at all. My sons, Kevin and Luke, have spent hours reading in the same room that I was writing in, and at other times they have made sure that I escaped from my desk. My partner, Alan, has spent hours reading and rereading the manuscript, giving me comments about wording. The times that Kevin and Luke spent sitting close by were most productive for me – those fun times were always refreshing, and Alan's constant loving support was most valuable: it is to them that I dedicate this book.

While I am indebted to all of these people, as well as many others who helped in my thinking, the statements made and the views expressed are solely the responsibility of the author.

1 Multimodal interaction

All interactions are multimodal. Imagine, for example, a simple two-person interaction, a conversation with a friend. During this interaction, you are aware of your friend's spoken language, so that you hear the verbal choices, the content, the prosody, and the pitch. You are also aware of the way that your friend is standing or sitting, the way that your friend is nodding or leaning back or forward; you are aware of your friend's facial expression, and clothing, just as you are aware of the environment in which this interaction takes place. If there is music playing in the background, even though you are not focusing on the music, you are aware of it. All of these elements play a part in this conversation. You may react to the words that your friend is speaking as much as you may react to your friend's facial expression or the posture that your friend is taking up towards you. You may speak quickly or slowly, depending on the music playing in the background or the given environment that the interaction takes place in.

Intuitively we know that we draw on all of these communicative channels or modes when interacting with others. We also know that we are aware of many things that surround us while we interact with others. Let us keep thinking about a conversation. No matter where it may take place, you are certainly aware whether other people are present in close proximity. Thus, if your conversation takes place at a table in a cafeteria, you are aware of others talking, eating, or passing by your table. You may not take much notice of these other people, because you are focused on your conversation, but you are aware of them nevertheless.

Interactional meaning

Generally it is assumed that we can communicate best through our use of language. Language seems to have the most informative content, which can easily be employed without a need for other channels. We may speak on the phone, write emails, or go to chat-rooms. In each case, we use language, either spoken or written, to communicate.

But when thinking about TV or the Internet, it is clear that we also communicate through images. Often, viewing an image may carry more communicative meaning than reading a description of the very same thing. We may even feel that the image has more "reality" to it than a written description of the same image would have. This realization questions the notion that the process of communicating is dependent upon language.

Just as moving images or still photos can communicate meaning to the viewer, nonverbal channels such as gesture, posture, or the distance between people can – and do – carry meaning in any face-to-face interaction. All movements, all noises, and all material objects carry interactional meaning as soon as they are perceived by a person.

Previously, language has been viewed as constituting the central channel in interaction, and nonverbal channels have been viewed as being subordinated to it. While much valuable work on the interplay between the verbal and nonverbal has been established, I believe that the view which unquestionably positions language at the center limits our understanding of the complexity of interaction.

Therefore, I will step away from the notion that language always plays the central role in interaction, without denying that it often does. Language, as Kress *et al.* (2001) have noted, is only one mode among many, which may or may not take a central role at any given moment in an interaction. In this view, gesture, gaze, or head movement may be subordinated to the verbal exchanges going on as has been shown in much research. However, gesture, gaze, and head movement also may take the superior position in a given interaction, while language may be subordinated or absent altogether. Alternatively, sometimes many communicative channels play an integral part in a given interaction, without one channel being more important than another.

While we all intuitively know that people in interaction draw on a multiplicity of communicative modes, and that people in interaction are aware of much more than just what they are focused upon, an analysis of such multimodal interaction brings with it many challenges.

Structure and materiality

One challenge for the analysis of multimodal interaction is that the different communicative modes of language, gesture, gaze, and material objects are structured in significantly different ways. While spoken language is sequentially structured, gesture is globally synthetically structured, which means that we cannot simply add one gesture on to another gesture to make a more complex one. In language, we can add a prefix to a word, making the word more complex; or we can add subordinate clauses to a main clause, making the sentence more complex. With gestures, this is not possible, since gestures that are linked to language inform about global content or intensity. Gaze, however, may be sequentially structured, and during conversation it often is. But, during other interactions, gaze can be quite random. For example, when you walk through the woods with a friend, your gaze may wander randomly, focusing on a tree, a rock, or nothing at all. Then there are other communicative modes, which are structured even more differently. As we will see, furniture is a mode, and when thinking about it, we find a functional structure. Chairs are usually located around a table, or a reading lamp is located next to an easy chair. Thus, different modes of communication are structured in very different ways.

Another challenge for the analysis of multimodal interaction is the fact that different communicative modes possess different materiality. For example, spoken language is neither visible nor enduring, but it does have audible materiality. Gesture, however, has visible materiality but is also quite fleeting. The mode of print has more visible materiality and is also enduring; and the mode of layout, thinking about furniture, for example, has highly visible materiality and is extensively enduring.

Awareness and attention

Our next challenge for the analysis of multimodal interaction is the need to explicitly link the analysis of interaction to an analysis of a person's awareness.

When conducting multimodal analysis of human interaction, we need to consider the human mind. I am partial to the notion of a duality of mind, as discussed in great detail by Chalmers (1996). He discusses the theoretical division of mind as the following two concepts: first, the psychological concept, which is the process whereby cognitive systems are sensitive to outside stimulation and result in a psychological change. This is the part of the mind in which people experience perceptions, thoughts, and feelings, but "it matters little whether a mental state has a conscious quality or not. What matters is the role it plays in a cognitive economy" (Chalmers, 1996: 11). Second, Chalmers speaks of the phenomenal concept of mind. This is the concept of mind as conscious experience or simply the state of awareness. While both concepts of mind often if not always co-occur, this division allows us to focus on just one part of consciousness.

Chalmers proposes that:

> A good test for whether a mental notion M is primarily psychological is to ask oneself: Could something be an instance of M without any particular associated phenomenal quality? If so, then M is likely psychological. If not, then M is phenomenal, or at least a combined notion that centrally involves phenomenology.
>
> (Chalmers 1996:18)

In interactional multimodal analysis, we are not much concerned with the perceptions, thoughts, and feelings that people are experiencing, but we are concerned with the perceptions, thoughts, and feelings that people are expressing. We can surmise that some perceptions, thoughts, and feelings that are expressed by someone are also somewhat experienced by that person, even though the actual experience and the expression of the experience should not be viewed as a one-to-one representation and may be as diverse as to contradict each other. We can also surmise that not every perception, thought, and feeling that a person experiences is expressed.

A part of conscious experience, namely *interactional awareness*, can be analyzed qualitatively. In order to do this, we analyze not only the messages that an individual in interaction sends, but also how other individuals in the interaction react to these messages. Thus, there is a constant tension between what a person consciously does and what that person expresses. Interaction, then, is the exchange of communicated (expressed, perceived, and thereby interpreted) experiences, thoughts, and feelings of participants.

Let us return to our example in a cafeteria, and imagine that there is a big window to the right of the table. When you gaze out of the window during the conversation, your friend may interpret this action as a sign of either boredom or deep concentration, or may not take any notice of it. Only through an analysis of you *and* your friends' actions can an analyst come to a conclusion about the communicative meaning that this action of looking out of the window has in this interaction.

In multimodal interactional analysis we are *only* concerned with what individuals express and others react to. We are *not* concerned with what people are actually perceiving, thinking, and feeling, which may sometimes be different and more complex than what they express. We are also *not* concerned with a person's intentionality, which sometimes may be different from what is expressed or different from what is perceived by others.

Multimodal interactional analysts set out to understand and describe what is going on in a given interaction. We analyze what individuals express and react to in specific situations, in which the ongoing interaction is always co-constructed. Furthermore, it is of utmost importance to realize that one and the same action – like looking out of a window – can have many different meanings, intentional or unintentional.

While we react to the words, gestures, facial expressions, etc. of others, we are rarely interested in what others are thinking. For example, when you visit a retail store to buy a present for your mother, and you talk to the sales person, you are not interested in what the sales person is thinking, but whether or not the sales person is showing you items that your mother would like. Considering what others are thinking is rare and usually comes about only in intimate situations.

Yet, what we do consider is an aspect of the phenomenal concept of mind. We consider whether a person is kind to us or shows anger, whether a person we interact with reacts in an appropriate manner or not, and whether or not somebody is paying attention to us. As humans, we are excellent at noticing whether others are paying attention, and we learn from early childhood onwards that we are supposed to realize whether we can approach another human being or whether the other person is occupied.

Thus, consciousness for the multimodal interactional analyst – just as for any participant in an interaction – means the analysis of another social actor's awareness. In the *Dictionary of Psychology*, we find the following definition of awareness:

> *awareness*: 1. **consciousness**; alertness; 2. cognizance of something; a state of knowledge or understanding of environmental or internal events.
>
> (Chaplin, 1985; emphasis **is** my own)

Awareness and attention can be used somewhat interchangeably, even though there are slight differences in their meaning. When looking at the *Dictionary of Psychology* again, we find attention to be defined as follows:

> *attention*: 1. the process of preferentially responding to a stimulus or range of stimuli; 2. the adjustment of the sense organs and central nervous system for maximal stimulation; 3. (Titchener) a state of sensory clearness with a margin and a focus.
>
> (Chaplin, 1985)

When you think about the definitions, you will find that you are certainly aware of something that you are paying attention to, and you also pay attention to something that you are aware of. But, awareness/attention comes in degrees. Let me refer once more to the *Dictionary of Psychology*:

> *attention level*: the degree of clarity of an experience ranging from **unconsciousness (total lack of awareness)** to **focal attention (vivid awareness)**.
>
> (Chaplin, 1985; emphasis **is** mine)

Consequently, when analyzing human interaction, we are concerned with only two aspects of the phenomenal concept of mind:

1 with the expressions of perceptions, thoughts, and feelings; and
2 with the different attention/awareness levels.

Certainly, these two aspects are combined in interaction, as expressions of perceptions, thoughts, and feelings are essentially communicated on different levels of attention/awareness. All participants in a given interaction react to the expressed aspect of the phenomenal mind of others, and it is this aspect of mind that is observable by the analyst.

Chalmers points out that:

> We often say that someone is conscious of something precisely when they are paying attention to it; that is, when a significant portion of

their cognitive resources is devoted to dealing with the relevant information. We **can** be phenomenally conscious of something without attending to it . . .

(Chalmers, 1996: 27, emphasis **is** mine)

A school crossing guard directing traffic

The following example, in which a police officer is directing traffic at a school intersection, illustrates these two concepts of the phenomenal mind.

The first image in Plate 1.1 (p. 8) shows a four-way intersection with a crossing guard directing traffic. Schoolchildren are gathering on the corner of the sidewalk close to the school bus. When focusing on the crossing guard, we see her communicating with the drivers and the children at the intersection in various ways, paying attention to them in varying degrees.

In the second image, she is focused upon the traffic turning left, pointing at drivers approaching from her front to turn. Simultaneously, she is stopping traffic on three sides: with her right hand, she stops the traffic to her right; with her back squarely positioned across the intersection, she stops the traffic behind her; and, with her bent left arm, she stops the traffic to her left. The crossing guard is paying attention to the three stopped flows of traffic, although she pays just a bit less attention to them than she pays to the flow of traffic turning left. Simultaneously, the crossing guard is aware of the children, who are gathering on the sidewalk, although she pays little attention to them.

The first image in the second row shows the crossing guard focusing her attention on the two flows of traffic that are now moving. She is stopping the other two flows by positioning her body squarely in the intersection. Certainly, she is also paying attention to these two flows of traffic, although to a lesser degree; and she is also aware of the children at the corner.

In the second image in the second row, the crossing guard has turned, stopping the traffic to her right with her hand. She is pointing to the front, motioning with her left hand to communicate to the drivers that they may now turn. The crossing guard's body is positioned diagonally, stopping two directions of traffic. Here, she focuses her attention on the drivers who are supposed to take a left, and while she pays less attention to the stopped traffic and the children, the crossing guard is well aware of them.

In fact, we can tell when she is shifting her attention from one section of the intersection to the next. This shifting always happens a moment before she turns to give the next part of the intersection her full attention. While such shifts of attention are discussed in detail in Chapter 6, I would like to point out that the shifts are of particular importance.

The first image in the third row shows that the crossing guard has stopped all traffic. She gazes at the corner where the schoolchildren have been waiting, and calls out: "*Walk! You may cross now!*" This is the first time that the crossing guard has used language to communicate. The second image in the third row shows the children crossing the street. In the first image of the last row the crossing guard is focusing her full attention on the children, while the last image shows that she has turned her attention back to the traffic.

This example illustrates how the crossing guard's focused attention shifts from one or two sections of the intersection to the next, while she is aware of the other parts of the intersection at various levels.

Structure of the book

Interaction is an everyday occurrence, and in each day-to-day interaction we use a multiplicity of communicative channels. In order to analyze interactions in their complexity, a theoretically grounded methodological framework is essential. Before setting out to delineate such a framework, in Chapter 2 I give an overview of a multiplicity of communicative modes. I introduce each mode separately by referring to some background literature and then explicating the mode with a real-time example. In Chapter 3, I discuss practical issues of multimodal transcription. I talk about the method of transcription and video analysis and give a step-by-step guide for accomplishing such transcription. Then I move on to the methodological framework, which makes it possible to incorporate numerous communicative modes in an analysis and links interaction to cognition.

In Chapter 4, the concept of modal density explicitly links multimodal analysis to the concept of awareness; and Chapter 5 demonstrates how we can identify various levels of attention/awareness of participants in an interaction. These levels of attention/awareness are heuristically placed on a continuum, to visualize these abstract levels.

Chapter 6 illustrates the semantic structuring devices that we all utilize in order to structure our own focused actions. We express these to the others present, which indicates that they have an interactive as well as a psychological function.

Chapter 7 utilizes the complete methodology for analyzing multimodal interaction, showing how our knowledge about each mode of communication, the concept of modal density, the levels of attention/awareness of social actors, and the semantic structuring devices all fit together.

In Chapter 8 I mull over the notion of interaction and conclude with what the proposed framework allows us to do. I discuss the affordances and the constraints of the model, before I discuss some new questions that arise from this methodology, ending the book with some ideas for new directions of research in a variety of fields.

In each chapter I have included a list of important terms and their definitions, and concepts and their explanations. These are useful as a study guide and as a quick reference. I also give some ideas of assignments that teach the student how to analyze interactions from a multimodal perspective.

Plate 1.1 A crossing guard communicating on different levels of attention/awareness.

Multimodal interaction:	*All* interactions are multimodal.
Interactional meaning:	*All* movements, noises, and material objects carry interactional meaning when they are perceived by an individual.
Structure of communicative modes:	Modes of communication may be sequentially, globally synthetically, or functionally structured, or they may appear to be quite random.
Materiality of communicative modes:	Modes of communication may possess audible materiality, visible materiality that is quite fleeting, materiality that is visible and enduring, or highly visible and extensively enduring materiality.
Awareness and attention:	In multimodal interactional analysis, we consider only the awareness and attention that individuals in interaction express and others react to.
	Actual experiences, thoughts and feelings and *expressions of* experiences, thoughts and feelings are not viewed as one-to-one representations.
	Awareness/attention comes in degrees, and a person may be phenomenally aware of something without paying much attention to it.

This book takes a look at the complexity of interaction by explicating a methodological framework of multimodal interactional analysis, which is squarely situated in practice. Multimodal interactional analysis grew out of interactional sociolinguistics, mediated discourse and nexus analysis, and multimodality in combination with the technology of video cameras and computers. I take from interactional sociolinguistics its focus on real-time interaction and language in use, from mediated discourse and nexus analysis their emphasis on mediated action, and from multimodality its highlighting of the importance of taking into account other semiotics such as music, color, and gesture.

In this book, I purposefully cross the boundaries between linguistics, nonverbal behavior, and the material world, in order to show that all three directions of research come together when we think about human interaction. My aim is to show the reader *how* to actually *perform* an integrative multimodal analysis of interaction without having to study each field in its vast complexity.

2 Communicative modes

Action:	Unit of analysis. Each action is mediated.
Lower-level action:	The smallest interactional meaning unit.
Higher-level action:	Bracketed by an opening/closing and made up of a multiplicity of chained lower-level actions.
	Often, we find several higher-level actions embedded in another, and/or overarching higher-level action.
Frozen action:	Higher-level actions, which are entailed in material objects.
Communicative mode:	A heuristic unit that can be defined in various ways. We can say that layout is a mode, which would include furniture, pictures on a wall, walls, rooms, houses, streets, and so on. But we can also say that furniture is a mode. The precise definition of a mode should be useful to the analysis.
	A mode has no clear boundaries.

Heuristic units

The first step to a multimodal analysis of interaction is a basic understanding of an array of communicative modes. Modes such as proxemics, posture, head movement, gesture, gaze, spoken language, layout, print, music, to name several, are essentially systems of representation. A system of representation or mode of communication is a semiotic system with rules and regularities attached to it (Kress and Van Leeuwen, 2001). I like

12   Communicative modes

to call these systems of representation *communicative modes* when I emphasize their interactional communicative function.

A communicative mode is never a bounded or static unit, but always and only a *heuristic* unit. The term "heuristic" highlights the plainly explanatory function, and also accentuates the constant tension and contradiction between the system of representation and the real-time interaction among social actors.

A system of representation – a writing system, for example – is usually thought of as a given system that exists in and by itself once it is developed. While such a system changes over time, we can describe the system in the form of dictionaries and grammars, showing the rules and regularities that exist. Taking this thought further, we could describe systems of representation like gesture, gaze, layout, etc. in a similar way to a written language, by developing certain dictionaries and grammars of these communicative modes.

Communicative modes and interaction

When observing an interaction and trying to discern all of the communicative modes that the individuals are utilizing, we soon notice that this is a rather overwhelming task. People move their bodies, hands, arms, and heads, and while the observer may try to understand the content of what is being spoken, they have already missed many important messages which each speaker is sending – intentionally or not – and the other speaker is reacting to through other modes. Yet, a multimodal interactional analysis is not as impossible as one may think. First, the analyst needs to become skilled at distinguishing one communicative mode from others. Then the analyst is ready to investigate how modes play together in interaction.

In this chapter, I give an overview of an array of selected communicative modes. These selections are by no means meant as a complete list, as there are many communicative modes that I do not address here, like facial expression, dress, object handling, and color.

Each selected mode is described in a separate section, giving the reader the opportunity to concentrate on one mode at a time. The first nine sections comprise the embodied and disembodied modes of communication that I discuss in this book, and the tenth section shows how all of these communicative modes play together in interaction.

In the first part of each section, I describe some function and/or regularity of a communicative mode, which is of particular interest to the study of interaction. Then, in the second part of each section, I draw on our knowledge about the system of representation, and illuminate it with a real-time example.

When working with real-time interaction, we discover that there is constant tension and contradiction between the system of representation and the event. Individuals in interaction draw on systems of representation while at the same time constructing, adopting, and changing those systems through their actions. In turn, all actions that individuals perform are mediated by the systems of representation that they draw on.

Unit of analysis

As I mentioned in the introduction, the differing structures and materiality of modes were challenges that needed to be overcome, as an integrative multimodal approach required a single unit of analysis that allowed for the communicative modes to be structurally and materially different.

In multimodal interactional analysis, the *mediated action* is the unit of analysis, and since every action *is* mediated, I will simply speak of the action as the unit of analysis. The *action* as unit of analysis, however, is still a complicated issue, because there are smaller (lower-level) and larger (higher-level) actions. Take, for example, a person uttering the words "*good morning.*" This is an intonation unit – the unit that discourse analysts rely on. But this intonation unit can also be defined as an action, and more specifically, as a lower-level action. Now, take a meeting among three friends, which can be called a conversation, a moment in time, or a social encounter. This meeting can also be called an action, however, and more specifically, a higher-level action.

This use of action as a unit of analysis may seem confusing at first sight. However, let us think about the specific example of a meeting among three friends – to illustrate the usefulness of this unit of analysis. The meeting is taken to be the higher-level action. This higher-level action is bracketed by an opening and a closing of the meeting and is made up of a multiplicity of chained lower-level actions. All intonation units that an individual strings together become a chain of lower-level actions. All gesture units that an individual performs become a chain of lower-level actions. All postural shifts that an individual completes become a chain of lower-level actions. All gaze shifts that an individual performs become a chain of lower-level actions, and so on. Consequently, all higher-level actions are made up of multiple chains of lower-level actions.

The chains of lower-level actions are easily understood when talking about embodied communicative modes like gaze, gesture, or spoken language. But disembodied modes can play just as important a role in interaction as do the embodied modes.

Modes like print – a magazine that participants are reading or that is just lying on a table for anyone to see; or layout – the furniture in a room, pictures hung on a wall, or a busy street with signs, buildings, and walkways, are disembodied modes. These modes can also be analyzed by using the unit of analysis, the (mediated) *action*. However, here the unit of analysis is the *frozen action*. Frozen actions are usually higher-level actions which were performed by an individual or a group of people at an earlier time than the real-time moment of the interaction that is being analyzed. These actions are frozen in the material objects themselves and are therefore evident.

When we see a magazine lying on a table, we know that somebody has purchased the magazine and placed it on the table. Thus, the chains of lower-level actions that somebody had to perform in order for the magazine to be present on the table are perceptible by the mere presence of the magazine itself. The same is true for furniture, pictures on walls, houses in cities, or a CD playing. Material objects or disembodied modes, which we are concerned with here because individuals draw upon them in interaction, necessarily entail higher-level actions (which are made up of chained lower-level actions).

We can think of lower-level actions as the actions that are fluidly performed by an individual in interaction. Each lower-level action is mediated by a system of representation (which includes body parts such as the lips, etc. for spoken language; or hands, arms, and fingers for manual gestures).

Higher-level actions develop from a sum of fluidly performed chains of lower-level actions, so that the higher-level actions are also fluid and develop in real-time. Every higher-level action is bracketed by social openings and closings that are at least in part ritualized. When the three friends get together for their meeting, the higher-level action of that meeting is opened up by the physical coming together of the friends and by ritualized greetings. Similarly, this overarching higher-level action will be ended by ritualized greetings and a parting of the individuals. Embedded within such a higher-level action, we find other higher-level actions such as a conversation between two of the three members, or another conversation among all three of them. Besides conversations, we may also find higher-level actions which develop from a sum of other lower-level actions in which there is little or no talk involved, like the higher-level action of consuming food and/or drink.

While lower-level and higher-level actions are fluidly constructed in interaction, frozen actions are higher-level actions, which are entailed in an object or a disembodied mode. To understand this concept, we can think about ice. Similarly to the freezing of water, actions are frozen in the material objects present in interaction.

When you are sitting in a cafeteria with a plate of food in front of you, and a friend comes by, your friend will know that you went through a chain of actions for the plate of food to be there. Thus, your actions of getting a plate of food in a cafeteria are frozen in the very plate of food that is now standing in front of you. These actions are no longer fluid, as you are not performing these actions of getting the food at this very moment. However, these actions are visible in frozen form in the materiality of the plate and the food on it.

There is usually more than one higher-level action frozen in a material object. For example, when you see a magazine lying on your friend's kitchen table, you will know that your friend bought the magazine and placed it there. These higher-level actions are the most *visible* frozen actions that are entailed in the magazine, because they are the most recent actions that an individual had to perform for the magazine to be present on that table.

There are also other frozen actions entailed in that magazine, one of which would be the production of the magazine itself. However, such higher-level actions as the production of a magazine are relatively distant in time and removed in place from the magazine's current position. This illustrates that the frozen actions which are closest in time and place to the ongoing interaction are the ones that individuals usually focus upon.

Assignment

Think about specific actions that you are performing at this time. How are these actions mediated? Which actions are lower-level actions, and which are the higher-level actions? Can you find frozen actions in your vicinity?

SPOKEN LANGUAGE

Intonation unit:	The unit of analysis, which is bracketed by inhaling.
Spoken language:	Generally, sequentially structured, but often there is also simultaneity of language, i.e. two or more people speaking at once. Simultaneous utterances are also sequentially structured.
Higher-level actions:	Specific utterances can help construct higher-level actions on various levels.

Talk in interaction

Spoken language is the mode that has received the most attention, developing rapidly in the last 30 years, and it is impossible to touch on its many concepts in such a short section as this. Therefore this is a fragmentary introduction, which includes the *intonation unit*, and three levels of discourse as viewed from a mediated discourse approach: three levels of higher-level actions.

Spoken language, although generally a sequentially organized mode, in which the smaller parts add up to larger parts, is not always and only utilized sequentially, but also simultaneously. Tannen (1984) shows how cooperative overlap, or simultaneous talk, builds and reflects the closeness of relationships, and Van Leeuwen (1999) shows that simultaneous talk is an important aspect of interaction.

16 Communicative modes

The lower-level action of most interest to multimodal interactional analysis is the intonation unit. As Chafe (1994) has pointed out, spoken language is uttered by speakers in intonation units. These units are physiologically conditioned by the need to breathe. Thus, each intonation unit is bracketed by the inhaling of air. Speakers do not speak in complete sentences, and speaking is often interrupted by false starts, pauses, and breaks. It is further colored by using *"hm," "ah,"* or *"uh,"* and, of course, by the many discourse markers like *"well," "oh," "but,"* or *"y'know"* (Schiffrin, 1987). Every intonation unit with all of the other sounds that a speaker may utter, has interactive meaning, and therefore, needs to be noted down in transcripts.

Sequencing of these lower-level actions (intonation units) creates, in part, the higher-level actions that individuals in interaction construct. Thus, people use language interactively on many different levels and for many different reasons. First, let us think about only three of the many different levels at which people can communicate by using language. To make this notion of different levels clear, let us think about questions.

A person may ask a question in order to receive specific information. Such questioning may be seen on a city street, where somebody is asking a passer-by for directions. Here, the level of discourse that appears to be most important is the sequentiality of specific turns at talk, the adjacency pair of question and answer (Schegloff and Sacks, 1973). Thus, the higher-level action that the individuals in this interaction construct is specifically built around the adjacency of question and answer. Once the second part of the adjacency pair is filled, when the direction is given, the higher-level action is complete.

Now think about a party at which a group of people are engaged in conversation. Suddenly, one person in the group asks a question that has nothing to do with the topic at hand. In turn, the group refocuses the conversation, trying to answer the person's question. Now, the question is functioning as the initiation of a topic shift. Here, we can see that the level of action initiated by the question is of a *higher* level than the question/answer pair in the last example. When a question functions as a topic shift, the interaction is not limited to the completion of a sequenced adjacency pair, but is rather extended in other directions.

Questions may be used in still other ways. Two people may be in a situation which may or may not involve conversation. Imagine two people who do not know each other, sitting in a waiting room at an auto repair shop while both are waiting for their cars to be fixed. One of the individuals may ask a question which has no specific answer. Here, the question functions as an opening to a conversation. This opening to a conversation has the potential to construct an even *higher* level of action than the topic shift in the example above, and the two people may be engaged in a long conversation following this conversation-opening question.

Spoken language, with its high degree of informative content, has been investigated from many different angles and from many different theoretical and methodological perspectives. In most of these perspectives, language is viewed as the primary mode of communication.

While language certainly is a very important mode, it is not always the case that it plays the primary communicative role. Language is one of many modes that people draw upon in interaction, and the actual role that language takes in a given interaction has to be determined through analysis.

In some interactions, language plays the superordinate role for a specific moment in time. Then, it plays a subordinate role for a while, before again taking on the primary role. Primacy of the mode of language – just like any other mode – may fluctuate at any given moment in any given interaction.

As language is the mode that has received most attention so far and therefore is best understood, I like to begin any multimodal interactional analysis by analyzing the spoken language first.

Dentist–guardian interaction

In this interaction, the dentist is giving a child dental treatment. Besides the dentist and the patient, an assistant and the child's mother are present.

Background

The child had sat down in the chair, while the dentist was exchanging greetings with the child and the mother. Then the dentist had engaged the mother in some conversation about dental care for another child. Once the child had settled in the chair and the assistant had placed a bib on his chest, the dentist moved the chair back and focused on the child's teeth.

Excerpt

After a while, the following exchange occurred, in which the dentist addresses the mother (see transcription conventions on p. 59):

(1)	*Dentist:*	is Hanau far from Frankfurt?
(2)	*Guardian:*	no, not far at all?
(3)		why's that.
(4)	*Dentist:*	I've got ah,
(5)		actually a friend
(6)	*Guardian:*	[mhm,
(7)	*Dentist:*	is ah,
(8)		head of the dental clinic there
(9)	*Guardian:*	[mhm,

18 *Communicative modes*

(10) *Dentist:*   at some point I hope
(11)   I'll be going over there,
(12)   to visit Brenda
(13)   and I was thinking,
(14)   well, if they weren't too far away
(15) *Dentist:*   THEN I COULD SEE THEM BOTH
(16) *Guardian:*   [THAT'LL WORK.

Analysis

This exchange is opened by the dentist with a marked topic-shifting question, addressing the guardian by asking: "*Is Hanau far from Frankfurt?*" Before this question, the topic of talk had been related to dental care only. The guardian's rising intonation in her answer in line (2): "*no, not far at all*." shows that she is surprised by the question, although she has no problem providing the information, as she comes from Germany. Then, this surprise is even more evidenced by the guardian's next utterance, asking "*why's that*" with lowered intonation in line (3).

With this question, the guardian invites the dentist to depict which conversational direction the dentist was opening up with her topic-shifting question in line (1), displaying curiosity.

The dentist starts her explanation in line (4) "*I've got*" and then indicates this as a false start with "*ah.*" She rephrases her start in line (5) with "*actually, a friend,*" and the guardian back-channels in line (6), saying "*mhm,*" indicating that she has followed the repair-sequence, overlapping slightly with the dentist's last word in line (5) "*friend.*"

Now, the dentist goes on, without a perceptible pause in line (7), saying "*is ah*" and line (8) "*head of the dental clinic there.*" Here, the guardian overlaps with the dentist when she mentions dental clinic, again back-channeling with "*mhm*" in line (9). These two back-channel responses by the guardian in line (6) and line (9) have a dual function: first, the exact placement of the back-channel responses, overlapping once with friend, and then with clinic, indicates that the guardian has understood the repair that the dentist performed in lines (4) and (5). Simultaneously, they indicate that the guardian is following the dentist's conversational direction.

Here, the dentist follows these indicators by laying out her thoughts, and, with that, her reasoning for having asked the question in line (1), in five very informative and clearly stated intonation units (lines 10 through 14). Here, she speaks of Brenda, who used to be her assistant and who recently had moved to Frankfurt.

In line (16), the guardian overlaps with the dentist in line (15), showing that she now knows where the conversation is going (as she also knew Brenda). The dentist keeps speaking in the same flow, but more animatedly than before. This is a clear case of cooperative overlap, as both speakers become more animated and keep speaking without interruption.

While I only analyzed the spoken discourse in this section, I take up this same example on pp. 38–41, analyzing the gaze of the dentist, showing that the actual exchange was much more complex than can be seen in the verbal exchange alone.

Assignment

Tape-record a conversation and transcribe a short section, which has a beginning and an end. Can you define the level of discourse at which the conversation is taking place? What are the interactional messages that the individuals are sending and/or receiving?

PROXEMICS

Proxemics:	The distance that individuals take up with respect to others and relevant objects.
Proxemic behavior:	Culturally conditioned and integrated with the higher-level actions performed as well as the environment in which the interaction takes place.
	Gives insight into the kind of social interaction that is going on.

Utilizing space

Proxemics is the study of the ways in which individuals arrange and utilize their space. We are concerned with the distance that an individual takes up in relation to others as well as to relevant objects. Hall (1966) notes that a social actor's "perception of space is dynamic because it is related to action . . ." (Hall, 1966: 115). The interest then lies in the relationship between the higher-level actions performed and the distances taken up by the participants.

As an example, think of meeting a friend who is standing at a bus stop. Meeting a friend is a higher-level action which is comprised of a multiplicity of chained lower-level actions. At the moment we are only concerned with the chains of proxemic lower-level actions. Thus, one chain of lower-level actions is made up of your proxemic behavior, and another one is made up of the proxemic behavior of your friend.

You walk up to your friend and stop, leaving a specific space between you and your friend. This initial physical positioning of you towards your friend consists of a chain of lower-level actions that you are performing. The space that you have taken up in relation to your friend indicates your social relationship and is appropriate for the higher-level action of meeting this friend at the bus stop.

Next, your friend may want to tell you a secret, taking a step towards you, decreasing the space between the two of you. This step towards you is now a lower-level action that your friend performs in order to talk to you in private. The new space that your friend is taking up towards you is then the appropriate distance to tell a secret.

Proxemic behavior is tightly integrated with the higher-level actions that are being performed, and at the same time, proxemic behavior indicates social relationships. Hall (1966) distinguishes four distances: intimate distance, personal distance, social distance, and public distance. He notes that proxemic behavior of this sort is culturally conditioned and entirely arbitrary, but is binding on all concerned. Intimate distance, personal distance, social distance, and public distance are never set values, but always and only general notions. We speak of ranges from close to far phases, when speaking of any one of these four distances to emphasize the range of possible spacing.

Thus, proxemic behavior is not arbitrary in a given situation among specific individuals, and gives insight into the kind of social interaction that is going on. It is possible to interpret the level of intimacy and/or formality of an interaction by investigating the distance that participants take up to one another. Hereby, it is necessary to keep in mind that the distance that participants take up to one another is further apart when individuals stand/sit across from one another, than when they stand/sit side-by-side. For example, personal distance can be as close as arms touching when people are standing/sitting side-by-side. This nevertheless depends on the culture and also upon the environment that the interaction takes place in. Generally, in closed spaces – a subway or a bus, for example – personal and social distance is much closer than in open space.

In interactional analysis, working with real-time, we discover that the individuals in interaction draw on the system of representation of proxemics that they have learned through socialization. However, the individuals are rarely – if ever – aware of such a system of representation being available to them. Individuals construct the mode of proxemics through their own actions, and we can learn much about the interaction going on if we are aware of the general proxemic behavior of the particular individuals under study.

When analyzing the mode of proxemics in interaction, we always need to remember that proxemic behavior is culturally habituated; and that, overall, while closeness tends to indicate intimacy and distance tends to indicate formality, the actual distances are completely arbitrary. Proxemic behavior is different in different cultures and subcultures, and it may be somewhat different for each individual. We therefore need to understand the proxemic behavior of a given culture/subculture and the individuals under study, before we can come to any conclusions about proxemic behavior in a specific interaction.

This necessary understanding of the individuals' proxemic behavior can be gained through ethnographic observation or through cross-examination of specific instances of interaction. Accordingly, we can observe video clips of one individual in many different circumstances interacting with many different people.

Once we understand the proxemic behavior of the individuals and/or groups that we are studying, we find that the study of proxemics gives us a great deal of insight into their interactions, because proxemic behavior is binding on all concerned.

An informal sociolinguistic interview

Exploring proxemic behavior:	Analyzing the distance of individuals towards others in interaction allows us to comprehend the individuals' understanding of the formality/informality of the occasion.
	Analyzing the distance of individuals towards objects is a first step to thinking about the many higher-level actions that an individual constructs simultaneously.
Higher-level actions:	Anna constructs the higher-level action of ironing (made up of many chains of lower-level actions such as taking a piece of clothing, placing it on the ironing board, flattening it with her hand, pressing it with the iron, folding it, and placing it on a pile of folded clothes); and the higher-level action of watching TV (again, made up of many chains of lower-level actions like lifting her head, focusing her gaze on the TV, etc.), while she is simultaneously co-constructing (with the interviewer) the higher-level action of being interviewed. While Anna is involved in even more higher-level actions, these are the central higher-level actions that are significant to the analysis of the interview.
With:	"A party of more than one whose members are perceived to be 'together'" (Goffman, 1981: 19).
Anwesenheit:	"A party of more than one whose main focus is not each other" (Norris, 2002b: 102).

For an informal sociolinguistic interview, the interviewer prepares some open-ended questions, but is also prepared and even inclined to cross the boundary between interview and conversation. In the following example,

I interviewed a German–Italian woman, whom I call Anna, about her self-perceived identity. The interview followed a long-term ethnographic study during which I spent many months with Anna and her family, focusing on Anna's personal, family, national, and transnational identity constructions.

The time of the interview was set by the interviewee, as I had let her know that I was available whenever she would have the time to talk for a while. She chose one mid-morning, during which her husband was at work, her oldest son in school, and her younger son in preschool. Her youngest child, whom I will call Katie, was the only other person present besides Anna and myself.

When I walked into the apartment, Anna was ironing. She had placed bundles of clothes on most of the chairs and pointed out that she had left one spot on the sofa for me to sit in. The TV was set to an Italian station, and Katie was sitting behind Anna on the floor, playing. I placed the tape-recorder on the chair closest to Anna, and then sat down in the spot that she had reserved for me.

Plate 2.1 shows the distances that Anna takes up with respect to Katie, the interviewer, the TV, and the ironing board.

When focusing on the participants present during this interview, it is noticeable that the distance between Anna and Katie is much shorter than the distance between Anna and the interviewer. While Anna and Katie are positioned back-to-back, their close proximity indicates a mother–daughter *Anwesenheit*. *Anwesenheit* is a German term for "presence," which only refers to human beings. This notion is similar to Goffman's "with," which is defined as "a party of more than one whose members are perceived to be 'together'" (Goffman, 1981: 19). However, while Goffman's "with" refers to a party whose main focus of attention is each other, the term *Anwesenheit* refers to a party whose main focus is not each other. Katie's *Anwesenheit* shapes Anna's actions during the interview to some extent, and the proximity between Anna and her daughter communicates the accessibility and awareness of mother and daughter.

Plate 2.1 Proxemics.

The distance between the interviewer and Anna is rather large. This distance was predetermined by Anna, due to her placing heaps of clothing on most seats and leaving one specific seat open. As we recall, Hall distinguishes between personal and social distance. For Anna, who is German–Italian (far) personal distance is exhibited between her and her daughter, while the distance that Anna takes up to the interviewer demonstrates (far) social distance. The social distance that Anna takes up to the interviewer demonstrates that she views this informal sociolinguistic interview as a formal occasion, which is even more apparent when investigating other communicative modes.

During the interview, Anna appears relaxed and confident; and, listening to the tape recording alone, one might quite wrongly conclude that she perceives the interview as an informal occasion, although her coherent string of utterances without many repairs and without much use of "*uh*" or "*ah*" points to the fact that she has thought about the interview beforehand (a point that she also discusses at the end of the interview). Nevertheless, Anna is talking freely about her self-perceived identity, and the interview is not strained or strictly memorized, either. Thus, the distance that Anna takes up with respect to the interviewer, which leads to the conclusion that this ostensibly informal interview is actually a formal interview for Anna, is also reflected in the spoken discourse.

Anna also takes up specific distances to relevant objects: the TV and the ironing board. As I mentioned above, Anna chose the time and place for the interview. Therefore, she also chose the actions of ironing and watching TV. She had positioned the ironing board at a certain distance from the TV, so that she would be able to look up from her action of ironing to watch the program. The distance that Anna takes up with respect to the ironing board is predetermined by her actions of ironing, and the distance she takes up with respect to the TV is predetermined by her actions of ironing and by visual space. The fact that Anna has positioned herself at these distances to these objects allows her to perform the actions she is performing. In turn, the actions that she is performing communicate information about her family and national identities.

Assignment

Observe an individual's proxemic behavior. For this, you will first want to observe people in an open space. People taking a walk in a park, standing at a bus stop, and walking in a busy shopping street or mall would be perfect situations. Then you want to look at enclosed spaces, like hallways, elevators, buses, or a room full of people.

Once you have conducted preliminary observations, look at one specific dyadic interaction and jot down your observations of the proxemic behavior of these two people. Be as scientific as possible, and keep in mind that

24 *Communicative modes*

you cannot interpret the meaning of their proxemic behavior by looking at just *one* interaction.

POSTURE

Posture:	The ways that participants position their bodies in a given interaction. People may display open or closed postures, and they display directionality through posture.
Postural behavior:	Gives insight into the involvement of participants with others.

Body position

Posture is the study of the ways in which individuals position their bodies. There are two important aspects to posture: first, the form of the body position, and, second, the postural direction that an individual takes up towards others. Dittman has described the open–closed position of arms and legs as hands and arms apart and knees separated for open, and arms crossed or folded and legs crossed for closed (Dittman, 1987: 55). However, there are other open and closed positions that an individual can take up. The interest for the interactional analyst lies in the relationship between the higher-level actions performed and the postures taken up by the participants.

Open and closed postures come in many varieties and degrees. A person may be standing in a fully open posture with limbs apart, or a person may express a completely closed posture with arms and legs crossed. However, body position is not only formed by the limbs, it is also formed by bending/straightening the torso, and is influenced by the lifting/lowering of the head. Thus, the complete body of an individual has to be considered in order to analyze the degree of any open or closed positions.

Similarly, directional positions of the body come in many varieties and degrees. As an example, think once more about the fictitious meeting between you and a friend at a bus stop. Imagine that your friend is facing the street and you are coming towards your friend from the right. As you approach and your friend recognizes that you are approaching, your friend will, most likely, move their body towards you. This directional move of your friend's body positioning may be completed to such a degree, that your friend's body turns to the right and is facing you. On the other hand, such a directional move may also be minute, so that your friend only turns the head and one shoulder to the right. Certainly, your friend can also take up any body position that lies in between these two.

While the perception of the open/closed body position of an individual and the individual's directional positioning as two aspects of posture is useful for analysis, these two aspects are always realized together. Thus, the friend at the bus stop, who only moves the shoulder and head to the right, opens the posture at the very moment that they direct their body towards you as you are approaching.

While the complete body has to be taken into consideration to judge whether the person is displaying an open or closed posture, positioning of the extremities is often specifically valuable for analysis. When a person is standing during an interaction, the position of the feet may give insight into the main focus of the participant. Similarly, when the participant is sitting, the location of the feet may give insight into the person's directional positioning.

In interactional analysis, working with real-time, we discover that the individuals draw on the system of representation of posture that they have learned through socialization. Individuals construct the mode of posture through their own actions, and we can learn much about the interaction going on if we are aware of the general postural behavior.

When analyzing the mode of posture in interaction, we need to remember that postural behavior is also culturally habituated. Postural behavior may be different in different cultures and subcultures and it may be somewhat different for each individual. Certainly, we can also find overlap in cultures and subcultures, just as we can find overlap in proxemic behavior in individuals. Before coming to any conclusions about the meaning of postural behavior of individuals in a specific interaction, we need to understand the postural behavior of a given culture/subculture and the individuals under study.

In order to analyze the mode of posture in interaction, a view from within the culture is very valuable, i.e. what the postural behavior of a participant means to the other participants in the interaction. This view from within a culture can best be gained through ethnographic research methods linked with *native interaction intuition*, since we all have native interaction intuition about the meaning of behavior in our own cultures and subcultures. But, one can also elicit native interaction intuition from the participants through playback methodology.

Generally, we can surmise that the directional positioning of the body towards others indicates an engagement – however remote – in an interaction, while the positioning of the body away from others communicates a disengagement – again, however remote – in a given interaction.

However, when an individual turns the body away from others, displaying disengagement through posture, it does not necessarily mean that the individual is unaware of the ongoing interaction. While they may signal disengagement, they may strongly focus on the interaction, which would be visible through other communicative modes. An example of this would be a parent watching several young children, sitting alone at a table eating dinner. While the parent may turn the body away from the children, they may pay special attention to all the ongoing sounds.

Speaking on a cell phone

Exploring postural behavior:	Each individual in interaction takes up a certain posture, which gives insight into the individual's physical positioning towards specific interactions that are going on.
Higher-level actions:	Sandra constructs two higher-level actions that are central to the analysis of this interaction. First, she constructs the action of speaking on the phone, and, second, she constructs the action of having coffee with a friend.
	Both higher-level actions have a clear opening and closing sequence; and the higher-level action of speaking on the phone is inserted into the higher-level action of having coffee with a friend.

The following example is taken from a long-term ethnographic study that I conducted in Germany. Here, a woman, whom I call Sandra, and her friend were sitting at an outdoor table of a coffee shop, when her cell phone rang. Sandra took the phone out of her purse, took up a new posture, and then spoke for about 15 minutes. The first image in Plate 2.2 shows Sandra's posture while she is speaking on her cell phone, exhibiting the same posture throughout.

The glasses with iced coffee on the table demonstrate that Sandra's friend is sitting to the right of her while she is speaking on the phone. During the phone conversation, Sandra's posture is closed, with her head slightly bent down, her right hand lying on her right leg, and her legs crossed. This closed posture communicates that she is not available for interaction with others in the café.

When viewing the specific arrangement of the closed posture, we see that Sandra's right arm blocks an interaction with her friend sitting to her right. Looking at Sandra's posture, we can envision the directionality of her feet as noted in the fieldnotes. Her right leg crosses her left leg, turning her torso to the left and away from the other person at the table. Sandra's right foot points into open space, and her left foot is aligned with the right. She holds the phone in her left hand, and her left shoulder is slightly bent backwards, and aligned with her torso. The directionality into open space, which is displayed in most of Sandra's posture, communicates to the person at the table that she is not available for interaction.

Sandra's head position is bent slightly to the right and thus is not aligned with the rest of her body. The head, as part of Sandra's posture, indicates to her friend at the table that she is aware of her presence. While, for the most part Sandra's bodily positioning – the closed posture as well

Plate 2.2 Posture.

as the directionality – puts her friend sitting at the table on hold, the position of Sandra's head nevertheless indicates some involvement with her friend.

The second image in Plate 2.2 shows Sandra and Anna eating dinner, when Anna receives a call on her cell phone. Here, Anna displays a closed posture with her forearms and shoulders close together and slightly bent forward. Anna's upper body actually displays an even further closed posture than Sandra's when she was speaking on her cell phone in the café (see the first image).

Yet, Anna has raised and slightly turned her head, gazing directly at Sandra, who is sitting across from her at the dinner table. Through the position of her head, Anna's posture is more open than Sandra's posture when she was speaking on her cell phone (see the first image). Anna's posture, opened towards Sandra as the participant in this interaction, demonstrates that she is clearly interacting with Sandra, even though she is speaking on the phone.

Assignment

First, observe postural behavior by looking at one individual at a time. How is the person standing or sitting? How are the extremities positioned? Is the person displaying an open or a closed posture?

Next, look at one specific dyadic interaction and note your observations on a piece of paper. You can do this exercise anywhere. People may be standing and talking on a street corner, or they may be sitting in a café. Note down how the two individuals in this interaction are positioning their bodies. Often a sketch – even with stick figures – can be very valuable.

GESTURE

Iconic gestures:	Possess a pictorial content, often mimicking what is conveyed verbally, describing specific objects or events, making them more vivid.
Metaphoric gestures:	Possess a pictorial content, however they present the invisible: an abstract idea or category. These abstract concepts are given form and shape in the imagery depicted in the motion and the space of the gesture.
Deictic gestures:	Point to objects or people in the physical world or to abstract concepts and ideas as if they had a physical location.
Beat gestures:	Look like beating musical time. Beats only consist of two movement phases: in/out or up/down movement and are short and quick.

Hand/arm movements

The communicative mode of gesture has received considerable attention in the literature. A gesture is a "deliberately expressive movement [that has] a sharp boundary of onset and that [is] seen as an *excursion*, rather than as a result in any sustained change of position" (Kendon, 1978: 69). In this section, I focus only on hand/arm or manual gestures.

Gesture is a global-synthetic mode, which means that gestures are constructed from whole to part. McNeill (1992) notes that the whole determines the meaning of the parts and one gesture can combine many meanings. However, gestures produced together do not combine to form a larger, more complex one. Thus, a gesture often has elements, including trajectory, but the parts always depend upon the meaning of the whole. The parts do not have an independent meaning (as opposed to the parts of a language which are meaningful, such as morphemes and words).

Hand and arm movements are often interdependent and concurrent with spoken language, slightly preceding the spoken discourse – to realize imagery. When a participant, for example, describes having seen a big door, the participant may use a gesture to illustrate the size and shape of the door just a moment before uttering the words "big door." Thus, a participant in interaction employs hand/arm gestures when speaking, and gesturing starts slightly earlier than the words expressing the same idea. It is probably not often useful to separate these kinds of gestures from the language with which they co-occur.

However, there are also gestures that do not coincide with spoken language, and others that co-occur but do not depict the same message that is conveyed in the occurring language. These are the gestures which have received much less attention. While they are composed just like gestures supplementing language, they accompany other communicative modes or depict meaning that differs from the language used. Before highlighting how gestures interact with other modes (see pp. 52–56), I focus on how to discern the movement phases of gestures and how to recognize the four types: iconic, metaphoric, deictic, and beat gestures.

Iconic gestures usually consist of three movement phases: the preparation, the stroke, and the retraction phase. Iconic gestures depict pictorial content and generally mimic what the individual communicates verbally. Such gestures often vivify the specific objects or events that the speaker is conveying verbally.

Metaphoric gestures usually consist of three movement phases: the preparation, the stroke, and the retraction phase. While metaphoric gestures also depict pictorial content, they portray abstract ideas or categories. Such abstract notions are given form and shape in the imagery portrayed in the motion and the space of the gesture.

Deictic gestures also usually consist of three movement phases: the preparation, the stroke, and the retraction phase. Such gestures often point to people or objects in the physical world, but they can also point to events in the past or the future, or point to ideas and notions as if they had a physical location in the world.

Beat gestures differ from these other three types of gestures in that they consist of only two movement phases: up/down or back/forth, which of course, can be performed in many different ways with fingers, hands, or arms. They look as if the performer is beating musical time in quick succession.

Language often plays a crucial part in the performance of gestures, and, without language, it is difficult to recognize whether a person is performing an iconic or a metaphoric gesture. Does the gesture refer to an object or specific event, or does it refer to an abstract concept? By viewing the gesture alone, it is usually not possible to come to a conclusion, because the two modes of gesture and language are here so closely linked that an analyst needs to refer to one mode to be able to understand the message in the other mode.

When looking at deictic gestures, however, we can often understand the message by viewing the gesture alone. When a person is pointing to someone, we often follow the stretched out arm with our gaze, even if we are not in earshot and cannot know what the person is saying. Therefore, while deictic gestures often occur with spoken language, these gestures can actually be understood without understanding the mode of language – at least to a certain extent. Here, then, we may say that deictic gestures are not necessarily as dependent upon language as are iconic or metaphoric gestures. Deictic gestures may also be performed without language altogether, for this reason.

Beat gestures are again different. Some beats are highly dependent upon the mode of language, taking on a function of emphasizing a certain word or notion, and thereby coherently integrating the overall discourse, while other beats indicate a higher-level communicative coherence (which will be discussed in detail in Chapter 6).

McNeill (1992: 83), building on Kendon (1972, 1980) describes gestures as occurring in a gesture phrase, which consists of one or more of the following movement phases:

1   *Preparation*, during which the limb moves away from the rest position to a position in gesture space where the stroke begins.
    Pre-stroke hold is the position that is reached at the end of the preparation.
2   *Stroke* is the peak of the gesture, at which point the meaning of the gesture is expressed.
    Post-stroke hold is the final position reached.
3   *Retraction* is the return of the hand to its rest position.

While the stroke is obligatory, all other phases are optional. Nevertheless, most iconic, metaphoric, and deictic gestures consist of three movement phases, the preparation, stroke, and retraction.

Interaction in an accounting firm

The following interaction between an accountant and his assistant was videotaped in the office of the accounting firm. The assistant had asked a procedural question regarding filling out a complicated and unusual part of a client's tax form.

The accountant walked over to his assistant's desk, leaned against another desk, and started to explain how to fill out the form that was lying on the assistant's desk. Here, I would like to focus on the deictic manual gesture that the accountant performs when he explains how to fill out the form.

In the first image of Plate 2.3, the accountant is holding some papers in his right hand, while he is slightly lifting the left corner of a piece of paper with his left hand. The assistant is sitting in her chair, gazing at the accountant's face.

Plate 2.3 Gesture.

The first image of the second row shows the preparation phase of the deictic gesture. The accountant has let go of the piece of paper and is stretching his arm out towards the form lying on the desk. Simultaneously, the assistant has lowered her head, and is now following the accountant's hand/arm with her gaze. The second image of the second row shows the stroke of the gesture. Here, the accountant has fully stretched his arm and his index finger, pointing at a specific place on the form. The assistant has moved her head and shoulders slightly, making it possible for her to look at the place that the accountant's finger is pointing at.

The first image in the third row indicates the post-stroke hold, showing that the accountant is holding the position of his outstretched arm and hand/finger in the position for a short period of time. The second image in this row displays the retraction phase of the gesture. With the accountant's arm retracting, the assistant is shifting, lifting her head, and the accountant and the assistant simultaneously move to a position that is similar to the starting point of this elaborate gesture phase. The last image shows the rest position of the accountant's left hand/arm, which is again touching the papers that he is holding with his right hand.

Assignment

Observe gestures that individuals around you perform. At the beginning of your observations you will realize that it is not always easy to distinguish which movement can be termed a gesture and which movement cannot. Similarly, you may have difficulty differentiating one gesture from another. Take your time and observe carefully.

Once you feel comfortable seeing gestures as units made up of parts, you will want to observe a dyadic interaction. Now, try to note down some gestures that are especially prevalent.

HEAD MOVEMENT

Head movement:	Bracketed by a break in movement.
Simple head movement:	Lateral, sagittal, or rotational.
Complex head movement:	Overlapping of two or more patterns.
Types of head movements:	Directional shifts (often one–two shifts) or deictic head movement (often three movement phases).
	Head beats, which are quick up/down or back/forth movements of the head (two movement phases).
	Postural shifts, which are discussed on pp. 24–25.
	Gaze shifts, which are discussed in pp. 36–38.

Positions of the head

Head movement is the study of the ways that individuals position their heads. Altorfer *et al.* (2000) have conducted extensive studies on head movement in conversation, and they distinguish between rotational (shaking the head), lateral (tilting the head to the right or the left), and sagittal (nodding) movements. While Altorfer *et al.* are using quantitative measurements and are focusing on the emotional side of behavior patterns, multimodal interactional analysts use qualitative measurements and are investigating the interactional meanings of head movement in everyday face-to-face interaction.

Individuals move their heads in many positions, and head movement in interaction has a range of functions from conventional to novel. The head can be moved up/down or back/forth to signal conventional or iconic meaning (in Western society, yes/no). Such movements would be simple sagittal or simple rotational movements. The head may be lowered or raised to close or open a posture, mainly through sagittal movement. The head can be moved to a wide angle and degree: to facilitate gaze, to point to something or somebody (deictic movement), and/or to display a change in focus. Such movements are often complex, with many positions intertwined.

Thus, head movement may be simple, meaning a clear lateral, sagittal, or rotational movement, or it may be a complex movement, in which two or all three movement patterns overlap. The extent of head movement differs in any culture and subculture, and even differs from one individual to another. As with any mode in interaction, it is necessary to understand the movements of the people that one is studying, in order to make any claims of meaning. Simultaneously, it is important to keep in mind that the same head movement may have a different meaning in different situations, as interactional meaning is always dependent upon the individuals performing the movement *and* the individuals interpreting it. Meaning is always co-constructed, and unintentional actions may be just as communicative as intentional ones.

Conventional head movements are important in interaction, and they are also the easiest to study. These movements have a clear one-to-one verbal counterpart: *yes* or *no*, and are often performed instead of a verbal message. Meaning for such conventional head movements can be assigned by analyzing their position within a conversation, where they often take the place of the second part of an adjacency pair.

Novel head movements are just as important in interaction; however, they are much more difficult to study. Such movements do not have a verbal one-to-one counterpart, and it is not always easy to distinguish head movement from other communicative modes.

There are two types of novel head movement that are of great importance to the study of multimodal interaction: first, the directional shifting of the head, or the deictic head movement; and second, head beats (or head tosses), which are quick up/down or back/forth movements of the head.

The movement phases for deictic head movements are similar to the movement phases of deictic gestures, and usually consist of three stages: a preparation, a stroke, and a retraction. The movement phases of the head beats or head tosses are similar to manual beat gestures, so that they only consist of two quick stages. While beats are generally up/down and back/forth, the actual direction or position of the head may vary. Individuals perform head beats by moving their heads up/down with a left/right slant (a sagittal movement with a lateral slant), or back/forth with an left/right slant (a rotational movement with a lateral slant).

The position and phases of head movements vary to a great extent, but one can determine whether a person is performing a head beat or a deictic head movement, because all head movements have clear boundaries. There are always pauses between head movements, even though they may be short. If an individual performs an up/down head beat, you will find that there is no movement before or after the beat. The same is true for deictic head movements, and, of course, also for conventional head movements.

Thinking of conventional head movements, we can often determine the strength of the message by the number of times that a person shakes or nods the head. Usually, the more often an individual shakes or nods between actually resting the head in one position, the stronger the message. Strength of novel head movements also presents important information, as I will discuss in detail in Chapter 6.

Only when analyzing head movement in interactional terms, is it possible to determine its meaning. The function that a head movement has for the individual performing it is no more important then the function that others in the interaction perceive, i.e. interactional meaning.

Interaction in a retail store

The following interaction between owner and designer was videotaped in a gift basket retail and distribution store. Both women were working behind a counter on different tasks. While the owner was reviewing the current order that was ready to be shipped, reading a list and putting it on a clipboard, the designer was filling gift baskets.

The women were working side-by-side on their own tasks for the most part of about half an hour. At one time, the designer had a question about the exact placement of a flower. At another time, the owner asked a question about an item that needed to be shipped.

In Plate 2.4, the store owner is standing to the left of the designer (to the right in the image). The designer is mostly hidden behind gift baskets, while we have a clear upper body view of the owner.

In the first image, the owner is looking at the designer, whose head is in a lowered position. This still image displays the rest position of the owner's head.

Plate 2.4 Head movement.

In the first image of the second row, the owner is rotating her head to the left and away from the designer, who has now lifted her head and is looking at the store owner's head. While we can see that the owner is holding a pencil in her right hand aiming to point, the designer cannot see the pencil, as it is hidden by the owner's head and hair. In the second image of this row, the owner has bent her head even lower and rotated it to the far left. Now, the designer has lifted her head further and is looking at the head movement, trying to follow what the store owner's head is pointing at. When looking at the pencil in the owner's hand, we can see that she is pointing upwards in the same direction towards which her head is pointing. The first of these still photos shows the preparation phase, and the second one displays the stroke (or the peak) of the deictic head movement.

In the first image of the third row, the owner holds her head in a post-stroke hold, holding her head in the position that it is in. Then, in the second image of this row, the owner moves her head in a quick retraction phase – the swiftness of which is visible in her flying hair. While the owner's right hand, which is holding the pencil, also rotates around, the pencil is no longer used as a pointer, but ends up as a tool to straighten out her hair. Throughout the retraction phase, the designer moves her head, lifting it slightly to better see what the owner had been pointing at.

The image in the last row shows the rest position that the owner's head takes up once this elaborate movement is completed. As the owner's head is reaching this position, the designer's head is rotating to the left to meet the owner's gaze.

Assignment

In order to discern head movements, you should begin by observing one person at a time. First, you should observe a person who is sitting or standing alone. You will see that there are long rest periods between movements. Try to use these rest periods to learn to jot down the movements as exactly as possible.

Next, look at one person in a dyadic interaction and again try to note down the head movements. Do not worry yet about the functions of these movements. Initially you need to learn to see head movements when they are being performed and then note them down quickly.

GAZE

Gaze:	The organization, direction, and intensity of looking.
	Gaze may play a subordinate role in interaction when people are conversing and are not engaged in other activities.

	Gaze may play a superordinate role when people are simultaneously engaged in other activities while conversing.
Structure of gaze:	Gaze can oscillate between sequentially structured and random, as it is integrated with the higher-level actions performed and the environment in which the interaction takes place.
	Generally, gaze is more structured when the interaction is also more structured.

Organization and direction of looking

The organization of gaze in interaction has received substantial attention. Kendon (1967) discusses the functions of gaze in conversation in detail and notes that the hearer gazes at the speaker more than the speaker gazes at the hearer, while the pattern of gazing is somewhat different for each position. He states that hearers give speakers fairly long looks broken by brief glances away, whereas speakers alternate looks toward their recipients with looks away from them of about equal length. Speakers typically look toward the hearer at the end of phrases. Goodwin (1981) examines mutual gaze at turn-beginnings and co-participation, as well as repair structures within spoken language, which are possible due to the mode of gaze. This literature suggests that gaze is to some extent sequentially structured, and that gaze is subordinate to language. Certainly, gaze in interaction is culturally agreed on, and varies not only from culture to culture and subculture to subculture, but also to some extent from one individual to the next.

Gaze can also be somewhat unsystematic. Imagine people going for a walk through a wooded area. They may focus their gaze upon parts of the trail: a particular tree, a rock on the side of the trail, or a particular flower growing in the distance. On the other hand, the gaze of a walker may be focused nowhere. The walker may be deep in thought, focusing the gaze somewhere in the middle distance, looking at nothing in particular. Or consider a person walking through an urban shopping street or mall, looking at the shop windows in passing without focusing on any particular item displayed. There may be an item that catches the person's attention for a while. Then they may look at other passers-by, and next may focus on one particular store that the shopper intended to walk into. If there are two or more people shopping together, they may randomly focus their gaze on shop windows, street signs, other shoppers, and also sequentially focus their gaze on each other (as discussed by Kendon, Goodwin, and others). The mode of gaze, thus, often alternates between a sequentially organized structure and a seemingly arbitrary structure.

When analyzing gaze, we find that this structuring of the mode can be placed on a continuum – where the sequential structure of gaze during conversation occupies one end of the continuum, and seeming arbitrariness of gaze occupies the other. The structure of gaze in interaction may oscillate from sequential structuring to arbitrariness, and back, with any point on the continuum possible.

When analyzing gaze in interaction, we have to be aware of the possibilities of gaze configurations. Interactions differ greatly and, with them, gaze distribution differs. Usually, the more structured the interaction, the more structured the gaze will be. When two people in Western society are engaged in conversation sitting or standing across from each other, gaze distribution will closely follow the structures described by Kendon and Goodwin. Similarly, gaze distribution will be structured in the same way if several people are engaged in one conversation – i.e. when one person at a time talks and the others are listening. However, the more the interaction deviates from these very structured conversations, the more the gaze distribution for each participant will oscillate between random and structured.

Many interactions involve more than two people and more than one focus of interaction. This makes the study of gaze difficult and also exciting. But what makes the study of gaze even more difficult is that we cannot be certain where a person is looking. Is it a middle-distance gaze or a long-distance gaze? Is the participant focused on a certain object or only on a part thereof? These are questions we as qualitative analysts cannot answer with certainty. However, as analysts we can observe what the individuals engaged in that interaction perceive.

As humans we are skilled at perceiving the gaze of others. Just think of the many times you have looked up only to see that somebody else is watching you, or the many times you have actually turned around because you *felt* someone's gaze on your back. Just as we perceive somebody's gaze, we can also quite aptly determine the gaze direction and gaze distance of others. All individuals in interaction perceive and in turn react to the gaze of other participants, and the interactive meaning of a certain gaze can be determined by the reaction of the other participants.

Besides our ability to perceive other people's gaze and observe the reaction to a specific gaze by others, the simultaneous use of other modes helps the analyst make sense of gaze in interaction.

Dentist–patient–assistant–guardian interaction

The structuring of gaze also depends on the other – not necessarily verbal – actions that a person performs. In order to illustrate this better, I now revisit the dentist–guardian interaction that I discussed on pp. 17–19 of this chapter. As mentioned there, the dentist and her assistant perform dental treatment on a child, while the dentist addresses the guardian, asking a topic-shifting question.

This time, we are focusing on the gaze of the dentist during that verbal exchange between dentist and guardian. The mother of the child is standing

Communicative modes 39

next to the camera, and, when you view the images in Plate 2.5, you see that we actually are analyzing a dentist–patient–assistant–guardian interaction. Gaze in this interaction is mainly structured by the dentist's actions that she performs in modes other than spoken language.

The first image shows that the dentist is looking at the guardian, while she is asking the question *"Is Hanau far from Frankfurt?"* Here, the dentist's direct gaze towards the guardian clearly indicates that the dentist is talking to the guardian, not to the patient, or to her assistant, and establishes mutual gaze at turn beginning, as discussed by Goodwin (1981).

This mutual gaze is brief and the dentist is shifting her gaze when the guardian answers *"no, not far at all?"* She is gazing intently at the child's teeth and at her own hands, manipulating the instruments, when the guardian continues with *"why's that."* Now the dentist says *"I've got ah,"* and then repairs this false start with *"actually a friend,"* and the guardian

Plate 2.5 Gaze.

back-channels with "*mhm.*" Throughout this false start followed by a repair, the guardian's back-channel, and the next intonation unit "*is ah,*" the dentist is highly focused on the patient. She is not paying very close attention to the talk. Yet, she is conversing with the guardian without a perceptible pause.

The first image in the second row shows that the dentist briefly makes eye contact with her assistant, while she says "*head of the dental clinic there,*" to which the guardian again responds with "*mhm.*" The assistant responds to the gaze by moving her hand holding a small container of toothpaste closer to the dentist.

At this point, the dentist is performing two separately sequenced actions simultaneously: she communicates with her assistant, so that mutual gaze established by the dentist is followed by a movement of the hand by the assistant; and she speaks her utterances addressed to the guardian, which are followed by a back-channel response. These two sequences of actions are independent from each other. The dentist is simultaneously communicating two distinctly different ideas with two different individuals. Each idea is addressed to only one of the individuals and is responded to by the one addressed.

The second image of this row illustrates that the dentist's gaze is now focused on the small container and her instrument, which she is dipping into the container. While extricating the toothpaste, the dentist speaks fluently without interruption, false starts, or repairs, saying "*at some point I hope I'll be going over there to visit Brenda and I was thinking, well, if they weren't too far away.*" Here, the dentist's manual actions do not take her full attention, giving her the opportunity to pay more attention to the ongoing conversation.

The last image shows that the dentist is cleaning behind the child's front teeth, gazing intently at the teeth and the instrument that she is manipulating, animatedly continuing her talk that is now overlapped by the guardian's utterance.

The dentist's gaze in this multiparty interaction is sequentially structured. In the first image, the dentist gives the patient a short break, making it possible for her to look at the guardian and initiate an exchange. Then, the dentist performs a number of actions on the patient's teeth, continuously gazing at what she is doing. As soon as these actions are completed, the next action sequence is initiated through gaze. Here, the dentist gazes at her assistant, giving her the necessary cue to move her hand forward, making it possible for the dentist to engage in the next action of picking up the toothpaste with her instrument. Here, the dentist's gaze is again focused on what she is doing with her instruments. Then the dentist returns her gaze to the patient's teeth.

While I pointed out that the dentist simultaneously communicates with the assistant and with the guardian in different modes, she is certainly also communicating with the patient in another mode, the mode of touch.

Thus, the dentist is communicating with all three participants simultaneously, utilizing different modes.

When analyzing the gaze directions of the dentist, we gain much insight into the structuring of gaze. The dentist's focus of attention is clearly observable when analyzing her gaze direction. Here, I have added the spoken language in the transcripts, to illustrate that the utterances and the gaze do not necessarily function together.

For the dentist, gaze is one of the main modes in this multiparty interaction. She cannot perform her actions without gaze. Everything that she does is structured by this embodied mode. She sits in a way that allows her to see the patient's teeth and the assistant's actions. Spoken discourse, while it is abundantly present, is playing a subordinate part for the dentist. However, for the guardian, the mode of gaze plays a subordinate role, while the mode of spoken language plays the superordinate role in this interaction. Thus, the role that a specific mode plays for the various participants in interaction may be different for each individual.

Assignment

Think of interactions in which gaze plays the primary role for one or more participants in an interaction and language is subordinated to gaze. Then go out and observe such interactions. How can you determine that gaze is more important in a certain interaction for a specific individual?

MUSIC

Music:	An embodied mode when individuals use instruments (including their voices when singing) to express their perceptions, thoughts, or feelings.
	A disembodied mode when people react to the music played by others (recorded or not).

Embodied or disembodied

Auditory modes like music or spoken language often appear to be more prevalent modes in interaction than the visual modes of communication, because it is easier for us to close our eyes or to change our focus than to shut out noise. When walking through a crowded street, we do not have to focus on the others present. We can focus on the street in front or nothing at all. But when a street musician is playing music in that street, we cannot easily disregard this music when we are close to the musician. Even if people appear to take no notice of it, they often incorporate the rhythm of the music into their movements.

For musicians, music is an embodied mode, which allows them to express their perceptions, thoughts, and feelings: communicating them to others present.

Just as musicians can express perceptions, thoughts, and feelings by employing the mode of music, everybody can utilize this mode in a disembodied way. Instead of playing musical instruments, people can play prerecorded music on the radio, a tape, or a CD. In today's world, this auditory communicative mode of recorded music is more prevalent than music used as an embodied mode.

Recorded music is played in many public settings. We only have to walk into a hotel lobby or the entrance of a large apartment building to hear some background music. There is music in the elevator, music in the dental office, and music in the grocery store. People, of course, frequently listen to music at home, and it is unlikely that somebody would have a party without playing some music. Music relaxes or stimulates the listeners, as it sets the mood and the pace of an interaction.

Music not only communicates to the listeners, listeners often react directly to the music, incorporating the rhythm into their embodied modes. The musical rhythm may be incorporated into the speech pattern, so that speakers listening to fast-paced music may speak just as fast, while speakers listening to slow-paced music may inevitably speak just as slowly. Similarly, the gestures, gaze patterns and other movements may be stimulated by music.

Unger-Hamilton *et al.* (1979: 12) point out "*dass Musik die ordnungslosen Schallereignisse der Umwelt in eine bestimmte Ordnung zwingen*" (that music forces the order-less noises in the environment into a certain order). Just as music can force noises into a certain order, music – if the mode is strong (an aspect of modes that will be discussed in detail in Chapter 4) – may also force movements into a certain order. Like any ambient sound – from traffic to birdsong in the woods – music is a mode to which people respond or entrain their actions.

Music as an embodied mode: a teenager playing a saxophone

This example shows a teenager, whom I will call Brian, practicing a new song on his saxophone for an upcoming concert. After a while, he pushes his music stand out of the way and improvises freely.

In the first image in Plate 2.6, Brian is utilizing the instrument to express his perceptions of the musical notes that are given in the book in front of him. His gaze is strictly focused on the book on his note stand, reading the notes as he plays. Brian's posture is slightly tense, displaying the amount of concentration necessary to read the notes and translate them into tones by pressing the right keys. Simultaneously, he is tapping his foot to keep the base rhythm for the song.

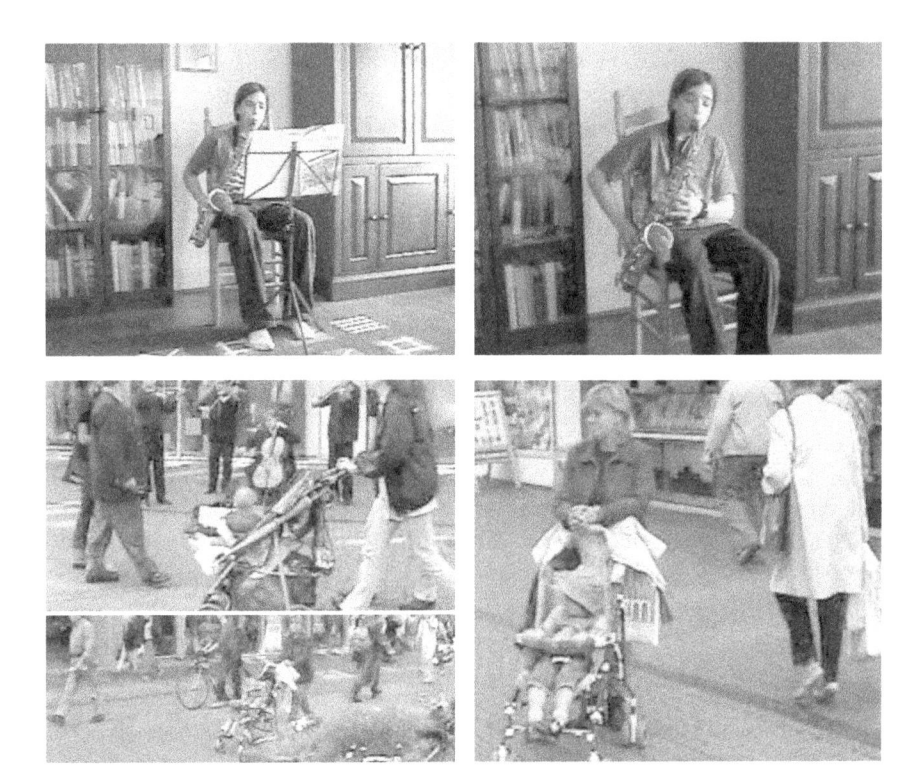

Plate 2.6 Music.

In the second image, Brian is improvising and expressing his own thoughts and feelings by playing the instrument. Here, his gaze is fixed in the middle distance, his posture is more relaxed, his notes are unrestrained, and his foot is no longer tapping along. He does not have to translate notes into finger movements that then allow him to produce desired tones, or to keep an expected rhythm. He utilizes the tones, and the rhythm that he is producing, merely to communicate his own thoughts and feelings. While his concentration was first focused on the outside: on musical notes and on playing a song correctly, his concentration is now focused within.

Music as a disembodied mode

The next example illustrates how people incorporate music that is played by someone else into their own movements. I took a video in a busy shopping street in a large German city. Street musicians were playing as people walked by. For the people in the street either listening to the music or just passing by the street musicians, the music is a disembodied mode.

The three other images in Plate 2.6 show that almost all the pedestrians who are walking closely past the musicians in the street are walking to the beat of the music. They have, most likely inadvertently, incorporated the rhythm into their step. In multimodal interactional analysis, we want to focus on the ways that people incorporate the mode of music – embodied or disembodied – into their actions.

Just as people react to ambient sounds, people respond to other ambient modes such as light, temperature, or the wind. As an example, think of people walking into a dark, cool cathedral with light diffused by stained glass windows. As soon as they walk in, their voices drop to a whisper.

Assignment

Listen to the background music in different settings like a grocery store, a disco, or a party, and watch how the people around you move about. Watch their step, their gestures, their head movements, and also listen to the pacing of their speech and their laughs. How loud does the music have to be for it to influence people's movements?

PRINT

Print:	An embodied mode when individuals use tools (pen, paper, computer) to express their perceptions, thoughts, or feelings.
	A disembodied mode when people react to the print developed by others (magazine, newspaper).
	However, the boundary between embodied and disembodied is always vague.

Written text and printed images

The communicative mode of print, as it is understood in this book, refers to written texts, including the language, the medium, the typography, and the content, when it is incorporated into the interactions. The mode of print also includes images in the printed media.

This mode may be employed by reading a magazine, writing a shopping list, or wearing clothes with writing and/or images printed on them. In multimodal interactional analysis, the focus is on the way that people in interaction use the mode of written text or images. People often read magazines together; they comment on a piece of news that they are reading in a newspaper or point to an image. Similarly, they may display and/or react to printed emblems on somebody's clothing.

Print is present in many settings, but, as a visual mode, the participants in interaction have to utilize the mode of gaze in order to incorporate this mode into their interaction. Unlike music, print can easily be shut out of a person's perception, and is deliberately utilized by participants.

Thus, in interactional analysis, we do not want to study the potential that the mode of print carries by simply being present in the environment; neither do we want to analyze the print media as such, but are only interested in how and when this mode is being utilized by participants in interaction.

The mode of print is multimodal in itself and "all aspects of materiality and all of the modes deployed in a multimodal object/phenomenon/text contribute to meaning" (Kress and Van Leeuwen, 2001: 28). However, instead of an analysis of the meaning within the print that is used, the focus here lies in the analysis of the meaning that the participants construct through the employment of the mode of print in real-time interactions.

Embodied and disembodied

Just as the mode of music can either be embodied or disembodied, depending upon how it is used by the participants in interaction, the mode of print can also be either embodied or disembodied.

While people are writing shopping lists and letters by hand, or school papers on the computer, these individuals are using the mode of print to communicate their perceptions, thoughts, and feelings. Here, people use the mode of print as an extension of their bodies, in order to communicate. Such embodied use of the mode of print can easily be located in an interactional context: a parent writes a shopping list, reading it out loud and, as they do so, asking the children if they can think of anything else; a person is sitting at a desk writing a letter, when a friend approaches and asks "*what are you writing?*"; two friends are sitting in their dorm room, writing term papers on their computers, commenting on what they have written.

Certainly, print is also a disembodied mode. We all read and speak about books, magazines, newspapers, and Internet pages. Print is rich in many different environments, and we only have to look around to see just how prevalent the mode of print is. When we employ the mode of print in interaction, commenting on a printed message, we employ it as a disembodied mode.

We may ask "*when does 'embodied' end, and 'disembodied' begin?*", and that is certainly a good question. Boundaries are fuzzy, but generally print is an embodied mode when a person is employing it as an extension of their own body, i.e. writing, drawing, or painting something. But once the object is created, it has taken on a life of its own and people utilize the created, printed object as a disembodied mode. Thus, the parent who is writing a shopping list is utilizing the mode of print in an embodied way until they finish writing it. Then, they may place the list into a wallet and only take it out in the store, when they utilize this same list in a *disembodied* way?

The embodied actions of writing have become frozen in the list. The list has become an object with a great degree of materiality, making it possible for the list to last for many years. This list exists without any further actions performed by the parent, and may also be used by other social actors. With these facts in mind, we can argue that the parent, when reading the shopping list in the store, is utilizing print as a disembodied mode.

However, when the parent reads the list in the store, they read it to remember their own prior thoughts. Thus, the list is nothing more than an extension of the parent's memory. With these facts in mind, we can also argue that the parent, when reading the shopping list in the store, is utilizing print as an embodied mode.

We see that the boundary between embodied and disembodied is fuzzy, but, while it is theoretically interesting to think about the ways that print – or any other generally disembodied mode – can be used by a social actor as an embodied mode, we do not need to worry about the actual boundary too much. There does not have to be a true boundary, and, as we can see from the above example, there isn't one.

So far, we have focused on the social actor, who is utilizing a mode. A person reads a magazine and the magazine can be viewed as the disembodied mode of print that the person utilizes. But, of course, we also need to think about the fact that all interactions are co-constructed. When viewed from this angle, each mode is always both *embodied and disembodied.* For example, at a specific moment in an interaction between two people, one person's lower-level actions are embodied (take posture, gaze, or gesture) for the performer and, at the same time, these same lower-level actions are disembodied for the person who "reads" these actions and entrains their actions to them.

Thus, all modes are both embodied and disembodied – depending on whether an action is performed or read and interpreted – and interaction is a constant shifting back and forth between embodied and disembodied. Furthermore, frozen actions are "read", just like somebody reads their own shopping list by reading an internal memory of what that (higher-level) action would mean if they had performed it themselves.

Interactions among friends

People often interact while employing, or by employing, the mode of print. The mode of print becomes an integral part of the very interaction. The images in Plate 2.7 make this notion more apparent.

The first image shows two friends engaged in conversation about some forms. Sandra has stacked the forms in a pile, not knowing how to fill them out or file them. She has asked her friend Marcus to take a look, and tell her what is important and what she should do with the forms; and she has handed them to him.

Plate 2.7 Print.

Sandra's and Marcus' posture; their proxemics to each other and the forms; their gaze; their slightly bent heads; and Marcus' hand movements while sifting through the forms, show that they are focused upon the mode of print. Sandra is watching as Marcus is trying to make sense of the forms and simultaneously advising her. The conversation is centered on the forms, i.e. the disembodied mode of print.

The first image in the second row shows two friends: Karen and Sandra, sitting at a table. Karen is reading a newspaper and the friends are simultaneously talking about a variety of topics, including their children, food, and news. While Karen's posture and gaze display that she is intently focused upon reading, the concurrent talk indicates that she only reads intently for short periods of time. During these times, she reads out loud. Karen's left arm leads us to assume that she shields any open interaction with Sandra; however, this assumption is wrong. Karen almost always supports her head with her left hand while reading. In the interaction, Sandra shows no sign that she interprets Karen's arm as an indication that Karen intends to focus on the newspaper alone. To illustrate that this posture is a natural one for Karen to take up when she is reading, I have added the second image in this row: in which Karen is reading a magazine, sitting alone, not interacting with anybody, and without anybody in sight to disturb her.

These two images illustrate how important it is for the analyst to understand the culturally, subculturally, and individually conditioned movements of each person under study. While someone who is not familiar with Karen's usual posture when she is reading might misinterpret the way she supports her head, Sandra is a good friend of hers, and the interaction shows that she interprets this posture as just something that Karen does – rather than reading special meaning into it. In the first image in the second row, then, print plays an integral part in the interaction – not a central one.

The last image in Plate 2.7 shows Diane sitting at a kitchen table, leafing through a magazine while conversing with a friend. At this moment, Diane is looking up at her friend, who is talking about her family. Diane is holding the page with her right hand and is involved in the conversation. When the topic comes to an end, Diane gazes back at her magazine.

At the moment when the picture was taken, the mode of print plays a peripheral part in the interaction. Diane's friend engages Diane in conversation, and Diane responds accordingly. However, when we analyze the complete 45 minutes that the friends spent together, we find that all conversational topics were introduced by Diane's friend, and that there are fairly substantial pauses between the end of one topic and the introduction of a new one. Therefore, we can see that the mode of print structures this interaction in a significant way.

Assignment

Observe your own use of print: for one day, write down all of the instances when you use print while interacting with others.

LAYOUT

> **Layout:** Interactions are structured by the layout that participants employ.
>
> While this mode appears to be extensive, participants in interaction usually employ only a small amount of a vast layout.

The setting and objects within the setting

The communicative mode of layout refers to the setting and the objects found within it. In multimodal interactional analysis, the focus is on how the participants utilize the layout and communicate through this mode.

Relevant setting

While all interaction takes place in some setting, the participants draw on the layout in specific ways. The images in Plate 2.8 show that participants draw on a seemingly broader or narrower layout, depending upon the interaction.

In the first image, three boys are standing at the seashore. Here, a vast layout surrounds them, and they can move freely in each direction without hindrance. The next image shows two boys walking along a path. Here, the children employ a layout that is constructed by paths and vegetation, giving them the option to choose among only four directions.

While the children can move freely in the first image and their possible movements are shaped by the layout in the second image, the children only employ a very small part of the given layout in each case. In the first image, the children are walking into the waves, their gaze focused not far in front of them. In the second image, the child to the left in the picture focuses straight ahead, and does not take much notice of what the path has to offer to the right or the left; whereas the child to the right is looking to the right, exploring the path in that direction with his gaze, while his feet show that he keeps going straight.

The first image in the second row shows people in a shopping street, and when we look at what each group of people does, we see that they all employ one small aspect of the given layout. Take the couple to the left in the picture, for example. They are focused on the big bear. No doubt, the child (for whom the woman is pushing the stroller) is exploring the bear very closely, as the man in the group is holding on to the big

Plate 2.8 Layout.

stuffed animal, making sure that it does not fall over. Thus, we can say that these people are only utilizing this small part of the layout – focused upon the bear and its immediate surroundings.

The second image in this second row shows two children in a barrel, trying to cross a pond. While the man-made pond is fairly large and is itself part of an extensive park, the boys are only utilizing a small area of the vast layout in this interaction. Here, they focus on the long pole that they use as a paddle – with which they have to push themselves forward. They do not take any notice of the park, or even of the other barrel that is trying to cross the pond. They utilize their own barrel, the long pole, and only a small part of the pond that directly surrounds them.

The images in the last row show enclosed spaces in which participants are interacting. The first image shows two women sitting at a table, conversing. While this room is part of a large house, the women are only utilizing the table and chairs.

The very last image shows two children sitting in a toy car which is placed in a toy store. They are only utilizing the car from this much larger layout, so that we can say that the toys and the candy in the background have no impact on the immediate interaction between the children.

When incorporating layout into a multimodal interactional analysis, the analysis focuses on the very aspect of the layout that the participants are utilizing at any given moment. Sometimes, a whole house plays a part in an interaction; sometimes a street is important in an interaction; but, most often, the layout that is utilized by participants in a specific interaction is quite narrow.

Assignment

Observe three groups of people in different settings. Take pictures of the groups, and discuss which aspects of the layout are relevant in each one of these interactions.

INTERCONNECTION OF MODES

Modes of communication:	Modes are interdependent upon one another in many different ways.
	The actual hierarchical structure that modes assume to one another may be different in any given interaction, and has to be determined through analysis.

Embodied and disembodied

Communicative modes are usually intricately linked and have no true boundaries, just as there is no true boundary between the embodied/disembodied distinction. Communicative modes are heuristic or explanatory units that allow analysts to dissect complex interactions and enable the analysis of small parts, before analyzing how these parts work together to construct the complexity of face-to-face interactions.

Meaning and meaning potential

Each mode discussed can give *some* insight into the interactional meaning of an overall interaction. Yet, when analyzing the modes separately, the analyst should be very reluctant to assign meaning to any one mode. Any lower-level action – such as a postural positioning, a head movement, or an utterance – entails a meaning potential that can only be determined by its environment. As an example, let us think of the word "tree." "Tree," in itself, carries a meaning potential, but its specific meaning in any one utterance is determined by the surrounding words. Thus, it could be a big tree or a small tree, a leafy tree or a pine tree, and each time we would communicate something different when using the word "tree;" and each utterance of a phrase such as "big tree" again carries a meaning potential that can only be determined by its environment within the utterance.

The same is true for all movements. On p. 33, I asserted that nodding of the head has a one-to-one verbal meaning ("yes" in Western society), and I explained that the nodding of the head often is positioned as the second part of a question/answer adjacency pair. However, people can nod their heads for different reasons, so that the same movement, located in a different context, takes on different meaning. As an example, let us imagine a group of people standing at a bus stop waiting for a bus. One bus comes, but does not stop. The next bus comes, does stop, but obviously is the wrong bus for these people. Nobody moves, and the bus drives off. The next bus comes and, like the first, does not stop. Now, as the bus drives past, one of the people in the group nods and another person says *"yeah, I can't believe it, either."* Here, nodding does not mean yes. In fact, the nodding by itself could not have been understood by the other person, but it was clear that the facial expression of the person who was nodding showed displeasure and disbelief.

As this example shows, each communicative mode is linked to other modes. One action in one mode alone has a meaning potential, but the actual meaning of any one action performed by a social actor in one mode cannot be determined without understanding the environment within which it is located.

Interconnection and hierarchical structures

Embodied and disembodied modes are closely interconnected, so that any one mode is usually interdependent upon others. While distinctions between modes are useful and even essential for analytical purposes, such distinctions are always and only heuristic.

Individuals in interaction usually do not utilize one mode completely separately, which we can observe when watching somebody speaking on the phone. Often, people speaking on the phone gesticulate, even though the person on the other side of the line cannot see the gestures. Here, spoken language and gesture are closely linked, and the person who is speaking expresses experiences, thoughts, and feelings by utilizing these interdependent modes. Of course, people do not only use the modes of spoken language and gesture. Each individual always takes up some proxemic distance and some postural alignment towards others and towards objects. Participants utilize the immediate layout surrounding them, so that the layout always structures at least part of the interaction. Simultaneously, all participants in interaction may move their heads and utilize the mode of gaze.

Head movement is obviously often linked to the mode of gaze, and gaze is often interdependent with head movement and spoken language. Gaze, head movement, and gesture also influence the postural position of individuals; and, since gaze and gesture are often interdependent upon the mode of spoken language, we can see that all embodied modes interconnect. Simultaneously, social actors need to employ embodied modes in order to utilize disembodied modes. Gaze is a necessary component when reading, and gaze, in turn, influences other embodied modes such as posture.

While gesture and gaze are often subordinate to spoken language, this hierarchical structure cannot simply be assumed. When analyzing multimodal interaction, we do not want to assume any hierarchical structure of the modes, but want to analyze what we see in the videotaped data.

Videotaped data are vital for the multimodal interactional analyst, as they give us the option to revisit the same interaction again and again, focusing upon one mode at a time and then analyzing their interplay. Only when focusing on the real-time interactions without preconceived notions of hierarchical structures of modes, will we be able to discern the true value of each mode in a specific interaction.

Theoretical and methodological assumptions inform the analyst: expanding or constricting the analysis to a considerable degree. As an analyst, one can only observe what the theory and methodology make it possible to explore. Therefore, multimodal interactional analysis takes a broad view of interaction.

Concurrently, multimodal interactional analysis takes into consideration what has been discovered about each communicative mode so far. Many of the modes have been studied in relation to language – showing how these modes are subordinated. This literature is extremely important and valuable, as it demonstrates how and when other modes are dependent upon the mode of language.

However, as illustrated on pp. 38–41, gaze is not always dependent upon the mode of language, even when these two modes coincide. The same is true for other embodied modes that may be dependent upon spoken language in some interactions. These same embodied modes may take on the superordinate role in other interactions, and still coincide with the mode of spoken language. Thus, the mere presence of spoken language does not indicate that it is the central mode in a given interaction.

In order to demonstrate the interdependence of the various embodied communicative modes discussed so far, let us revisit the sociolinguistic interview from pp. 21–23 and the interaction in the accountant's office from pp. 30–32.

An informal sociolinguistic interview

The first image in Plate 2.9 shows Anna ironing during the sociolinguistic interview. In the second section of this chapter, discussing the mode of proxemics, I described the way in which Anna had placed heaps of clothing on all but one seat, which she declared to have left open for the researcher. Thus, the interviewee had prearranged the mode of layout, manipulating the mode of proxemics so that the proximity between her and the interviewer *felt* right to her. I say "felt right," because the mode of proxemics is culturally learned and binding on all concerned. People always feel more comfortable taking up a specific proximity to others in specific instances.

Certainly, the piles of clothing and the empty seat are not the only aspects of layout that are relevant in this interaction. The objects and their arrangements throughout the room communicate – having taken on the form of frozen actions. The leather chairs, the heavy, dark furniture, the piano, the rugs, the pictures on the walls, the plants, the curtain-less windows, are all of communicative value for the interviewer: informing about the social actors living within this space and also about the interactions that are going on within it.

Layout takes part in the integrative meaning-making of an interaction. Since Anna had piled clothes on all available chairs and had left room on the couch for just one person to sit, she had structured the interview before it had taken place. Visible in the layout, we find that the distance to the researcher, and Anna's posture and alignment, were pre-positioned before the actual event.

Anna's posture is clearly interdependent with her proxemic behavior and her use of layout, as she has positioned her body in such a way that she can perform the action of ironing without straining or having to move unnecessarily. Her back is straight, and her head bent, allowing Anna to move her gaze from her left hand to the piece of clothing and the iron in her right hand.

Anna's postural position allows her to gaze slightly to the left, to look at the TV, or slightly to the right, to make eye contact with the interviewer. Since Anna is standing, and the interviewer is sitting, Anna does not have to move her head in order to see her.

Looking at Anna's feet, we see that they are turned slightly to the right. They are not aligned with the rest of her bodily posture, but point away from the ironing board. Anna's feet point to the seat in which the interviewer is sitting. Thus, part of Anna's posture is structured by her actions

Plate 2.9 Interconnection of modes.

of ironing and watching TV, while another part of her posture, the positioning of her feet, is structured by the interview.

Anna's gaze follows her actions of ironing, and the images on the TV screen, but it is structured by her engagement with the interviewer. Once in a while she peeks behind her, while keeping an eye on Katie. She shifts her gaze from one action to another, synchronizing it with the other actions that she performs, and when she looks at the interviewer, she does not place the iron on a new piece of clothing, but rather performs an action on the ironing board that does not require her to utilize the mode of gaze.

The following transcribed excerpt of a brief section of this interview shows that Anna's gaze is structured by the mode of spoken language.

(1) Anna: (ironing and gazing down) I intensely cultivate
(2) (ironing and gazing down) friendships.
(3) (lifting the iron) that is extremely
(4) (shifting gaze to interviewer) important to me

Here, gaze is sequentially structured by the utterances, and the mode of spoken language takes the central position. Anna looks at the interviewer at the end of the phrase in line (4), while she has been looking at her manual actions of ironing when gaze was not necessary for the fluency of the conversation. Simultaneously, the action of ironing is here subordinated to the action of speaking.

The gaze shift towards the hearer, essential in focused conversation, structures Anna's action of ironing, so that she lifts the iron off the piece of clothing before she shifts her gaze to the hearer. This example stands in contrast to the dentist–patient–assistant–guardian interaction on pp. 38–41 of this chapter, in which gaze took on the central role for the dentist.

Interaction in an accounting firm

In the second image, the accountant is pointing at a form which is lying on his assistant's desk. He has moved his upper body forward in order to reach the form with his outstretched index finger. His head and gaze are aligned with the outstretched arm, so that his whole upper body is engaged in this action of pointing. He simultaneously utilizes print; proxemics to the form and his assistant; posture; head movement; gaze; gesture; and spoken language, saying "*you put it here*," to answer his assistant's question.

All of the modes utilized by the accountant play an equally important role at this moment. The stroke of the deictic movement, expressing the meaning that can roughly be translated into "*here*," coincides with the words "*put it*," and thus precedes the equivalent message sent by the mode of spoken language. Without a deictic gesture, this utterance cannot be interpreted correctly.

Rather than looking at the gesture–posture–head movement–gaze deictic message as an appendix to language and viewing language as the central mode, language is at this instance simply a part of this meaning-making aggregate. The accountant uses a gesture–posture–head movement–gaze–utterance deictic meaning aggregate to communicate with his assistant, which is only possible through his use of the mode of layout, proxemics, and print. Here, language takes on no particular intensity, as the modes are tightly interconnected and together send a coherent message.

Assignment

The next time that you speak to your friends – ready to tell them something that you have experienced and in some way feel strongly about – try to speak without gesticulating. Keep your hands/arms in a rest position, and observe yourself. What happened? Discuss in class how you felt.

The next time that you eat lunch with somebody, try not to look at the person at all. Keep your gaze fixed on your plate, but do talk. Observe what happens.

Now watch a one-minute dyadic interaction on video, but, while observing all participants, focus especially on one individual. You will have to watch this interaction many times. Take advantage of the pause button, and note down which embodied and disembodied modes the participants rely on, and how these modes are interconnected. Then watch the interaction again, and try to discern if and/or when the modes are hierarchically structured.

3 Multimodal transcription

Some basic research questions:	How/when are communicative modes utilized separately?
	How/when are communicative modes interdependent?
	Do individuals express their experiences, thoughts, and feelings by employing several modes simultaneously in a synchronized and/or a contradictory fashion?

Transcription beyond language

In the last chapter, you were asked to watch a videotaped one-minute dyadic interaction; to note down which embodied and disembodied modes the participants relied on; and to discern if and when the modes were hierarchically structured. Undoubtedly you would have realized just how difficult the assignment was, when you worked on it. Such an assignment is nearly impossible to complete without a fully fledged multimodal transcription system.

But, very functional transcription systems are already available. In linguistics, and particularly discourse analysis, analysts have developed a way of hearing spoken language in intonation units, making the transcription process relatively easy. Linguists have developed transcription systems that are easily readable and understandable, by only adding the amount of detail that is necessary for a particular analysis. Some of the systems have been developed for quantitative analysis and others for qualitative analysis.

Multimodal interactional analysis is a qualitative methodology, as the research interest is of a qualitative nature. Qualitative discourse analysis is well developed, and often analysts add descriptions of nonverbal behavior in such transcripts, using the mode of language.

When looking at an interaction between a teacher and her students in a first-grade English–German bilingual classroom, it becomes apparent that transcription of such classroom discourse only begins with the transcription of the spoken utterances and the inclusion of nonverbal behavior.

The following exchange occurred when a teacher was working with a group of four students. All students in this group are native English speakers with limited ability to express themselves in German. Here, the teacher explains the word *"Graben"* ["moat"] without telling the students overtly. The teacher (T) and each student (Bob, Joe, Jim, and Jon) have a handout with an image of a castle and a moat around it in front of them. The teacher has turned her handout around for the students to see what she is pointing at.

Transcription conventions:

German utterances:	in italics.
Translations:	[in square brackets]
Descriptions:	(in parentheses)
Emphasis:	in CAPITALS
Overlap:	indicated [by these brackets

In the following excerpt, the teacher is pointing and speaking, when Bob suddenly focuses on something very different in his handout:

(1) T: *das ist Wasser* [that is water]
(2)   *was da rund rum ist* [which is all around there]
                     (pointing to the water)
(3) Bob: A GUY
(4) Jim: mountain. (looking at T's pointing finger)
(5) Joe: ground. (looking at T's pointing finger)
(6) T: *nein passt mal auf,*   [no look here,]
(7)   *hier das ist die Mauer ja,* [here that's the wall right,]
                     (pointing at the wall in the picture)
(8) Bob: a guy (almost inaudible)
(9) Jim: ⌈ (postural shift)
(10) Joe: ⌊ (gaze shift to Bob, then to Bob's handout)
(11) T: ⌈ *hört mal zu,*   [listen,]
(12) Jon: ⌊ (postural shift and gaze shift to Bob)
(13) T: *das ist die Mauer* [that's the wall]
(14) Jim: (gaze shift to Bob, then to Bob's handout)

(15) T: und da rund rum ist noch was,
              [and there around there is something else,]
(16) Bob: I JUST found a GUY!
(17) Joe: (pointing at own handout) A GUY right HERE
(18) Jon: (gaze shift to Joe's handout/Joe's finger) that's a guarder
(19) T: (gaze shift to Joe's pointer, then Bob) ja, da IST einer
              [yes, there IS someone]

In lines (1) through (15) the teacher follows her agenda of trying to get the students to understand the word "*Graben*" ["moat"]. While talking, the teacher notices that the students are shifting their focus, and reminds them to listen in line (11). The students' shift in focus is apparent in their postural shifts; their gazing to Bob and to the image in his handout, trying to figure out what exactly Bob is looking at; and, of course, their spoken language.

Bob is excited that he found a guy, Joe and Jon chime in and the teacher acknowledges in line (19) that there really *is* a guy, whom she had not focused on before (which is apparent in her intonation of *ist*). Here she shares the children's excitement of having found a person in the picture. The teacher's refocusing to what is interesting to her students results in a conversation or a contingent discourse that is closely anchored in the experiential world.

In a setting like this, the images play as much of a role as the spoken language and the nonverbal behavior. The students' gaze direction, their pointing to certain parts of an image, their facial expressions, and their postural shifts, all communicate to the teacher – just as the teacher's gestures, facial expression, and body posture communicate to the students. All of these communicative acts can be transcribed. While this is possible by using only language as the mode of transcription, transcripts become much richer when we incorporate images. Such images allow us to perceive details that we cannot easily distinguish in a transcript that only utilizes language.

When trying to answer some basic multimodal interactional questions as indicated at the beginning of this chapter, we see the need for multimodal transcripts to help visualize and present the ongoing face-to-face (inter)actions.

Multimodal transcripts allow the visualization of participants' lower-level actions, so that the analyst has visual records of the ongoing interaction, providing them with documents for analysis. Subsequently, multimodal transcripts allow the analyst to present their findings to others.

The processes of *transcribing for analysis*, and *transcribing to explicate the analysis*, are complex. The latter follows naturally from the former, so that the transcripts to present an analysis grow out of the many transcripts that first allow that analysis of a complex interaction.

METHOD OF VIDEO ANALYSIS

Multimodal transcripts:	Facilitate the analysis of complex (inter)-actions.
	Allow the presentation of complex multimodal analyses to others.

Methodological steps

Multimodal analysis requires multimodal data, and a video camera is currently the best tool to collect records of the audio and the visual aspects of real-time interactions.

Ethics:	In the US, issues about ethics in human research have recently been discussed widely. In academic institutions, research falls under the regulation of the Institutional Review Board (IRB), which regulates any human research that is conducted in the US and/or by US researchers anywhere in the world. While the IRB was established to regulate medical research, all human subject research is regulated by this board.
	The research that is conducted in the social sciences is certainly of a different order to medical research, and the need for such regulation is highly debated
	In the social sciences it is common practice to always conduct research in a highly ethical way, and participants are asked for permission.
	I always have the participants fill out a form in which they agree to be videotaped and to give me the right to use their pictures in publications.
	I always stay in touch with my participants, calling them up with questions if necessary or doing playback sessions (in which the participants can give me their view of what was going on in a particular interaction).
	Then, I always put together a CD for each participant that includes their video clip(s) and the section(s)/paper(s) in which I use their images. This is my way of *giving something back* to the participants.
	For an interactional analyst, it is of utmost importance to work together with your participants. Such working-together, of course, can only be achieved by using the highest ethical standards.

Data collection

Data collection is always interlinked with theoretical, methodological, and analytical decisions that influence the analysis, but are made long before review of the data. Such decisions relate to what is actually recorded and what the analyst chooses to leave out; to the camera position; and the supplementary data collection. Although a video camera can record face-to-face interaction quite well, a video camera can never record everything going on around the interaction that is being filmed. The camera angle is limited, and the positioning of the camera always focuses on a certain section of the interaction, to the exclusion of others.

Supplementary data – such as fieldnotes – come in very handy for later analysis. Such fieldnotes should include aspects of the surrounding environment that the video camera does not catch. For example, if we are taping a family dinner and the camera is focused on the table, but there is a dog sitting next to the door, we need to note that fact down. We may not analyze the tape until much later, and we may have forgotten all about the dog by then. However, it is possible and even likely that some of the participants are actually reacting to the dog in some way.

Data log

When collecting video data, I recommend logging each tape the same day that it is recorded. The sooner that one fills out the log, the easier it is. Such a log should start out with the date and some fieldnotes – a description of the nonrecorded setting and any mention of other factors that may have influenced the interaction. We note down as much as we can, and try not to worry about whether or not something that we are noting down is actually influencing the interaction that we are studying. Often, one cannot determine the actual significance of a dog by a door, or outside noises, until one analyzes the tape later. We may also note down things that turn out to be irrelevant to the participants, but may seem relevant to us at the time of jotting them down. However, that is also something that we will be able to discern later. More is always better in this case.

Besides this description, we log the number and names of the participants, the time of day, the time on the tape, and the length of the interaction. Then we describe the interaction in our own words. If we have recorded a dinner, we include a description of what the participants are eating, as they will most likely refer to some of the food by using specific demonstratives, without naming the food that they are referring to. The topics of discussion which are most prevalent in the interaction should also be noted in the log.

A sample data log is given below. As we will see, the description should include our view of aspects of the interaction. Whether or not this is relevant information will not become apparent until one analyzes the interaction. Students are often surprised by just how useful their own insights are when they are analyzing the events in detail, and they also realize that they have forgotten these tiny details of prior interactions that are relevant.

Sample data log	
Recorded:	June 2, 2003
Time:	6:30–7:15 p.m.
Tape # 1:	From beginning of tape
Interaction:	Family dinner
Participants:	Mother, father, Julie (1½), David (5), Monica (11)
Food:	Curried chicken, rice, mixed green salad
Topics:	School day (Monica) Sports event (David) Work issues of mother Work issues of father
Description:	The family dog moved about between the door and the kitchen. Although nobody addressed the dog, Julie in particular kept following the dog with her gaze.
	David often looked out of the window, because his friends were playing ball outside. He also shifted in his seat a lot; it seemed that he would rather have joined his friends.
	The father was distracted in the beginning. He had received an unpleasant phone call before he sat down for dinner, and still seemed preoccupied with the call.
	Monica had had a wonderful day at school and couldn't wait to tell her father about her A in a math test. Yet, the father's reaction was slow (because of the call, I think), although he takes up this topic again later and his reaction is positive and makes Monica happy.
	Julie did not nap even though she had not slept much the night before, and she is very cranky. The mother seems to hurry to get Julie to bed early, although she never says anything about Julie's need for sleep.

Video data

Once the interaction is recorded, and before transcribing it, we have to transfer the video to a computer. Depending on the computer system, there are various ways to do that, and I will not go into detail here.

64 *Multimodal transcription*

Multimodal interactional analysis relies on qualitative methods, and the video data need to be organized on the computer in order to accommodate this type of analysis. The best way of organizing video data is by transferring one interaction as one clip (i.e. the above dinnertime interaction would be one clip). Hereby we have to be careful to keep a log of each clip in a separate file, using some of the same information as in the data log, making it possible for us to easily find particular interactions and the matching descriptions.

Thus, the clip log for the dinnertime interaction that is illustrated in the data log above should include the following information:

Recorded: June 2, 2003
Time: 6:30–7:15 p.m.
Tape #1: From beginning of tape
Interaction: Family dinner
Participants: Mother, father, Julie (1½), David (5), Monica (11)
Topics: School day (Monica)
Sports event (David)
Work issues of mother
Work issues of father

As soon as the data are converted into computer-based clips, one can play and replay the interactions in order to select representative samples, and we are ready to transcribe specific instances.

Method of transcription

Transcribing video data is a complicated undertaking, and always involves multiple methodological steps. In the beginning, we want to find a brief instance of about 30–45 seconds, as the process of transcribing multimodal data is extremely complex. Goodwin emphasizes the process of transcription and representation of multimodal analyses:

> The complexity of the phenomena involved requires multiple methods for rendering relevant distinctions ... any transcription system must attend simultaneously to two separate fields, looking in one direction at how to accurately recover through a systematic notation the endogenous structure of the events being investigated, while simultaneously keeping an eye on the addressee/reader of the analysis by attempting to present relevant descriptions as clearly and vividly as possible.
> (Goodwin, 2001: 161)

The task of multimodal transcription is a task of translating the visual and audio aspects into some printable format. Video captures help in this process, as the images themselves communicate modes that are not easily translated into language. One such example is the mode of color, which is used in magazines as a highly elaborated mode, and yet, as Kress and Van Leeuwen have noted, it is not easily translatable. Similarly, exact body posture takes many words to describe, while an image illustrates a posture much more clearly and easily. The mode of (particularly recorded) music, on the other hand, is still not easily translated.

Multimodal transcription is a constant interplay between analysis and method of description, and, of course, is always based in theoretical assumptions. The task of a multimodal transcript is not to analyze the images that are incorporated, but rather to use the images to describe the dynamic unfolding of specific moments in time, in which the layout and modes like posture, gesture, and gaze play as much a part as the verbal.

These multimodal transcripts, like any transcripts, reflect the theory of the researcher. Communicative modes are taken to be equally important within the interactions. However, the images, due to their salience in the multimodal transcripts, highlight the visual aspects within interaction. The verbal is positioned in relation to aspects of other modes, and is thus de-emphasized. Spoken language in these transcripts is presented as waves, emphasizing prosodic effects of speech.

In traditional discourse analysis, nonverbal aspects and features of the setting are usually taken as context. In order to show their importance in interaction, these communicative modes are highlighted within these multimodal transcripts. At the same time, the prominence of spoken language is generally taken for granted in the field of discourse analysis, making it essential in a multimodal analysis to de-emphasize spoken language. By de-emphasizing spoken language, we are not taking away the importance of spoken language, but are rather accentuating the other communicative modes that are as essential in interaction as spoken language.

Embodied and disembodied modes of communication are employed by social actors in order to communicate complete messages, which often integrate several conflicting messages. An individual can, for example, convey solidarity and dominance simultaneously. While visual modes of communication are difficult to interpret without interpreting the mode of spoken language, spoken language is also difficult to interpret to its fullest extent without interpreting other accompanying modes.

STEP-BY-STEP TRANSCRIPTION

Multimodal transcripts entail numerous transcripts of any one interaction. During transcribing, communicative modes are first kept separated (as far as that is possible), and transcripts display spoken language, images, and/or descriptions. In a finished transcript, images are combined with speech – displaying the most important aspects of the interaction.

66 *Multimodal transcription*

In order to illustrate *how* to transcribe, I have devised a step-by-step guide for multimodal transcription. First, we complete a transcript for each communicative mode; then combine two or more; and finally, combine all of our individual transcripts to present a complete transcript.

In this guide I first introduce how to transcribe each mode. This *how-to* information is followed by practical examples, although I do not show each step there. Rather, I show some transcripts for one mode alone; and show a transcript for two modes; and sometimes, I just provide a description of how to transcribe a mode.

The practical example draws on a one-minute-long section of a video clip, showing a web-designer working from her home while she is watching her little girl. The transcribed interaction shows the web-designer speaking on the phone with a client at a moment when she does most of the talking. Simultaneously, she is watching her daughter: picking her up and putting her back on the floor.

Spoken language

Some conventions:	• Punctuation reflects intonation, not grammar.
Spoken language:	• ⎡Brackets show overlap: ⎣two voices at once.
	• CAPITALS indicate emphatic stress.
	• Numbers in parentheses ( ) indicate length of pauses in seconds.
	• — marks a glottal stop or abrupt cutting off of sound.
	• 0:00 indicates the minute and second of the beginning of an utterance.
	• Speaker changes (and noises) are marked by the time in the clip.

Spoken language is the mode that is transcribed first. The reasoning behind this is twofold: first, spoken language has a high information value; and second, due to our educational training, which places great importance on the mode of language, we are generally more inclined to consciously make sense of what a speaker is *saying* than to notice what a speaker is expressing in other modes. Here, we can choose from a multitude of current transcription conventions. I prefer to use conventions from a variety of sources, including the systems designed by Gail Jefferson (Sacks *et al.*, 1974: 731–733) and Tannen (1984); and I have added the notion of

A web-designer on the phone – spoken language

In a verbal transcript we provide the line number for later reference, then the name of the speaker, followed by the utterance. At every point when another speaker begins speaking (or is making a noise), we also provide the time of the clip in minutes and seconds, and sometimes in milliseconds when that is crucial for the analysis. Recording the exact time of speaker changes allows us to match and combine transcripts more easily later.

Certainly, we transcribe the spoken discourse from general to specific, so that we will first only have a broad transcript without much detail, that we can then develop further, providing the overlaps, the pitch, and the intonation at the end of an utterance. I will leave out these broader steps and only present a detailed transcript of this minute of interaction.

(1)	5:06	*Web-designer:*	when you're trying to publish,
(2)			I think,
(3)			it tries to grab that one page,
(4)			that you made changes to
(5)			so
(6)			I was hop—
(7)			I was thinking,
(8)			if you
(9)	5:14	*Baby:*	UH UH AH,
(10)	5:15	*Web-designer:*	[that if you have that
(11)	5:17	*Baby:*	⎡ UH UH AH,
(12)	5:17	*Web-designer:*	⎣ if you try to change
(13)			you would know,
(14)			if your publishing had worked,
(15)			I don't know if that's correct though.
(16)			I'M NOT REALLY SURE.
(17)			hhh I guess what I'm saying
(18)			⎡ is try to publish it,
(19)	5:33	*Baby:*	⎣ aAHH
(20)		*Web-designer:*	hh and then we'll SEE. (4)
(21)			whAT are you doing?
(22)			she's sucking on her fingers,
(23)			she's sucking on her fingers
(24)			and I just picked her up hh (3)
(25)	5:54	*Baby:*	AH
(26)	5:54.45		I'm I guess,
(27)			I got off the phone to you,

68 *Multimodal transcription*

(28) and I fixed that problem,
(29) and just thought, (2)
(30) 6:00 *Baby*: UH UH UH
(31) 6:06 *Web-designer*: do you ahm,
(32) OK it's FIXED.

Proxemics

Some conventions: **Proxemics**	First we provide an initial still image that shows the distance that the participants are taking up to one another and to relevant objects (we start this visual transcript at the same time in the clip as the verbal transcript).
	Then, we provide images for each change in proxemic behavior by the participants and mark the time in minutes and seconds (milliseconds) of the clip.

When transcribing proxemics, we visualize the distance that participants take up to others and to relevant objects. Often, the distance that participants take up to others does not change much throughout an interaction. When we are investigating a dinnertime interaction, for example, everybody takes up a position around the table, and does not move much. However, there are also instances when this distance changes during an interaction.

In the case where there is no change in the participants' proxemic behavior during the interaction that we are studying, one video capture of the participants may be enough. However, if the participants move about in the setting, we note this down by taking a snapshot of every completed move. Here, we also record the exact time in the clip when the movement is performed. These still images can then be transferred to a document and placed in order, according to the time.

Posture

Some conventions: **Posture**	First we provide an initial still image that shows the posture that the participants are taking up.
	Then we illustrate every postural change by each participant, and mark the time in minutes, seconds, and milliseconds of the clip.

When transcribing posture, we focus on one participant at a time while watching a brief segment of recorded tape, noting the exact time in seconds and milliseconds of when a postural shift occurs. As with audio transcription, we move from broad transcription to more detailed transcription. The first transcript should indicate which participant changes their body posture at which time in the clip.

Next, we take snapshots of each postural shift – looking at one individual at a time. Postural shifts are often one–two shifts. This means that a person shifts their posture from one position that they had taken up for a while to another. Therefore, we usually have to take two snapshots to illustrate the movement. Sometimes, postural shifts are accomplished through a middle step, which I call a mid-shift hold, in which case, we illustrate this shift in three images.

Throughout the transcription process, we discover that the embodied communicative modes are intricately intertwined and very difficult to keep completely separate. However, by focusing on the specific mode of posture – or any other communicative mode – during transcription, we learn how posture is linked to gesture, gaze, and spoken language.

There will also be other movements that are very difficult to place. For example, when the web-designer picks up her daughter, as illustrated below, she does not really change her distance to the little girl. Also we cannot say that the web-designer is shifting from an open to a closed posture when she is bending down to pick up the child. Yet, this is certainly a noteworthy movement and needs to be illustrated. Once the mode of proxemics and the postural behavior of all participants are transcribed, it is time to combine these two transcripts.

A web-designer on the phone – proxemics and posture

Plate 3.1 demonstrates a combined transcript of proxemics and posture for the interaction of the web-designer speaking on the phone with her client while she is watching her daughter.

Gesture

Some conventions: *Gesture*	We illustrate the onset or rest position, then the stroke or highest position, and then the retracted or rest position of the gesture; and the highest and lowest position for a beat.
	Some gestures should also be illustrated by showing the mid-points of the preparation and/or the retraction. If the gesture includes a post-stroke hold, we indicate it with a separate image.
	We always mark the exact times of the stills in the clip.

70 *Multimodal transcription*

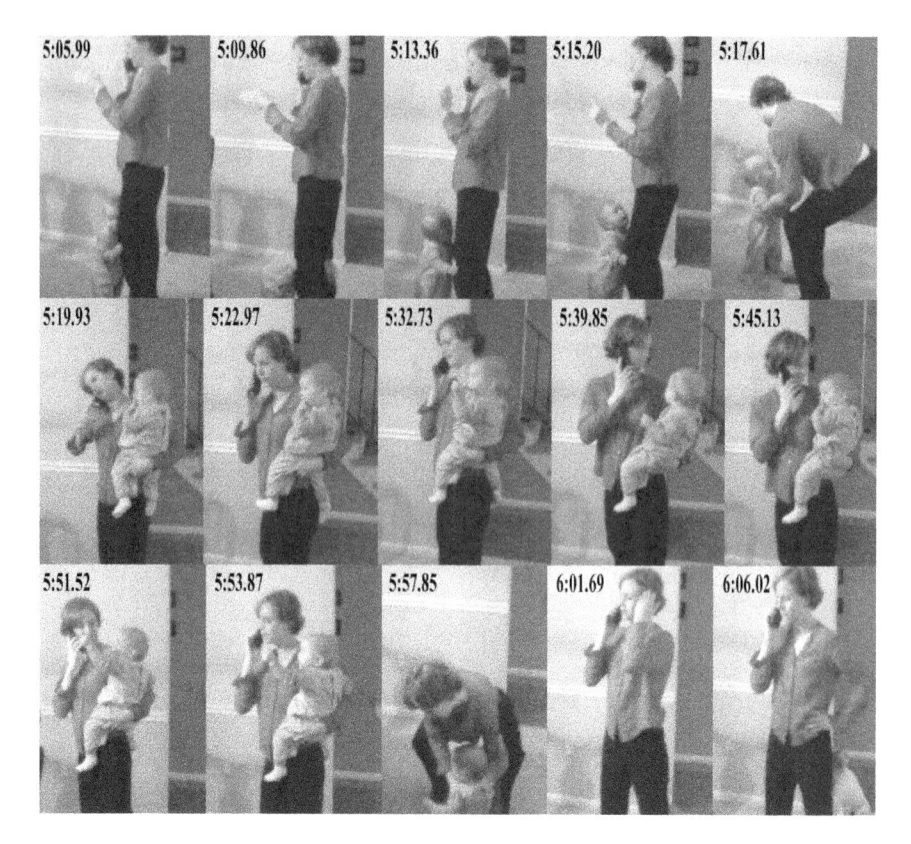

Plate 3.1 Transcript: proxemics and posture.

All iconic, metaphoric, and deictic gestures should be transcribed by showing (at least) the onset, the stroke, and the retraction of the gesture. Often it is also valuable to show the mid-point of a phase.

Beat gestures often come in twos or threes. Certainly, not every beat has to be illustrated, as the beats are usually almost exactly identical. Illustrating the highest/lowest points of the up/down or back/forth movement once, and indicating the number of times that the individual performs the gesture, are sufficient. Beat gestures can be performed with the head or the shoulders at the same time as a person performs a beat gesture with the hand/arm or finger. When this happens, these movements are usually synchronized, so that two still photos will show all of the beats that are being performed by the same person.

A web-designer on the phone – gesture

Plate 3.2 shows a transcript, illustrating the communicative mode of gesture in the interaction.

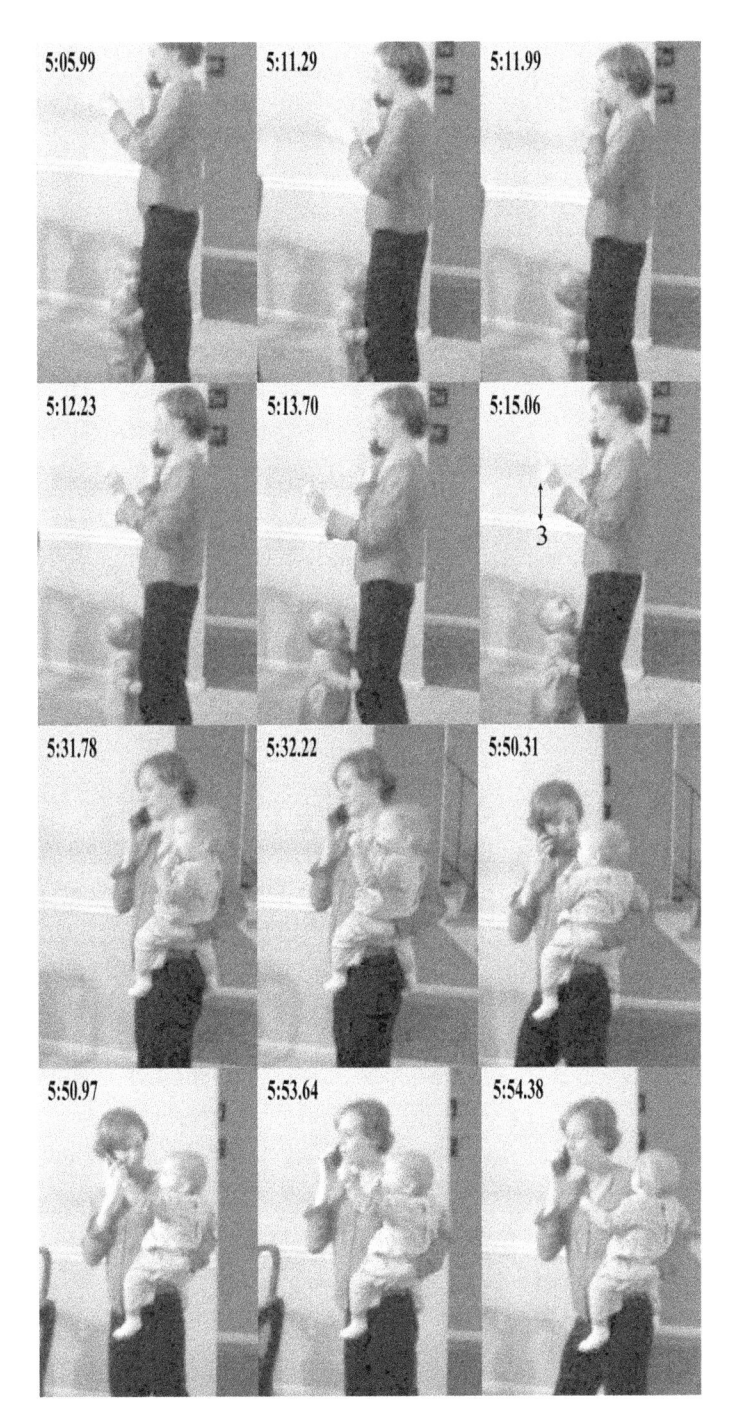

Plate 3.2 Transcript: gesture.

Head movement

Some conventions: *Head movement*	We illustrate the rest position and then the newly taken up position of the head for each participant.
	Some head movements are of a deictic, iconic, or metaphoric nature, and should be illustrated in three images.
	Some deictic head movements include a post-stroke hold, which is indicated with a separate image.
	The exact times of the stills in the clip are indicated in the transcript.

Head movement is transcribed by indicating the rest position followed by the furthest point of the movement. Many head movements have a clear one–two phase, so that an individual who has taken up a head position will change it to a different one.

If a participant is nodding (sagittal movement) or shaking the head (rotational movement) there often are several nods or shakes, and we illustrate one nod or shake and the quantity of the movement.

Gaze

Some conventions: *Gaze*	We illustrate any change in gaze direction that can be perceived.
	Often, gaze is organized by structured interaction, as described by Kendon and Goodwin.
	Just as often, participants look in one direction for a while, then change the direction and look in another direction for a while.
	Again, the exact times of the stills in the corresponding clip are indicated.

By now, we have noticed that we are taking stills at the same time in our clip, but for different reasons. This overlap will become even more apparent now that we are looking at gaze.

Participants gaze in the same directions as the positions of their heads allow, and many of the stills that were taken initially will show that this is true. Yet this cannot be assumed, and we do want to put together a gaze transcript that illustrates where the participants are looking, indicating every directional change with an image and the exact timing.

Certainly we cannot determine with certainty what an individual is gazing at. But, since we are interested in the interactional value of gaze, we need to focus on the participants and determine how they themselves react to each other's gaze. Once head movement and gaze of all participants are transcribed, these two transcripts are combined.

A web-designer on the phone – head movement and gaze

Plate 3.3 demonstrates a transcript that combines the two modes of head movement and gaze in the interaction.

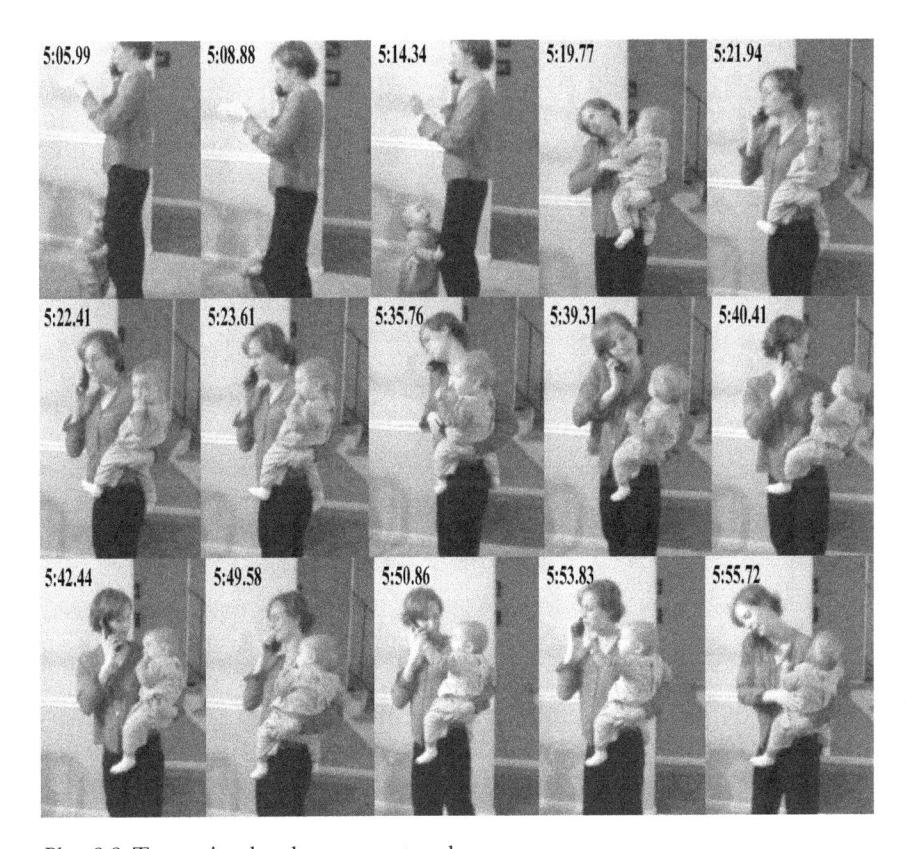

Plate 3.3 Transcript: head movement and gaze.

Music

Some conventions: **Music:**	
Embodied	We add musical notation to the images at the correct times.
Disembodied	We indicate the exact time of the onset and end of the music in the transcript (if this is relevant) by adding a description box above the stills.
	The description box has to indicate the type and rhythm of the music, and may indicate some of the lyrics (if they are relevant).

When transcribing music as an embodied mode, we use musical notation in the transcript. However, when transcribing music as a disembodied mode, we determine what is most important about that music.

In many interactions, people are listening to background music, and often a brief description of the music – indicating the type and the rhythm of the music – is as much as can be done. We want to watch carefully if the participants are moving, gesturing, or speaking in the rhythm of that music, as such rhythmic coordination demonstrates that the participants are utilizing that mode, and this needs to be indicated in the transcript. At other times, we may want to transcribe some of the lyrics.

Print

Some conventions: *Print*	We add an image that shows how the participants are using printed media. Such images usually fall under fair use.
	When adding an image of printed media that shows the pictures/text of a magazine, CD-ROM, or the like, we need to obtain permission.
	Instead of a particular picture or text, we can add a description of the print in a textbox.

Print should be visualized if it is important in an interaction. Although the visualization of printed material is certainly easy enough to do by simply taking a picture of it, the mode of print brings with it other problems when it comes to transcription.

When transcribing print, we have to be aware of the copyright laws that pertain to it. Are we taking an image of a magazine page that clearly shows an image or an article in the magazine? If so, this requires permission. Or are we showing a person reading a magazine where the images or print in the magazine are not clearly determinable? In this case, use of the printed material possibly falls under fair use (to find out more about fair use and copyright laws in the US see: http://www.copyright.gov/fls/fairuse.html).

Sometimes, it is useful to obtain permission, because a particular piece of print needs to be illustrated to show that it is linked to the interaction. Other times, a description of the printed material is enough for the analysis, which then does not entail the permission process and/or fee. I have also found that permissions may be rendered for free as long as you are using images or text for academic purposes. This, however, is something that you should not assume. Each time that we are using an image of a picture or text, we need to contact the primary source and establish their copyright policies.

Often print takes an integral part, so that a participant is actually reading a newspaper or a magazine – referring to something that is seen in the printed media. If that is the case, one can simply transcribe what the participants are reading or saying, since that is the part in the magazine or newspaper that is most relevant to the interaction.

Layout

Some conventions: *Layout*	Relevant layout for the interaction is usually visible in other still images.
	When participants draw on an extended layout, we visualize this with an additional still.

The layout often does not need to be transcribed separately, as the setting and the objects that participants are utilizing in the interaction are usually visualized in most of the stills. We only need a separate image if the participants in the interaction draw on aspects of the layout that are not shown in other images.

A complete transcript

Some conventions: *Final transcript*	We assemble the final transcript according to the timed utterances, gaze and postural shifts, gestures, and so on. There is much overlap in the images of the various singly transcribed modes, telling us much of the intricacy of an interaction, and we want to note these observations in a separate document.

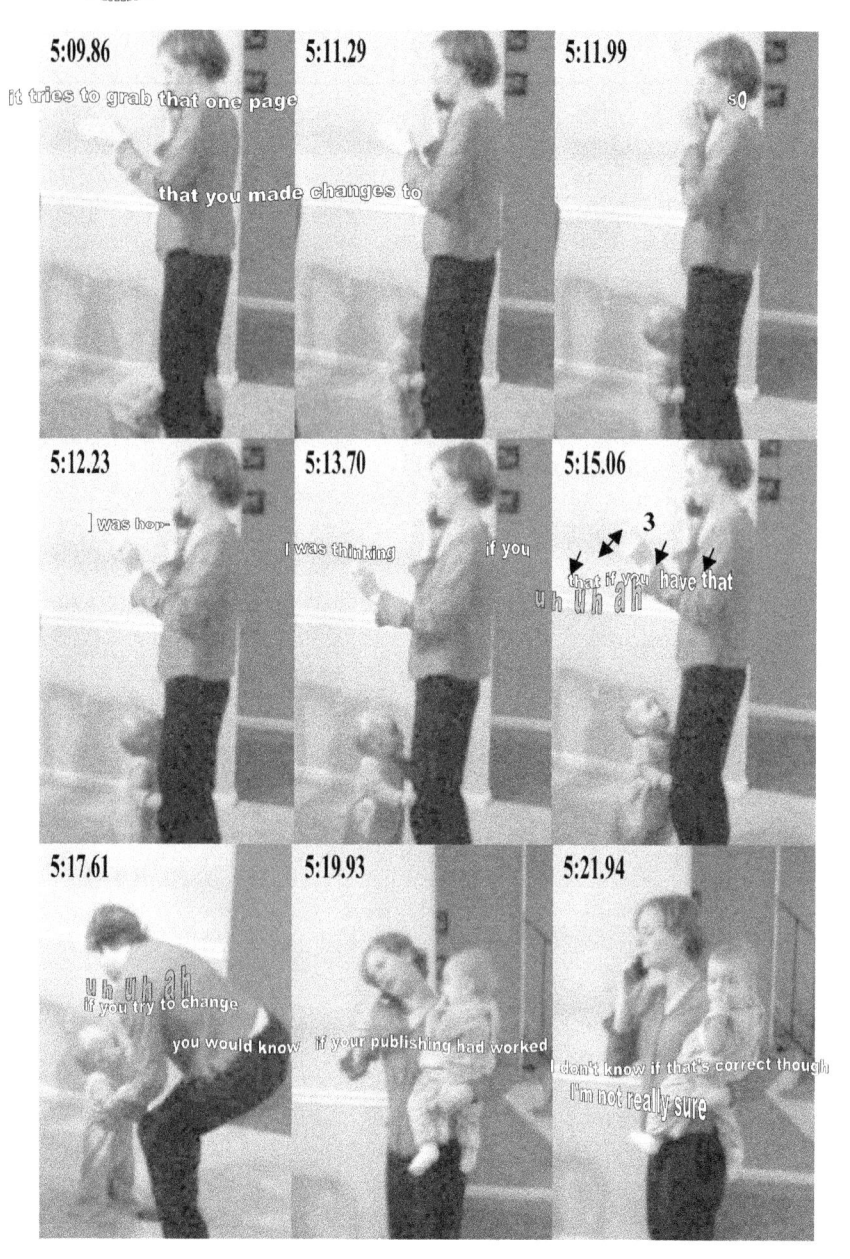

Plate 3.4 Multimodal transcript.

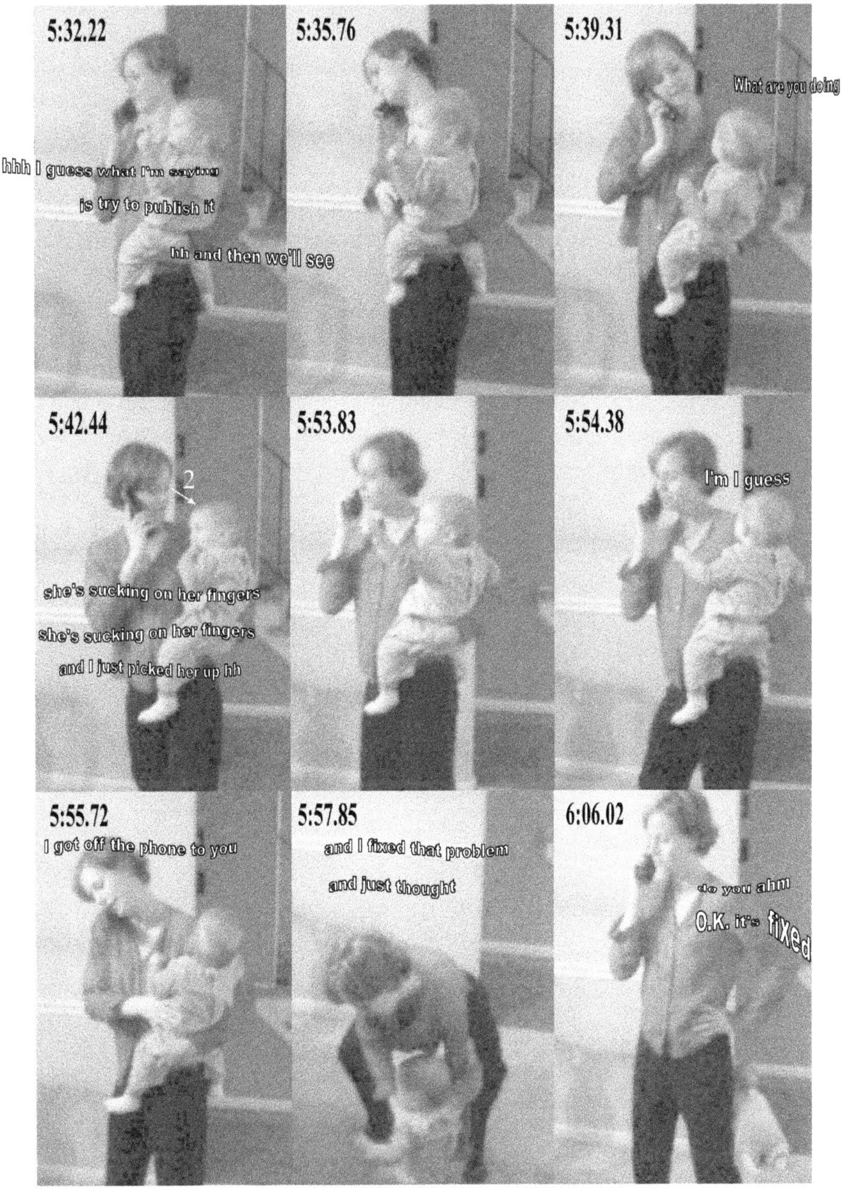
5:32.22
hhh I guess what I'm saying
is try to publish it
hh and then we'll see
5:35.76
5:39.31
What are you doing
5:42.44
2
she's sucking on her fingers
she's sucking on her fingers
and I just picked her up hh
5:53.83
5:54.38
I'm I guess
5:55.72
I got off the phone to you
5:57.85
and I fixed that problem
and just thought
6:06.02
do you ahm
O.K. it's fixed

78 *Multimodal transcription*

> In the final transcript, arrows and numbers can sometimes be substituted for several images that show specific movements. We visualize the rising and lowering of intonation by transcribing utterances as curves; pitch by size and boldness of letters; pauses by spaces between letters or utterances; and overlap by closeness/touching of utterances. Speakers are distinguished by utilizing different colors or fonts.
>
> Translations, if necessary (which may also include word-for-word translations depending upon the focus of study) should be given in a textbox as close as possible to the actual utterance. In a (if necessary, color-coded) translation box, we mark the utterances as spoken language by not capitalizing the beginning; use a diffferent line for each utterance; and do not use punctuation marks as the prosodic effects, which are not truly translatable, are visible in the original language of the speaker in the multimodal transcript.

The assembly of a complete transcript is our last step. Here, we combine all prior transcripts, including the spoken language one, and this final transcript reflects the actual interaction as clearly as possible, excluding unimportant images.

Each step in the transcription process is also a step in the analysis. Therefore, we do not delete the single-mode, dual-mode, etc. transcripts, but rather refer to them again later during further analysis.

Furthermore, when transcribing, we always note our insights in a separate document, which we draw on during the final transcription process, when combining transcripts, as well as during further analysis.

A web-designer on the phone – final transcript

Plate 3.4 illustrates a final transcript.

Assignment

Now look again at the one-minute-long interaction that you were describing for the assignment in the last chapter, and complete all of the transcripts as discussed above.

4 Modal density

MODAL DENSITY THROUGH INTENSITY OR COMPLEXITY

Modal density:	Can be achieved either through modal intensity or modal complexity (or both).
Modal intensity:	The more intensity or weight that a mode carries, the higher the modal density.
Modal complexity:	The more intricately intertwined the multiple modes are, the higher the modal density.
Weight of a mode:	The weight of a mode can be determined by the higher-level action.
High modal intensity:	A mode that changes the higher-level action if the mode is discontinued always comprises *high modal intensity*.
Medium modal intensity:	A mode that changes the higher-level action only slightly if the mode is discontinued comprises *medium modal intensity*.
Low modal intensity:	A mode that does not change the higher-level action if it is discontinued comprises *low modal intensity*.

Modal density refers to the modal intensity and/or the modal complexity through which a higher-level action is constructed.

The intensity, weight, or importance of specific modes in interaction are determined by the situation, the social actors, and other social and environmental factors involved. Therefore, the weight of any specific mode changes from one interaction to the next, and may change within an interaction.

80 *Modal density*

The complexity and multiplicity of modes in interaction is dependent upon the participants' lower-level actions that construct the higher-level actions. Any higher-level action is constructed through interplay among a multiplicity of communicative modes. Social actors draw on certain embodied modes such as spoken language, gaze, gesture, posture, and proxemics. At the same time, the social actors may employ disembodied modes, such as listening to recorded music or reading magazines together.

Modal density may also be achieved through the interplay of several moderately intense modes. The number and weight of the modes is always dependent upon the actual situation. Thus, during a phone conversation, spoken language is a highly intense mode, since it is the one mode that allows the participants to communicate on the phone.

The concept of modal density is the key for the study of multimodal interaction. Let us first explore this notion by thinking about transcription and the questions that we encounter there.

Question the obvious:	In multmodal interactional analysis we want to explain the subject matter that is generally perceived as obvious.
	Every time we think that *we know* what is going on in an interaction, we ask ourselves *how* and/or *why* we know.

Some questions

When constructing a multimodal transcript, it soon becomes obvious that participants in interaction draw on a multiplicity of communicative modes that are often tightly interlinked and interdependent.

The final transcript of the web-designer speaking on the phone with a client while simultaneously watching her daughter shows that the web-designer is focused upon the phone call. She only shifts her focus to the baby when the client apparently has asked what the little girl is doing.

The questions that we have to answer are: *how* do we know? and *what* is it in the interaction that makes this observation appear to be so obvious? Certainly, her focus becomes manifest in the web-designer's spoken language, which is the primary mode that connects the web-designer to her client.

But, if we take spoken discourse as our primary and only communicative mode that appears to be relevant, we will miss the fact that the web-designer is continuously interacting with her daughter by utilizing different communicative modes. Throughout the transcribed minute of interaction, it is evident that the web-designer is aware of her daughter, and is communicating this awareness to her daughter. Thus, the web-designer is actually engaged in two interactions simultaneously: she speaks on the phone with her client; and she interacts with her daughter face-to-face.

Furthermore, the one time when the web-designer turns to her daughter and says: "*what are you doing?*" with a rising intonation on the "*what*", she is not actually speaking with her daughter as much as she is trying to answer the sudden personal question of her client. Yet the little girl takes the web-designer's apparent attention shift as a true shift, and the web-designer in turn quickly negates this interpretation.

Now, we have to ask *why* the little girl interprets her mother's action as an attention shift, and *how* we know that she makes this interpretation, and also *how* we know that the web-designer negates this interpretation. When thinking about modes, actions, and the phenomenal mind, we will be able to answer these questions.

Modes and actions

Higher-level actions:	Participants perform higher-level actions by constructing chains of lower-level actions. Each mode utilized builds such a chain of lower-level actions.
	Simultaneously performed higher-level actions have an impact on one another.

Participants in interaction always draw on a multiplicity of communicative modes and, as Kress *et al.* (2001) have noted, communicating is achieved through all modes separately and simultaneously together. This notion emphasizes the communicative function of each mode, and at the same time highlights the fact that modes are in constant interplay.

Individuals draw on a multiplicity of communicative modes in order to facilitate the performance of higher-level actions, which in turn are constructed out of an array of chained lower-level actions. As an example, the higher-level action of speaking on the phone with her client that the web-designer engages in is partly constructed through the chained utterances. When viewing all of the actions that the web-designer is performing, we see that she is constructing this higher-level action by utilizing many more modes than just spoken language.

In other words, the web-designer is not only constructing this higher-level action through chained utterances, but also through chained postural shifts, chained gestures, and so on. This illustrates that a participant draws on various communicative modes. Concurrently, each utilized mode is constructed in interaction through chains of lower-level actions, and all of these chains combined construct the higher-level action that the participant performs.

In this example, we can easily discern which modes the web-designer utilizes for which higher-level action. She speaks to the client, gestures in accordance with her speech, and gazes into space while concentrating on the client. Simultaneously, she picks up the little girl, holds her in her arms, and places her back on the floor. Both higher-level actions are easily separable, while at the same time we can also easily determine that one higher-level action impacts on the other.

When revisiting the audio transcript from line (6) to line (12) (p. 67), we find that the web-designer utters a number of false starts:

(6)			I was hop—
(7)			I was thinking,
(8)			if you
(9)	5:14	Baby:	UH UH AH,
(10)	5:15	Web-designer:	[that if you have that
(11)	5:17	Baby:	UH UH AH,
(12)	5:17	Web-designer:	[if you try to change

These false starts occur at the same time as the web-designer's daughter is getting restless, and we see how the interaction with her daughter directly impacts on the interaction with her client. The same is true later, when the client asks about the little girl (in lines 21–26). This inquiry, although seemingly surprising to the web-designer, follows some noises that the baby had made.

The phenomenal mind and modes

| **The phenomenal concept of mind:** | Participants in interaction employ communicative modes: interactively expressing perceptions, thoughts, and feelings (intentionally or not). |

In the introduction, I stated that a multimodal interactional analysis has to be linked to an aspect of the phenomenal concept of mind, since we are interested in investigating what people in interaction express and perceive. All interactions are co-constructed by the participants, allowing analysts to perceive the expressive behavior of one individual in the expressive behavior of another.

In the multimodal transcript, the baby perceives the web-designer's turning her face towards the child as focal attention. In reaction to this perceived focal attention – and as an attempt to engage in focal attention with her mother – the baby points to the lamp, saying "*ah.*"

Part of the phenomenal concept of mind is that aspect of mind with which participants in interaction express their perceptions, thoughts, and feelings; and other participants react to these expressions. Thus, when the web-designer turns her face, gazes at her daughter, and employs higher pitch in her utterance, she expresses focal attention – intentionally or not – and the daughter perceives this expression of focal attention.

Modal density 83

The question we want to ask ourselves now is: *how* is it possible for the little girl to perceive her mother's turning towards her as focal attention? The little girl had been held for a while, and the web-designer was employing the modes of touch and proxemics in the interaction with her daughter. Now, she gazes at the child, and asks *"what are you doing?"* employing slightly higher pitch in the word *"what."*

Here, the direct gaze of her mother and the higher pitch in one of the words take on high intensity for the baby, making it possible for the child to perceive her mother as paying focal attention to her. In the next section, we will discuss this concept of *intensity*.

Modal density through intensity

High intensity:	A mode that takes on primacy in a certain (inter)-action takes on high intensity.
	Any mode can take on high intensity.
	At times, several modes jointly take on high intensity.
Interconnection among modes:	All modes that a participant in interaction utilizes are intricately interconnected, so that the interaction may change if one mode is added, discontinued, or simply used differently.
A mode takes on high intensity:	• If other modes are structured by this mode.
	• If the higher-level action that is being performed by the participant through the use of this highly intense mode would not be possible in that way if the mode had not been intensified.
	• If all embodied modes of the participants(s) are focused upon this one mode.

Communicative modes can take on particular *intensity* in specific interactions. In the example of the web-designer speaking on the phone, the mode of spoken language is strongest. Although she also utilizes other communicative modes, these modes carry much less intensity. For example, she does not have to stand during the phone call. One could argue that her postural behavior is therefore of little importance to the phone conversation. Gaze and pitch, on the other hand, are of great importance in the interaction with the baby, which means that these two modes take on high intensity for the little girl.

This certainly seems plausible enough, but here, we again need to ask ourselves *how do we know* when certain modes take on high intensity, while other modes that are equally utilized take on lower intensity? We find the answer to this question either in the expressions of other participants or in a shift of expression by the participant utilizing the highly intense mode(s).

The web-designer's client presumably responds to the utterances of the web-designer, just as the web-designer reacts to the utterances of her client. This give-and-take in spoken discourse demonstrates the intensity of the mode in this interaction. Clearly, neither the web-designer nor the client is directly reacting to the other's postural stances or gestures. Therefore, these modes take on little intensity in the interaction. I intentionally say *directly reacts*, because indirectly these modes do impact on the mode of spoken language. As discussed in Chapter 2, p. 28–32 and 52–57, gestures are often intricately linked to spoken language, and enable the individual to express themselves more clearly and fluently. Similarly, an individual's postural stance influences the verbal stance taken up to the addressee.

Likewise, the heightened intensity of the higher pitch in one word and the simultaneous direct gaze by her mother to the little girl is perceptible in the baby's actions. Some examples below illustrate *how we know* when a mode takes on particular intensity in an interaction.

Layout and music taking on high intensity

Sandra is setting up her computer while she is listening to music on a CD, i.e. she employs the mode of music as a disembodied mode. In this instance, the researcher is sitting in the same room, at a desk located across from Sandra, reading a book. Sandra is sitting on the floor reading labels on attachments or parts in the instruction booklet, and attaching the pieces. Once in a while, she engages the researcher in her work, asking a question. Sandra's four-year-old son is playing in the hallway, which she has turned her back to. Here, I illustrate her actions from two different camera angles. First, the camera is located next to the desk, showing Sandra from the front; and then the camera is located next to the CD player, showing her from the side.

In the first image of Plate 4.1, Sandra is pointing at a label that is fixed to the side of a computer part. Sandra's motions are synchronized with the music, demonstrating that she utilizes this disembodied mode.

The first image shows that Sandra has positioned a box, some small pieces, and an instruction booklet in close proximity to her body. For 17 minutes she works in the position that is illustrated here, only moving her arms and head slightly to grasp a new attachment, to place it back into the box, or to read the instructions.

Sandra's concentrated actions are only possible in this way because of the layout that she has constructed around herself. The box is located in her peripheral vision, so that she actually throws items back into the box without having to gaze at it directly. The cables and the instruction booklet are placed in front of her on the floor, so that she can see the cables and read the instructions without having to move her body or pick something up.

> Music: German hard rock
> Singer: Male, deep voice
> Lyrics: *Mama, ich hab letzte Nacht ins Bett gemacht*
> Mama, I wet my bed last night

hört das eigentlich irgendwann mal auf

well is that ever going to stop

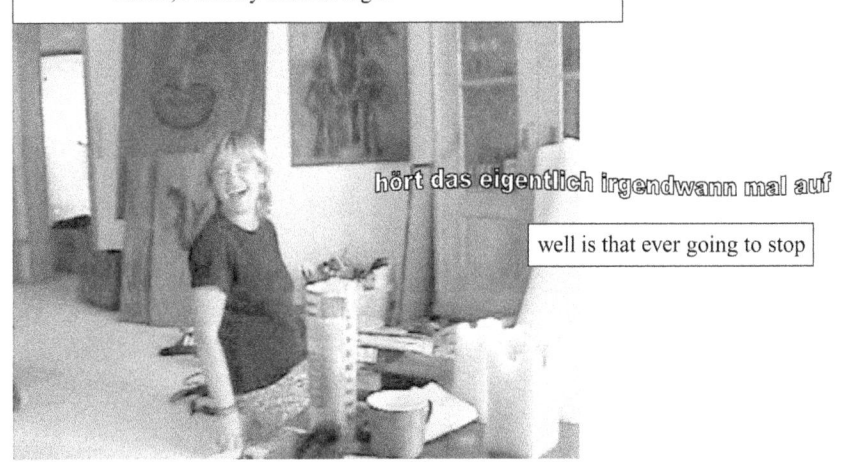

Plate 4.1 High modal density: layout and music.

Thus, the layout of these items and their positioning in the setting take on high intensity. Only because of this layout, Sandra can work in this position for 17 minutes.

The second image shows that Sandra has thrown her upper body and head far backwards, thereby opening her posture, facing the CD player (and the camera), and is laughing out loud.

The box above the image explains that the music that is playing is of the hard rock genre, with a deep male voice singing "*Mama, I wet my bed*

86 *Modal density*

last night." Sandra laughs out loud because her four-year-old son did wet his bed the night before. The lyrics are particularly funny, as Sandra's experiential world and the deep male voice singing these words are in stark contrast. We can see that the music suddenly takes on high intensity for Sandra. She stops working on her computer, has a good laugh, and says, still in a laughing tone: "*well is that ever going to stop*" – directly reacting to the music that is playing.

Examples of modes taking on high intensity

The images in Plate 4.2 provide examples, illustrating moments in interaction in which one mode takes on high intensity.

Plate 4.2 Modal density: high density.

Modal density 87

Both images in the first row of Plate 4.2 illustrate how *one mode* can structure other modes employed, thereby taking on high modal intensity. The first image shows that music takes on high intensity for the people surrounding the street musicians. Some people are dancing; others are swaying to the rhythm of the music. The second image illustrates a moment in which gesture has taken on high intensity. One of the people in the group is pointing, and everybody starts moving in that direction.

The second row of images in Plate 4.2 illustrates that the higher-level action that is being performed by the participant through the use of a highly intense mode would not be possible in that way if the mode had not been intensified. The first image in the second row shows a little boy disturbing his mother while she is shopping, although she had told him to wait next to the cart. Here, the mode of posture takes on high intensity. The second image shows a group of children playing. Their close proximity makes this game possible, and proxemics takes on high intensity in this interaction.

The last row of images in Plate 4.2 illustrates that all embodied modes of the participant(s) are focused upon one mode. The first image in the last row shows Anna writing a shopping list – the mode of print taking on high intensity. Anna's posture, hand/arm movements, and gaze, as well as her proximity to the table and to the piece of paper, are focused upon this mode. The second image in the last row shows a father and his infant gazing into each other's eyes. Here the mode of gaze takes on particular intensity.

Modal density through complexity

Modal complexity:	The interplay of many different communicative modes.
	A higher-level action is not drastically altered when a mode is changed or discontinued.
Modal complexity is achieved:	When the modes that participants draw upon, constructing a higher-level action, are intricately intertwined.

Although any mode can take on high intensity, often participants in interaction employ high modal complexity when performing a higher-level action. Modal complexity refers to the interplay of numerous communicative modes that make the construction of a higher-level action possible.

Let us once more think about the conversation between you and your friend in the cafeteria (from Chapter 1). You are sitting with a plate of food in front of you, your friend comes by, and you talk about your day. This interaction is quite complex when you consider that you are utilizing the modes of spoken language, proxemics, posture, gesture, gaze, head movement, music, and layout. In fact, you are utilizing an even greater range of communicative modes that can also easily be included, such as facial expression, dress, and color.

Often, *what* you are speaking about matters less to the interaction than the tone that you employ. Your posture, your smile, and your gaze all communicate together in synchrony. This is what I mean by modal complexity. There is not one mode that is more important than many other modes, and not one mode that structures this interaction more strongly than any other mode. You can choose to talk about many topics or not to talk much at all; you can stand up and walk with your friend, changing the layout, having the music fade away while you leave the cafeteria. None of these changes impact strongly on the higher-level action of conversing with your friend, and such a higher-level action is constructed through modal complexity – without one communicative mode taking on particular intensity.

Examples of modal complexity

Plate 4.3 shows some examples of participants in interaction employing modal complexity.

In the first image, two women are engaged in conversation. They are sitting at a table, once in a while looking at magazines, and speaking about a variety of topics. Every so often, one of them gets up to check on their children, who are playing in the yard. The women are employing the communicative modes of spoken language, proxemics, posture, gesture, gaze, head movement, print, music, and layout. No one mode takes on particularly high intensity, and all modes are complexly interlinked.

The second image in the first row shows an accountant speaking with his assistant. They are engaged in conversation about tax procedures. Some of their talk refers to the form which the accountant is holding in his hands; while some other talk refers directly to various clients. In this moment of interaction, the accountant and his assistant utilize the modes of spoken language, proxemics, posture, gesture, gaze, head movement, print, and layout. All modes are intricately intertwined, and the change in one mode does not transform the interaction to any great extent.

In the first image of the second row, a mother is playing with her infant. They are holding hands, gazing into each others' eyes, while the baby is making delighted gurgling sounds and the mother says "*ahh.*" Mother and child are employing the modes of proxemics, posture, gesture, gaze, head movement, and layout in a complexly interlinked way. A change of one mode again does not drastically alter the interaction of play, which is constructed through the use of all of these modes together.

In the second image of the second row, two women in a retail store are working side by side. They are both involved in their own work, while they are also helping each other every so often. They employ the modes

Plate 4.3 Modal density: modal complexity.

of spoken language, proxemics, posture, gesture, gaze, head movement, and print. Furthermore, they employ the modes of object handling, color, and dress. Modes fade in and out throughout the interaction, but the higher-level actions of working side-by-side evolve without a drastic change.

In all of these instances, the participants draw on a complexity of communicative modes that all help in constructing the higher-level actions that they perform. A change in one mode does not substantially transform the higher-level action that is being constructed, and all modes that the participants draw on are intricately interlinked. While modes may fade in and out of an interaction, the involved interplay of the modes brings about high modal complexity.

Modal density through intensity plus complexity

Modal complexity and modal intensity can also combine. A hierarchically structuring mode, which is an intense mode that structures other modes in an interaction, may jointly function together with other complexly interlinked modes.

Plate 4.4 shows a boy, whom I will call Peter, playing his guitar. He is using sheet music, tapping his right foot in rhythm, and simultaneously answering his father's question of whether he always has to tap his foot

90 *Modal density*

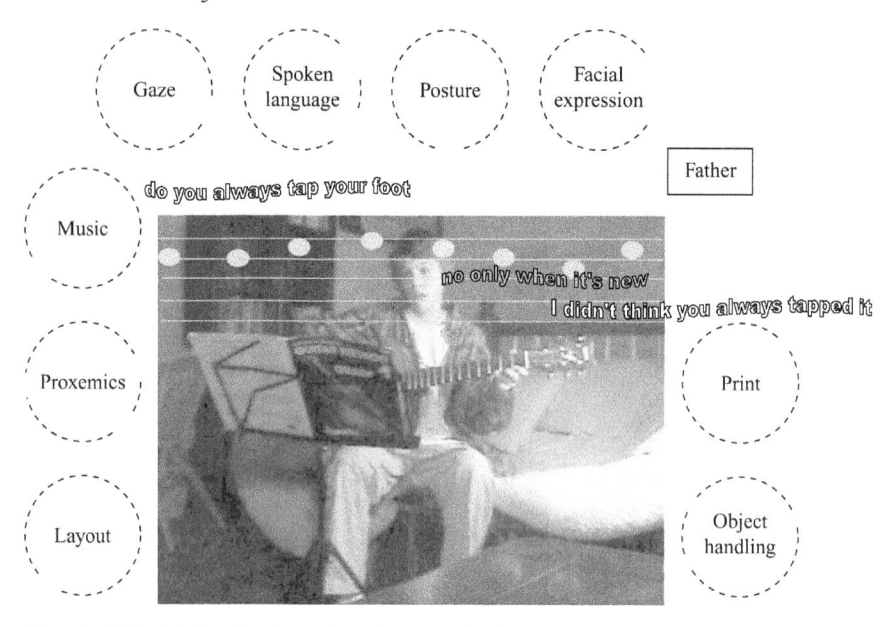

Plate 4.4 Modal density: intensity plus complexity.

in order to keep the rhythm. Here, Peter utilizes the modes of spoken language, proxemics, posture, gesture, gaze, head movement, print, music (embodied), and layout.

The modes that Peter utilizes are tightly interlinked and this communicative moment comes about because of the interplay of these modes. However, at this moment, several of the highly interlinked modes also take on high intensity for Peter. He is playing his guitar for his father, who is sitting in a chair across and to the left of him. Therefore, we can say that the interaction that is going on is Peter's performance of a new song for his father. This higher-level action can only be constructed if Peter is playing his guitar, utilizing music as an embodied mode, and performing a song that he is learning. The mode of music, therefore, takes on high intensity.

Peter is playing notes from sheet music, and he could not play the song that he is playing without reading the printed notes in front of him. Thus, the mode of print also takes on somewhat higher intensity in this instance, as Peter could not construct the higher-level action if we removed the mode of print.

Peter takes up a specific posture, and he has positioned himself in a certain distance to the music stand – utilizing the layout of chair and stand in order to make it possible for him to easily read the sheet music. Here, posture, proxemics, and layout all take on somewhat higher modal intensity, making it possible for Peter to perform.

At this point of the performance, the following brief exchange occurs between Peter and his father:

(1) *Father:* do you always tap your foot.
(2) *Peter:*   no only when it's new
(3) *Father:* I didn't think you always tapped it.

Although Peter answers his father's question, this utterance has no impact on the higher-level action. Instead of speaking, Peter could just as easily shake his head, shrug his shoulders, or simply tighten his lips, and none of these lower-level actions would have impacted on his higher-level action of performing. Therefore, spoken language does not take on much intensity for Peter in this instance.

While Peter employs music, print, posture, proxemics, and layout rather intensely, we can imagine him changing his posture by standing up, and we can still imagine him being able to perform for his father. Similarly, if we take away the sheet music, Peter may just play a song that he can play without employing the mode of print, or he may start to improvise. Again, his higher-level action of performing for his father would still be possible. Therefore, most modes take on medium intensity for Peter in his performance, and they are not as intense as the mode of spoken language during a phone conversation. However, the mode of music takes on high intensity in this interaction, because Peter cannot perform this higher-level action without this mode.

While embodied modes can generally be viewed as having more weight in an interaction than disembodied modes, disembodied modes can outweigh some embodied modes at certain times. Just as music achieves high modal density in the example above, music also takes on much weight in a dance hall. The weight or intensity that this disembodied mode carries can usually be read off of the social actors' embodied modes, the proxemics to the other dancers, and the movements involved.

Intensity of modes is determined by the actions of a social actor, and may be different for various social actors in the same setting. For example, the music takes on high modal density for the dancer, but much less modal density for a social actor, who is engaged in conversation while the music is playing and others are dancing.

Modal density and attention/awareness

Perception and modal density:	Participants in interaction perceive a multiplicity of lower-level actions drawing on a wide range of modes – several at once and/or numerous in quick succession.
	Every participant reacts to the perceived lower-level actions of the other participant(s) whereby they are co-constructing the interaction.

92 *Modal density*

Modal density indicates the level of attention/awareness that a social actor places on a certain mode – just as it indicates the level of attention/awareness that a social actor places on a certain higher-level action. As I mentioned above, the music takes on high modal density for the dancer, while it takes on much less modal density for the person who engages in conversation. This also means that the person dancing pays much more attention to – and is much more aware of – the music than the person who is talking.

Take the mode of music away, and the dancers stop moving. This demonstrates that the dancers could not perform the same actions when the mode of music is discontinued. On the other hand, when people are conversing in a dance hall, their conversation may be rhythmically organized with the beat of the music: they may gesture in accordance to the rhythm; they may shift their postures and heads in rhythmic motions; and their talk may be rhythmically structured to the beat of the music – speaking fast and loud when fast and loud music is playing, or speaking slow and softly when slow and quiet music is playing. Yet, take away the mode of music, and the higher-level action of conversing will not be greatly altered. The participants will find their own rhythm, which will be in some harmony with the setting and each other.

Interactional perception

Certainly, as humans, we can only perceive snippets of available communicative information at any one instance. However, we can perceive a range of bits and pieces of information in very quick succession, and often it takes a while before we come to a conclusion about what other social actors are doing. When entering a dance hall, we may gaze at the dancers for a few seconds, and then at the people sitting and chatting, before choosing the direction to move in and/or higher-level action to engage in.

Perception of multiple modes that participants are utilizing is not instantaneous, and is surely interconnected with our prior experiences and the psychological concept of the mind. So, when I speak of our ability to discern modal density, either in the form of modal intensity or in form of modal complexity, I do not mean to imply that this understanding results from instantaneous perception. Rather, our ability to discern the modal density that participants in interaction utilize emerges from successive quickly organized perceptions that allow us to compose the viewed interactions in a kaleidoscopic fashion. In this way, participants, as well as analysts, can read the intensity and complexity that modes take on for a particular social actor in a specific social situation from the social actor's actions.

Now, let us once again return to our example of you and your friend talking in the cafeteria. I had said earlier that you are aware of your friend's posture, proxemics, gesture, gaze, head movement, dress, and so on. Here, I would like to point out that nobody constantly moves their heads, changes their posture, gestures, or even speaks during a conversation. While all of these modes are utilized by the participants in an interaction, and there is great symmetry among the modes, no mode is unremitting. Every mode is organized by pauses. As discussed in Chapter 2, head movement can be discerned by the pauses previous to and following the movement. Similarly, gestures take place from a rest position and end at a rest position, and utterances are bracketed by in-breaths. These pauses between the lower-level actions do not all coincide. Gestures slightly precede the verbal utterance of the same idea, and gaze is structured around phrase endings in conversation.

Therefore, we do not need to perceive every mode simultaneously during interaction. Rather, we perceive a certain amount of modal information in quick succession. While it may appear that we focus on an interaction, we actually focus on small parts of an interaction – swiftly shifting this focus.

When you are talking with your friend, you may focus upon the mode of dress at the very beginning of the interaction, possibly before your friend even reaches your table. You may react to this mode without being consciously aware of it, or, if the mode of dress is in contrast to your expectation, you may address this fact. When your friend speaks, you may listen to the utterances, gazing at your plate, and look up when it is almost your turn to speak.

This illustrates that we do not perceive all modes all of the time during interaction. Such constancy is not only impossible, it is also not necessary. Once you have perceived what your friend is wearing, you do not need to focus upon that mode again, as this perception stays in your mind. Similarly, once your friend has sat down at the table in a specific spot, you no longer need to focus upon the mode of proxemics, as it is now a given. Your conversation will be constructed with the mode of proxemics as one mode, and only if this mode is changed will you take note of it again. Up until then, you naturally react to the given proxemics that your friend has taken up, without a need to focus upon it any further.

The phenomenal mind

Phenomenal mind:	Participants in interaction react to the expressions of perceptions, thoughts, and feelings of others, constantly interpreting others' lower-level and higher-level actions.

The part of the phenomenal mind which we are concerned with here is that heuristic notion of mind that expresses perceptions, thoughts, and feelings. This is the only part of mind that we as participants and as analysts can interpret, as nobody can perceive what another person is truly perceiving, thinking, or feeling.

Misinterpretations are frequent in interaction, and such misinterpretations result in repair structures. If a friend asks you *"why are you so sad?"* you may answer *"oh, I'm not, I just don't feel well."* Such exchanges occur often in interaction, because a participant interprets a facial expression or a posture in one way, while the actual thinking and feeling of the other person does not coincide with that interpretation. However, such misinterpretations are just as frequently repaired as they occur, and, as I stated above, interaction would not be possible without our constant interpretation of others' lower-level and higher-level actions.

Attention / awareness

> **High modal density equates to a high level of interactional attention/awareness.**

So far, I have mainly discussed focused higher-level actions of participants in interaction. These focused higher-level actions are constructed through high modal density: either by employing high modal intensity of one or more modes, or by employing high modal complexity through a multiplicity of intricately intertwined communicative modes. When participants engage in focused interaction, they pay great attention to the interaction and simultaneously demonstrate that they are highly aware of it.

In interaction, all participants constantly interpret the level of attention/awareness that a social actor places on a higher-level action. While people engage in focused interactions all day long, it is quite rare that they *only* engage in focused interaction. However, one cannot engage in two focused interactions simultaneously, and I take up the notion of levels of attention/awareness in the next chapter.

Assignment

Take notes of three focused interactions that you engage in, and think about the notion of modal density. Following each interaction, try to answer these questions:

- Which modes did you utilize?
- What was the weight of the modes?
- Did you employ high modal density through modal intensity or through modal complexity?

5 Levels of attention/ awareness

> **Levels of attention/ awareness:** A participant in interaction can engage in several simultaneous higher-level actions on differing levels of attention/awareness.

A participant in interaction focuses on a higher-level action by employing high modal density. Conversely, the individual's employment of high modal density allows other participants (and the analyst) to perceive the individual as being engaged in focused (inter)action.

One level of attention/awareness

Let us once again return to the hypothetical conversation that you are having with your friend in the cafeteria. You are sitting at a table: your friend approaches, sits down, and the two of you engage in conversation. You perceive your friend's lower-level actions, and your friend perceives your lower-level actions. Together, you co-construct a focused interaction in which the utterances are sequentially structured; the gestures and the gaze are intertwined with and structured by the spoken discourse; and your talk is influenced by the layout and the background music. Both of you perceive the other to be highly engaged in this higher-level action of conversing, and other people around you also perceive that both of you are involved in focused interaction. Such a perception of the focused interaction is due to the high modal density that both of you employ.

Two levels of attention/awareness

Let us now return to the example of the school crossing guard in Chapter 1. I showed that the crossing guard is either engaged in focused interaction with the drivers by directing the traffic at the four-way intersection, or she is engaged in focused interaction with the schoolchildren by directing them to cross the street.

When the crossing guard is directing traffic, she is certainly aware of the schoolchildren gathering at the corner of the intersection. Similarly, when directing the children to cross the intersection, the crossing guard is aware of the traffic that is accumulating.

Here, we can easily discern two levels of attention/awareness. While the crossing guard shifts her focal attention from directing the cars to directing the children and back again, she simultaneously engages in two higher-level actions on different levels of attention/awareness. In other words, when the crossing guard is directing traffic, she is engaged in focused interaction with the drivers, while she is simultaneously engaged in interaction with the children at the corner: making sure that they are safe. Her engagement in the interaction with the children at this time is not as focused as her interaction with the drivers, but is clearly ongoing.

As soon as the crossing guard shifts her main attention to the children, she engages in focused interaction with them, directing them to cross the street. Simultaneously, the crossing guard is keeping an eye on the traffic, and she interacts with the drivers, although she does not give them her focused attention at this time.

Three levels of attention/awareness

Next, let us think about the web-designer. She speaks on the phone with her client, engages in interaction with her daughter, and reacts to the researcher – who videotapes the interactions.

Here, the web-designer is involved in focused interaction with her client, employing high modal density, which results mostly from the high intensity of spoken language. Concurrently, she is engaged in interaction with her daughter. However, she is not engaged in focused interaction with the little girl, and the one time that the child misinterprets her mother as giving her focused attention, the web-designer quickly negates this interpretation through her action of turning her head away from the child. The web-designer interacts with her daughter on a different – and not very focused – level of attention/awareness. She is obviously paying attention to the child, as we can see when she picks her up, holds her, and places her back on the floor. However, she does not focus on the little girl, and even though the interaction with the child interferes with the focused interaction with her client at some points, the web-designer does not shift her focused attention to the child during the call.

Simultaneously, the web-designer is engaged in interaction with the researcher, who is videotaping her; although she does not pay attention to the researcher, she is certainly aware of the researcher's presence.

Here, we can discern three levels of attention/awareness that the web-designer employs simultaneously. But, *how do we know?*, to question the obvious. The answer to this question can be found in the concept of modal density. The web-designer clearly employs higher modal density in the higher-level action of speaking on the phone than she employs in the higher-level action of interacting with her daughter, or in the higher-level action of interacting with the researcher.

Foreground, mid-ground, background

Foreground:	The higher-level action that a participant highly attends to and/or highly reacts to, and/or highly acts upon, is in the *foreground* of their *attention/awareness*.
Mid-ground:	The higher-level action that a participant attends to in some degree and/or reacts to in some degree, and/or acts upon in some degree, is in the *mid-ground* of their *attention/awareness*.
Background:	The higher-level action that a participant is only decreasingly aware of, disattends, and/or does not react to, and/or does not act upon, is in the *background* of their *attention/awareness*.

Foreground, mid-ground, and background distinguish three levels of simultaneous awareness of a person in interaction. These notions are merely of a heuristic nature; they are not distinct points of attention/awareness, and are simply functioning in an explanatory sense.

In multimodal interactional analysis, we view interaction as the construction of several higher-level actions which are happening at various stages or on various layers of a person's consciousness. We discern the levels of attention/awareness that particular individuals place on certain higher-level actions by investigating the modal density employed.

Foreground–background continuum

Foreground–background continuum:	The continuum highlights that interaction is fluid: demonstrating that the three stages are not fixed entities at which participants in interaction perform higher-level actions.
	Higher-level actions can be heuristically placed on such a continuum for explanatory reasons.
	Depending on the interaction, higher-level actions may be performed at these theoretical points of foreground, mid-ground, and background on the attention/awareness continuum, or at any point between foreground and background.
	There can be more or less than three stages.

98 *Levels of attention/awareness*

When analyzing interactions in real-time, we often find that participants work with differing notions of what to foreground, mid-ground, or background. While we certainly can find many interactions in which the participants focus on the same higher-level action, we can find just as many interactions in which the participants' foregrounding (mid-grounding and backgrounding) of actions is mismatched.

A participant in interaction usually is aware of several higher-level actions, displaying awareness and/or relative unawareness through the employment of various degrees of modal density. The higher-level actions that a social actor actively attends to through the employment of numerous communicative modes are located between the fore- and the mid-ground, while the ones that are constructed and are largely out of the awareness of the social actor are located in the background of the continuum.

A methodological framework

A methodological framework:	The heuristic model of a *modal density foreground–background continuum* allows the recognition that any individual in interaction is simultaneously engaged in several higher-level actions.
	These simultaneous higher-level actions are constructed through the employment of a multiplicity of communicative modes.
	The notion of modal density is essential to hierarchically structure the various higher-level actions.
	The notion of a foreground–background continuum of attention/awareness levels is essential to hierarchically place the various higher-level actions in heuristic positions.

The heuristic concept of a modal density foreground–background continuum of a social actor's levels of attention/awareness is depicted in the following graph in Figure 5.1.

The graph in Figure 5.1 shows the *x*-axis illustrating the decreasing levels of attention/awareness of an individual in interaction, and the *y*-axis demonstrating the amount of modal density employed. This model, *the modal density foreground–background continuum*, is a methodological tool to represent simultaneous higher-level actions that one individual constructs at a particular moment in interaction (Norris, 2002b, 2003b).

The curve in the graph indicates that a decrease of modal density equates to a decrease in expressed attention/awareness of the individual. This

Levels of attention/awareness 99

```
Modal
density
   ↑
   |‥.__
   |    ‾‥._
   |         ‾‥._
   |              ‾‥._
   |                   ‾‥._
   |                        ‾‥·‥._
   |                                 ‾‥._
   |_____→ Decreasing
                                       attention/awareness
   Foreground    Mid-ground    Background
```

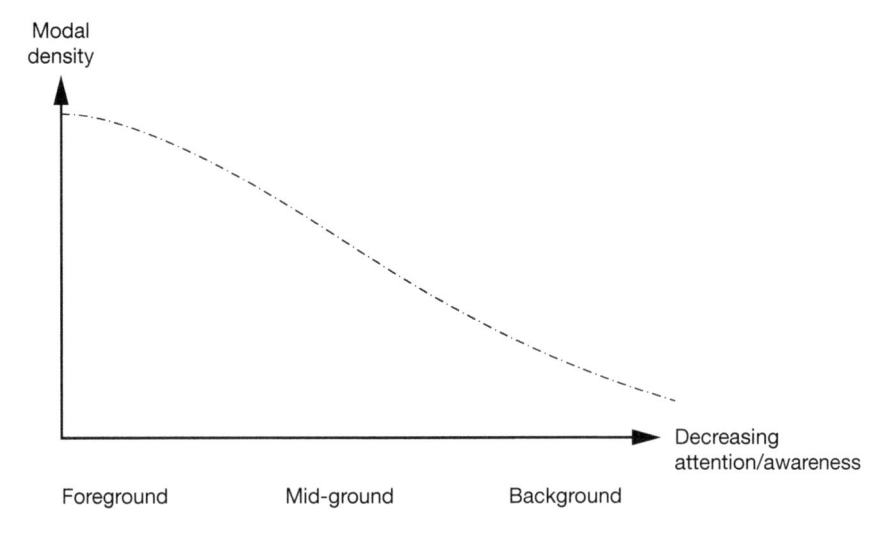

Figure 5.1 Modal density foreground–background continuum.

curve is only an approximation. Therefore, I indicate with a dotted line the way in which it illustrates the relationship between modal density and attention/awareness levels.

In this graph, the attention/awareness levels of a participant in interaction are placed in relational positions. These relational points may seem similar in illustration, but in reality, and also depending on our focus of analysis, these points may vary to a great extent from one interaction to the next.

Situations differ, and participants utilize different communicative modes and a variety of modal densities to communicate. While some higher-level actions entail a very high level of modal density to be in the foreground of a person's attention/awareness, other interactions entail less modal density to be distinguished as focused interaction.

Transcription and simultaneously performed higher-level actions

The modal density foreground–background continuum:	This heuristic model, which depicts the different levels of attention/awareness paid to simultaneous higher-level actions, corresponds to the multimodal transcripts depicting the same interaction.

The modal density foreground–background continuum is a methodological tool that allows us to illustrate the simultaneous higher-level actions that we are investigating in a particular moment in interaction.

Such visualization is not unlike any other transcription process. When transcribing the communicative mode of spoken language, we listen carefully; add all of the important aspects that are necessary for the analysis; and essentially dissect the utterances to a degree that average listeners cannot achieve within interaction. Thereby, we translate the spoken word into some written form. Such transcriptions are of great value, as they allow us to analyze the discourse. Similarly, in multimodal transcription, we dissect and translate videotaped interactions into a fairly small number of still images, plus words, arrows, and other necessary explanatory items. This translation of video clips makes it possible for us to analyze the complexity of interaction.

The graph that I call the modal density foreground–background continuum functions in tandem with a multimodal transcript. We place the simultaneous higher-level actions that a participant engages in on the continuum: dissecting and translating the actions into a visual format. Such a visual depiction of simultaneous higher-level actions makes it possible for us to analyze and present them.

Relevant higher-level actions

The modal density foreground–background continuum:	This heuristic model helps the analyst to focus on relevant simultaneously performed higher-level actions.

Which higher-level actions are relevant depends not only on the interaction, but also on the focus of study. If we are investigating an interaction in a retail store, we will choose among a number of higher-level actions – discounting others as irrelevant. We may want to analyze the higher-level action of a sales person who is engaged in focused interaction with a client, while the sales person is simultaneously engaged in higher-level action separately with both the owner of the store, and another employee. These would be three interactions that are simultaneously constructed. But instead, we may want to analyze the higher-level actions that the sales person is engaged in that are peripheral to the customer–sales person interaction. Here, the sales person may be engaged in the higher-level action of ordering, or in a higher-level action of stacking products, or even in the higher-level action of cleaning products in the store.

Either way, we can position the higher-level actions that are relevant for the focus of study on the modal density foreground–background continuum. Such heuristic positioning of the higher-level actions that a person is performing simultaneously, helps the analyst to intensify the analytical focus, and, at the same time, makes it possible to present this analytical focus to others.

Method of analysis

Following Western ideology, the modal density foreground–background continuum conveys that the multimodal analysis including focused and less-focused as well as unfocused aspects of interaction, begins at the point where the foreground–background axis meets the modal density axis. This point represents the focus of attention/awareness of the participant.

Generally, we have been trained to analyze focused interactions, or, as I like to call them, the foregrounded higher-level actions. This tendency to focus on the foregrounded higher-level actions is utilized in this methodological framework, and the analysis proceeds along the foreground–background axis from left to right, from the focal point of attention/awareness to the unfocused aspects of interaction.

The focal point of attention/awareness is usually most apparent in the interaction. Once this foregrounded higher-level action has been discovered, we move on to the next discernible higher-level action that the participant is engaged in. However, discerning simultaneous higher-level actions is not an easy task.

In order to illustrate how to discern simultaneously performed higher-level actions, let us look at a practical example in which Sandra simultaneously performs six higher-level actions.

Six simultaneously performed higher-level actions

Sandra and Anna own a catering business together. In the following example, Sandra and Anna are meeting in Anna's apartment to write a shopping list for an upcoming event. During this meeting, Sandra's two children and Anna's three children are present, together with the researcher. While Sandra and Anna are working, Sandra receives a call on her cell phone from a close friend whose mother is in the hospital undergoing a major operation. In Plate 5.1, you see a multimodal transcript of a brief excerpt of this complex interaction, in which I specifically focus on Sandra.

Sandra and Anna have been occupied with their meeting for about six minutes. In the first image of the transcript in Plate 5.1, Sandra is writing a shopping list – adding all items that Anna mentions. The second row of images shows Sandra first looking up briefly: looking at her younger son who is speaking with the researcher, before returning her gaze to the list. At this time the phone rings.

The third row of images shows Sandra speaking on her cell phone, and the fourth row of images illustrates Sandra looking up at Anna while on the phone, saying "*yes, I'm still listening,*" and then starting to write again, while speaking on the phone.

Plate 5.1 Transcript: six simultaneous higher-level actions.

Foregrounded higher-level action: writing a shopping list

In the first image of the transcript in Plate 5.1, the complex employment of embodied and disembodied modes conveys that Sandra is foregrounding the higher-level action of writing the list. She employs embodied modes such as proxemics (to Anna), proxemics (to the piece of paper), gaze, posture, and the disembodied mode of print. All modes are intricately intertwined, and the employment of one mode is not possible without at least some of the others; and a change in one of these modes would result in a change of the higher-level action. This intricate interplay of various communicative modes reflects the high modal density employed.

Foregrounded higher-level action: speaking on the phone

When Sandra receives a call, she answers the phone, and speaks with her friend about her friend's mother's operation.

The first image in the third row of the transcript depicts Sandra foregrounding the higher-level action of speaking on the phone. Here, Sandra is sitting in the same position as before and, although her posture has not changed much, her gaze has become unfocused, displaying a middle-distance gaze. In addition, her right hand motion has become unfocused, and Sandra is moving the piece of paper in front of her slightly back-and-forth. Conversely, the communicative mode of spoken language has taken on high intensity. This high intensity of language reflects the high modal density employed, and the high modal density in turn indicates that Sandra is foregrounding the phone call at this time.

When Sandra gazes at Anna in full gaze, saying: "*ja ich hör trotzdem zu*" ["yes I'm still listening"] in the first image of the fourth row, Sandra has shifted her focus. Here, Sandra has lowered and focused her right hand and is ready to write: again employing high modal density through high modal complexity and intensity. Thus, as depicted in this image, Sandra is again foregrounding the higher-level action of writing a shopping list with Anna.

The spoken language has lost some of the intensity in the construction of the higher-level action of speaking on the phone, as Sandra is speaking with Anna and she is simultaneously listening to her friend on the phone.

While, at times, Sandra foregrounds the higher-level action of speaking on the phone, she quickly shifts between foregrounding the phone call and the writing of the list. Thus, one of these higher-level actions is foregrounded, while the other is only slightly further back (but still very close to the foreground) in Sandra's attention/awareness.

Mid-grounded higher-level action: playing a game

While Sandra is engaged in the two higher-level actions of writing a shopping list with Anna and speaking on the phone with a friend, alternately foregrounding one of them, she is also engaged in the higher-level action of playing a game with the two older boys, whom I call Shawn and David.

In the second image of the second row in the transcript, Anna's son, Shawn, is dropping off a letter, placing it into Sandra's direct vision next to the shopping list (as indicated by the arrow). In the first image of the third row, Sandra's son David picks up the letter and places it back on the table, and, in the second image of this row, Sandra has picked it up and glances at it. In the first image of the fourth row Sandra has moved the letter to the other side of the table (a movement that is indicated by the arrow in the second image of the third row), and Shawn, who has moved to the other side of the table, is picking up the letter, while David watches delightedly.

Whereas this interaction is foregrounded by the two boys involved, Sandra does not focus on this interaction. She takes the letter, gazes at it, and moves it concentrating on the phone conversation and writing a shopping list. Sandra is paying much less attention to the presence of the two children and their game; however, she is taking part in the interaction and is paying *some* attention to it.

The modal density employed for the higher-level action of playing this game is lower for Sandra than the modal density that she employs to construct the higher-level actions of writing a shopping list and speaking on the phone. Nevertheless, Sandra does employ the mode of proxemics to the boys; the mode of object handling by picking up the letter and moving it to the other side of the table; and the mode of touch when David touches her arm. She also utilizes the mode of gaze, looking at the letter and presumably reading the few words that are printed on it.

Certainly, as in any interaction, the employment of communicative modes is co-constructed. When David moves close to Sandra, she also intensely employs this mode of proxemics and employs the mode of touch to some extent, even though she has not moved and has not actively touched David. The employment of a mode does not have to be active in the sense that the social actor has to *carry out* a specific lower-level action in order to utilize a mode. When David moves very close to his mother and touches her arm, she no doubt perceives this closeness and touch.

Here, Sandra's communicative action can be read off of her motionless state. In other words, Sandra allows her son to display intimate distance and touch. Since Sandra does not reject these actions, she communicates that she engages in interaction with him through these modes. However, we see in the transcript that Sandra does not employ extensively multiple or complexly intertwined modes of communication to construct this higher-level action of playing a game with Shawn and David. Therefore, this higher-level action can be placed in the mid-ground of Sandra's attention/awareness continuum.

Modal density can be different for each participant involved in a higher-level action. David and Shawn, for example, utilize much higher modal density in the game than does Sandra.

Higher-level action between mid-ground and background: watching the younger boys

While Sandra is writing a shopping list, speaking on the phone, and playing a game with Shawn and David, she is also watching the two younger boys. This higher-level action is visible in Sandra's gaze in the first image of the second row in the transcript. There, Sandra is watching her younger son.

Although Sandra takes little notice of the two boys, she is aware of their games and their positions within the room. Later on in the interaction, at a point that I have not transcribed here, one of the boys opens the patio door and Sandra interferes immediately. At another time, the boys play a little too roughly, and again Sandra interferes. These interferences with the boy's actions illustrate that Sandra is aware of them, listening to them, but she pays little attention to them for the most part.

Here, in this piece of the transcript, Sandra employs medium to low modal density in the construction of this interaction. Therefore, we can say that the interaction between Sandra and the two younger boys can be heuristically placed between the mid-ground and the background on the modal density foreground–background continuum. Such placement is only possible by analyzing the other higher-level actions that Sandra is engaged in. When we think about her engagement in the higher-level action of playing a game with Shawn and David, we can perceive that she pays less attention to the younger boys. Therefore, we have to place this interaction further back on the continuum.

The modal density foreground–background continuum is a heuristic and methodological tool that allows the relational positioning of the simultaneous higher-level actions. While this continuum represents that there are many different stages of attention/awareness, there is no one-to-one correlation between an actual consciousness and the graph.

Higher-level action between mid-ground and background: interacting with the researcher

Sandra is also engaged in interaction with the researcher. The researcher is present, videotaping the interactions, and speaking and playing with the children. While Sandra pays very little attention to the researcher, Sandra is no doubt aware of her presence. In the second image of the third row and the first image of the fourth row, we can see the researcher walk past Sandra and Anna. The close proximity between Sandra and the researcher suggests that Sandra is aware of her. The modal density that Sandra employs is very low for this higher-level action, and we can place it even further toward the background in the modal density foreground–background continuum.

Higher-level action in the background: meeting with Anna in her apartment

Although Sandra employs many communicative modes to construct the higher-level action of meeting with Anna, she pays no attention to this higher-level action. Sandra pays no attention to the fact that she is sitting in Anna's apartment, in one of Anna's chairs, writing on Anna's paper with Anna's pen placed on Anna's table. She also pays no attention to the fact that Anna's dog spends most of the time lying under the table.

The higher-level action of meeting in Anna's apartment is completely backgrounded, disattended to, and not acted upon. Yet, all of the higher-level actions heuristically placed on all other points on the modal density foreground–background continuum could not be possible in this way, if the meeting was taking place in a different location. *While this higher-level action is backgrounded, it actually structures the other higher-level actions in this complex multiparty interaction.*

Essentially, this backgrounded higher-level action is of a *higher level* than the five other higher-level actions. While a visualization of embeddedness of action is also possible, a placement of all higher-level actions on one continuum demonstrates that the individual *is* performing the actions simultaneously, and that the higher-level actions (even though theoretically of a different dimension) are structured in a person's consciousness.

Here, in multimodal interactional analysis, we are mainly concerned with the human being in interaction. In other words, we want to realize how a person hierarchizes various higher-level actions in their own minds, and how the person displays this structure through the employment of communicative modes. *Our theoretical issue is to hierarchize the importance of higher-level actions for an individual in interaction, and not to hierarchize the various levels of actions.*

Modal density circles

Modal density circle:	A methodological tool that allows the visualization of the modal density that a participant employs when constructing a higher-level action.
	Like any methodological tool, a modal density circle is a heuristic device to aid in analysis and presentation.
	Communicative modes are depicted as dotted intermittent circles to illustrate the fact that modes are not bounded units.
	The dimensions of the circle illustrates the heuristic weight that a mode in a specific interaction carries.

Levels of attention/awareness 107

The modal density circles shown in Figure 5.2 depict the six higher-level actions that Sandra engages in simultaneously.

Modal density circle (a) depicts Sandra's employment of a multiplicity and complexity of interdependent and interplaying communicative modes to construct the higher-level action of writing a shopping list with Anna. Here, high modal density is developed through complexity and medium intensity of the modes.

Modal density circle (b) depicts Sandra's employment of the highly intense mode of spoken language to construct the higher-level action of speaking on the phone with her friend. Here, high modal density is developed through the intensity of this one communicative mode.

Modal density circle (c) depicts Sandra's employment of several communicative modes to construct the higher-level action of playing a game with Shawn and David. Here, medium modal density is developed through high modal intensity of proxemics and the modes of object handling, gaze, and touch.

The dimensions of the circles are dependent upon the intensity of the modes employed (i.e. Sandra's proxemics to David is closer and therefore more intense than Sandra's proxemics to Anna in the last three images of Plate 5.1). The less importance a social actor places on certain modes to construct the higher-level action (and the less importance other participants place on those modes in co-construction of this higher-level action), the smaller the modal circles in the drawing.

Modal density circle (d) represents the modal density that Sandra employs to construct the higher-level action of watching the two younger boys. Here, mid–low modal density is achieved through mid–low complexity of her use of gaze, proxemics, layout, and spoken language to construct the higher-level action. Sandra's use of any of these modes to construct this higher-level action is sporadic and brief. She gazes up for two seconds, and mostly listens to the children, speaking infrequently with them (however, each time demonstrating that she has been listening to some extent), and the children walk past her or play fairly close by. None of these modes are employed with great intensity, and neither are they complexly interlinked.

Modal density circle (e) indicates the back–mid-grounded interaction with the researcher. This higher-level action is even further backgrounded than the higher-level action depicted in (d). Here, Sandra employs proxemics, gaze, and layout in the construction of the higher-level action of interacting with the researcher. Throughout this multiparty complex interaction, Sandra is aware of the researcher, but pays no attention to her. This interaction is constructed primarily through proxemics, indicating an *Anwesenheit* (as discussed in Chapter 2, pp. 21–22), and the given layout of the room that this interaction takes place in. The researcher's *Anwesenheit* no doubt shapes Sandra's actions to some extent, and the distances between Sandra and the researcher, even though changing slightly throughout the interaction, communicate accessibility and awareness.

(a) Foregrounded higher-level action

Modal density achieved through modal complexity

(b) Foregrounded higher-level action

Modal density achieved through modal intensity

(c) Mid-grounded higher-level action

Medium modal density achieved through medium complexity and some intensity of one mode

(d) Mid-to-backgrounded higher-level action

Mid–low modal density achieved through mid–low complexity

(e) Back- to-mid-grounded higher-level action

Low to medium modal density achieved through low to medium complexity

(f) Backgrounded higher-level action

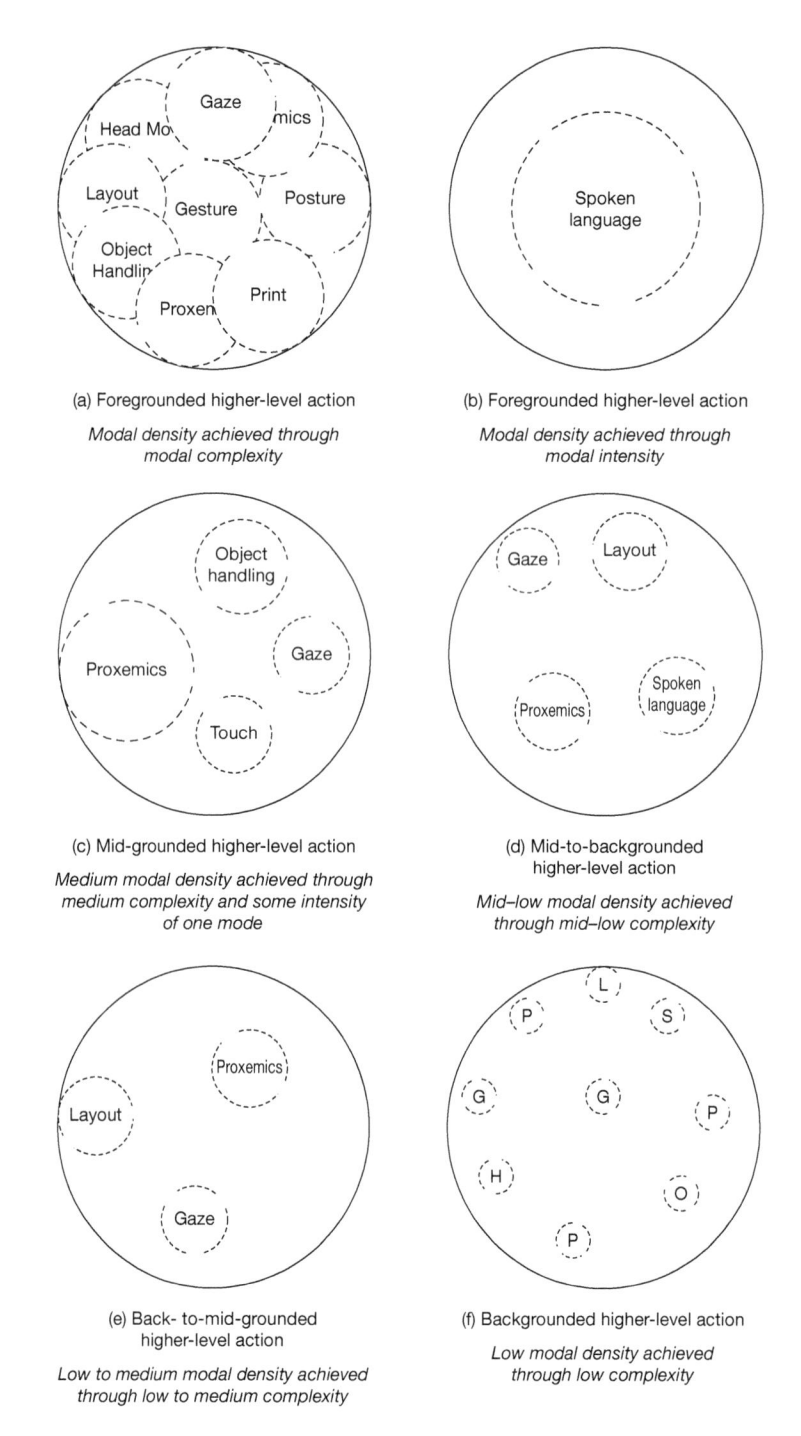

Low modal density achieved through low complexity

Figure 5.2 Modal density circles as heuristic tools to visualize the density employed for specific higher-level actions.

Levels of attention/awareness 109

Modal density circle (f) depicts Sandra's employment of layout, print, posture, proxemics, gaze, gesture, head movement, and spoken language to construct the higher-level action of meeting with Anna in her apartment. Her use of all of these modes (and many more: including dress, color, and object handling) is continuous throughout the interaction. Yet, Sandra does not pay any attention to the construction of this higher-level action, and therefore this higher-level action can be visualized through a multiplicity of employed modes that do not take on much intensity.

The modal density circle helps to illustrate how a social actor utilizes a multiplicity of communicative modes without paying any attention to the higher-level action that is being constructed. A backgrounded higher-level action such as "meeting in Anna's apartment" demonstrates that high modal density *does not* necessarily come about because of a high number of communicative modes involved. Modes can never be counted. A mode is only a heuristic unit, and the number of modes utilized does not give insight into the level of attention/awareness that an individual in interaction employs to construct a specific higher-level action.

Modal density circles force us to think about higher-level actions as being constructed through multiple modes. With such considerations, we realize that the employment of a mode does not have to be actively constructed by a social actor; modes are impossible to count; and modal density circles allow the presentation of the modal density of any higher-level action.

Modal density foreground–background continuum

Modal density foreground–background continuum:	This allows us to heuristically visualize simultaneous higher-level actions that a person constructs.
	Higher-level actions are hierarchized and relationally placed on the continuum of a person's descriptive attention/awareness levels.
	In multimodal interactional analysis we are interested in the person's structuring of different higher-level actions. Generally, we are not much concerned with the differentiation of levels of higher-level actions, even though we do want to be aware of the various levels, as they may give us further insight into interaction. Often, the backgrounded higher-level actions are of a *higher* level than the other higher-level actions that a person performs simultaneously. This demonstrates that the backgrounded higher-level action

110 *Levels of attention/awareness*

> often structures the other higher-level actions performed. Let us think of a group of people going to the movie theater. They all perform several simultaneous higher-level actions while they are in the theater, and, once they have entered, they background the higher-level action of visiting a movie theater. Yet, all participants behave in a certain way because they are constructing this higher-level action, and all other actions are structured by this one action.
>
> While backgrounded higher-level actions are disattended, they are not completely out of the awareness of a participant.

When placing the six hierarchized higher-level actions that Sandra (co)constructs simultaneously on a modal density foreground–background continuum, we visualize the levels of attention/awareness that Sandra employs for each action.

Figure 5.3 illustrates the importance that Sandra places on each simultaneously performed higher-level action. When reviewing the transcript in Plate 5.1, we see that the modal density foreground–background continuum illustrates the third and fourth rows of the transcript, since in the first two rows Sandra is not speaking on the phone.

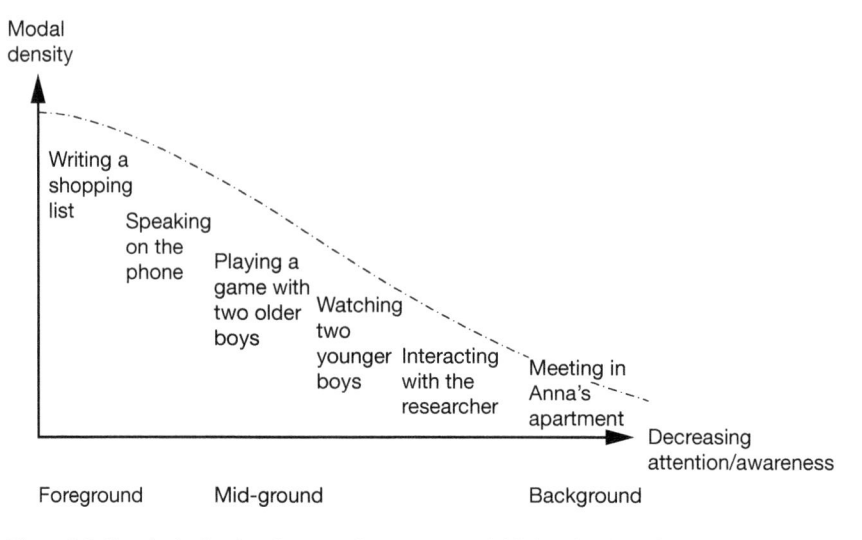

Figure 5.3 Sandra's six simultaneously constructed higher-level actions placed on a modal density foreground–background continuum.

Sometimes, foregrounded, mid-grounded, and backgrounded higher-level actions (and all higher-level actions in between these points) shift very quickly, and the participants in interaction are well aware of such shifts. But *how do we know?* The next chapter discusses multimodal structuring devices.

Assignment

Walk into a building or an open place where there is much activity going on, and try to find a place to sit. Now close your eyes and try to discern how many different sounds you can hear. If you are in an open area, you may hear people speaking (and this counts as one kind of sound), you may hear cars (again one sound), you will hear footsteps, and so on. Once you have counted the number of sounds that you can make out, try to hierarchize them. Which one is loudest?, which one quietest? Take notes about your discoveries and share them later in your class.

Then open your eyes and look around very carefully. Discern as many visual modes as you can, and think about color and layout (you may want to divide the mode of layout into furniture, buildings, etc.). Which one is the most powerful mode?, which one the least important? Again, take notes and discuss your findings.

Once you have learned to hierarchize modes in the environment, observe people in multiparty interactions. Focus on one person and discern how many higher-level actions the person is involved in.

6 Semantic/pragmatic *means*

Multimodal interactional analysis

Multimodal interactional analysis:	A holistic analysis of the multiple real-time sequential and simultaneous communicative processes that participants engage in.
Communicative semantics:	A type of semantics that underlies our holistic and multimodal interaction.
Pragmatics:	"The study of the relation of signs to interpreters" (Morris, 1938: 6).
Face-to-face interaction:	Generally, the interactions that people engage in when they are within clear line of sight of each other.
	This type of interaction is usually differentiated from phone or computer-mediated interaction.
	In multimodal interactional analysis we do not differentiate between face-to-face and mediated interactions, as all interactions are mediated, and many entail aspects of both.

Multimodal interactional analysis is an approach to a holistic analysis. The importance of each mode in a real-time interaction is integrated exclusive of the presupposition that any one mode is inherently more important than another; and the importance of a mode is always established by investigating the given modal configuration.

When speaking of *semantics*, I consider here a communicative type of semantics, and when speaking of *pragmatics*, I consider a communicative type of pragmatics, both of which underlie our holistic and multimodal interaction. Semantics allows us to realize the general meaning of communicative structuring devices, while pragmatics allows us to realize the specific meaning of such devices in use.

While the framework of multimodal interaction is essentially a framework of face-to-face interaction, the original use of the term "face-to-face" is significantly broadened by the possible inclusion of all modes – embodied and disembodied. In Chapter 3, I described the web-designer speaking on the phone with her client as a face-to-face interaction. I also included Sandra's cell phone call in the face-to-face interactional analysis in the last chapter. Yet, a phone conversation cannot really be termed a face-to-face interaction in the original sense. *Why* then do I not differentiate between a phone conversation and a face-to-face interaction? The answer to this question is found in our multimodal analysis and in the general notion of mediation.

Every action – lower- or higher-level – is mediated. The higher-level action of speaking on the phone is mediated by an object: *the telephone*. But, the higher-level action of the web-designer interacting with her daughter while former is speaking on the phone is also mediated. This higher-level action is mediated by various communicative modes and the bodies of the participants.

Participants often engage in interaction with several individuals simultaneously, through the use of various communicative modes, and we no longer have to distinguish actual face-to-face interaction (which is mediated in many ways) from other mediated interactions (which are mediated in many of the same ways as well as by the phone or the computer).

Ruth Finnegan (2002) emphasizes that the process of communicating:

> may be more, or less, purposive, organized and conscious; more or less mutually influential or recognizable; work simultaneously or sequentially on multiple levels . . .
>
> (Finnegan, 2002: 29)

The methodological framework of multimodal interaction allows us to investigate this fluidity and multiplicity of interaction described by Finnegan. Interaction – or the process of communicating – is complex and mediated by many physical objects in addition to embodied modes. When we investigate how participants make sense of this complexity, we find an underlying communicative semantics.

Communicative semantics/pragmatics

| **Communicative semantics:** | Multiple sequentially and simultaneously structured communicative processes are in a dialogical relationship to a communicative semantics. |

114 *Semantic/pragmatic* means

	We are particularly concerned with beats and deixis, as such lower-level actions structure the foregrounding and backgrounding of higher-level actions that a participant is simultaneously engaged in.
Communicative pragmatics:	Since we are analyzing interactions in real-time we are analyzing how participants *use* these lower-level actions.

A communicative semantics is a systematic organization of the complex of interactive meaning, which is both simultaneously and sequentially structured, and helps people indicate the level of attention/awareness that they place on certain higher-level actions.

Communicative semantic structure is made up of *pronounced* lower-level actions. I call these pronounced lower-level actions *means* in order to differentiate between the signals and the modes that they belong to. The *means* that are discussed in this chapter fall into two categories: the category of beats and the category of deixis.

I speak of *means* as having semantic property, when I emphasize their function of structuring meaning; and I speak of *means* as having pragmatic property, when I emphasize their interactive structuring function. Certainly, *means* have both properties at the same time; however, it is analytically worthwhile to distinguish between the two.

Beats

Beat- and deictic-type *means*:	Participants utilize many different pronounced beat- and deictic-type lower-level actions to structure their foregrounding of higher-level actions.
	Means are somewhat individualized. Some participants prefer one type of *means* over another, so that we may find a person who utilizes more eyebrow flashes than other *means* to structure their focused attention/awareness.
	The pragmatics of these *means* are interaction-dependent in the sense that an individual may utilize an elaborate deictic head movement rather than an eyebrow flash to indicate a shift in foregrounded higher-level action, because the other participants are not in a position to notice a facial *means*.

Some *means* of signaling a shift in higher-level action are beat-type lower-level actions. As we recall from Chapter 2, pp. 28–29, beats only consist of in/out or up/down phases, and have the same form regardless of the discourse content. They are generally seen to have a structuring function.

In language and gesture, beats have been demonstrated to be highly dependent upon language: taking on the function of emphasizing a certain word or notion, and thereby coherently integrating the overall discourse. Conversely, beats can indicate a higher-level communicative coherence – or communicative semantics – by indicating the foregrounding or backgrounding of higher-level actions that a social actor in interaction performs.

Such pronounced beat-type lower-level actions are not language dependent, and can be performed with other parts of the body as well as with the hand/finger. They take on meaning similar to deictic-type lower-level actions, in that they point to a shift in foregrounded higher-level action.

Deixis

The term "deixis" comes from the Greek word *deiktikos* and it means *pointing, indicative*. On pp. 28–30, I discussed deictic gesture, on pp. 32–37 deictic head movement, and on pp. 56 deictic gaze. Deictic lower-level actions – no matter which mode is utilized – can easily point to the positions or orientations of entities or events in the real world. They can also point to the level of attention/awareness that a participant in interaction places on a certain higher-level action. When an individual performs a deictic lower-level action that points to the foregrounding or backgrounding of a higher-level action, this deictic lower-level action is highly pronounced and structures the attention/awareness levels of the person. Therefore, such pronounced lower-level actions function as *means* in communicative semantics.

Within interaction, we study the *means* in relation to the participants. Here, the pronounced lower-level actions function as *means* in communicative pragmatics.

The phenomenal mind and means

The phenomenal mind:	Each participant in interaction expresses their experiences, thoughts, and feelings, and, at the same time, all other participants in the interaction are generally able to perceive and interpret (at least some of) these expressed experiences, thoughts, and feelings.
Semantic means:	*Means* structure meaning beyond words and sentences and also beyond the mode of language through multiple communicative

116 *Semantic/pragmatic* means

	modes in systematic ways. Here we speak of *communicative semantics*.
Pragmatic means:	*Means* are used by social actors, and they are used in interaction with other social actors. *Means in use* structure real-time ongoing interactions beyond words, sentences, and language. Here we speak of *communicative pragmatics*.

As outlined in Chapter 1, and discussed further in Chapters 4 and 5, some aspects of the phenomenal concept of mind have to be taken into consideration when studying multimodal interaction. While I have illustrated that participants in interaction can engage in several higher-level actions simultaneously, we also know that a participant is only able to focus on, or foreground, one higher-level action at a time (Baars, 1988; Raskin, 2000; Jones, 2003).

Focused attention requires the highest involvement of the participant, and foregrounded higher-level actions are clearly structured by semantic *means*. These *means* are the most important semantic/pragmatic features for our multimodal framework, as they help the participant in interaction discern an individual's shift in foregrounded higher-level action. While participants appear to discern such shifts in focus that other social actors carry out without being consciously aware of it, we can learn to consciously discern the shifts of foregrounded higher-level action of the participants under study.

How do means function?

Function of *means*:	*Means* are used by the performer to structure their own consciousness: organizing their own foregrounding of higher-level actions.
	Means can be used by the performer to communicate their shift in focused action, which indicates that the *means* simultaneously have an interactive function.
	Means can function to structure someone else's consciousness: structuring the other's foregrounded higher-level action.

Every time an individual shifts their focused attention, they structure this shift by employing a *means* just before the shift occurs. In other words, an individual consciously shifts from one foregrounded higher-level action to the next, and marks this shift through a *means*. The *means* has a dual function in interaction, as all interaction is co-constructed by the participants:

1   A *means* functions semantically by marking the end of a foregrounded higher-level action (or the beginning of a new higher-level action), facilitating the organization of higher-level actions in the performer's own mind.
2   A *means* functions pragmatically by communicating the upcoming occurrence of a shift in foregrounded higher-level action to the other participants.

The way in which *means* can be analyzed in real-time interactions can most easily be understood by looking at some examples.

Real-time examples

Analyzing real-time examples:	When analyzing real-time examples, we can sometimes read the meaning of the *means* from the reaction (indicating the perception) of other participants.

Deictic head movement

Before looking at some new examples, let us revisit the example in Chapter 2, pp. 34–36, where I discuss the deictic head movement. The reason that head movement is of particular importance for multimodal interactional analysis is that participants in interaction often use the head to indicate a shift in foregrounded higher-level action.

Here, the owner of a gift-basket shipping-and-retail store performs a pronounced deictic head movement, which actually indicates her foregrounding of the higher-level action of engaging in conversation with the designer. But *how do we know?* As we recall, the owner and the designer had been working side-by-side. The owner was reviewing the current order that was ready to be shipped, while the designer was filling gift baskets.

While the owner indicates a shift in foregrounded higher-level action through her elaborate deictic head movement, an analyst can read the actual interactional impact of this shift from the designer's reaction to the *means* which the store owner employs.

The images in Plate 2.4 illustrate that the designer could not help but notice such a pronounced head movement which the store owner performs in her peripheral vision. The preparation phase of the head movement precedes the spoken utterance "*is that the same as this?*", the stroke coincides with "*that*", while the retraction phase occurs with "*the same as,*" and the end of the movement coincides with a glance at a specific basket and the utterance "*this?*"

118 *Semantic/pragmatic* means

The deictic movement has a dual function:

(1) a shift in higher-level action; and
(2) pointing to baskets.

In the previous 25 minutes, the owner has employed unpronounced lower-level deictic-type actions without shifting her foregrounded higher-level action. Here, she utilizes a pronounced deictic head movement – indicating a shift.

The answer to the question *how do we know?*, however, does not lie in the store owner's head movement alone, but rather in the reaction of the designer, who perceives the head movement as a shift. The designer starts to focus on the store owner in reaction to the pronounced deictic head movement, and shifts her attention from filling gift baskets to interacting with the owner – by first following the owner's deictic movement with her gaze and then entering into conversation with the owner. The women had been working on their own tasks before the head movement occurred. While the owner had asked questions during that time, the questions did not lead to a shift in the women's foregrounded higher-level actions. Only once the elaborate head movement occurs, do they engage in focused interaction. Not only do the women now talk about particular baskets, but the designer walks around behind the counter, looks up at the first basket that the store owner referred to, and then takes a look at the other basket. The whole time, the women are discussing a certain type of basket and are fully engaged in this higher-level action.

This description illustrates that the owner has shifted her foregrounded higher-level action from checking the list to interacting with the designer. While prior questions that the store owner asked resulted in short answers like "I'm not sure" by the designer, this question, linked with the elaborate head movement, demands a shift in higher-level action from the designer. Now, the designer abandons her foregrounded higher-level action of filling baskets, and foregrounds the higher-level action of interacting.

Deictic leaning towards an object/participant

Analyzing real-time examples:	We can often read the meaning of a *means* from the higher-level action that the performer engages in.
	If an individual employs a *means* to foreground a new higher-level action, the *means* clearly marks the end of a foregrounded higher-level action and the beginning of a new one.

Semantic/pragmatic means 119

In the following example, the lower-level action of leaning towards an object and a participant in a pronounced way, indicates a shift in higher-level action.

Anna and Sandra have been sitting at a kitchen table. Anna has been reading a gourmet magazine, trying to find new ideas for their next catering event; and Sandra has been speaking about her personal life. Sandra is currently going through a divorce, and is worried about the sale of her house. While Anna listens to Sandra, she does not respond to her troubles, but rather is pointing out certain kinds of cheeses and speaks about what she has just read in the magazine. While Sandra listens to Anna, she does not respond to her talk about the magazine, but rather is concentrating on her personal problems. A brief multimodal transcript in Plate 6.1 illustrates this moment of interaction.

The first image in Plate 6.1 shows that Anna is sitting close to the table, demonstrating a closed posture, holding her head in her left hand, and leaning over the magazine. Sandra, on the other hand, is sitting as far back from the table as the table and bench allow. Both women have remained in this position for about 15 minutes. Then Sandra shifts topics from her personal problems to a memory of a personal experience and moves forward as she speaks, as illustrated in the second image of Plate 6.1.

In the first image of the second row, Sandra has moved further forward and, in the second image, Sandra leans far forward. She holds this position for a few seconds before she moves slightly back again, as illustrated in the last image. Here, Sandra has moved back, placed her right elbow on the table, and propped her head into her right hand. She is now gazing at the magazine and, from here on, discusses with Anna which items they

Plate 6.1 Semantic/pragmatic *means*: deictic leaning towards an object/participant.

120 *Semantic/pragmatic* means

could use for their next catering event. This higher-level action of reading the magazine stays in the foreground of both women's attention/awareness for the next 10 minutes.

The movement phase, from her rest-position in the first image of the first row to the stroke of the deictic leaning in the second image of the second row takes 3.11 seconds. Sandra then holds the leaning position in a post-stroke hold for a comparatively long 5.07 seconds, before she retracts in 2.93 seconds to take up her new rest-position. The time that this leaning takes – 11:11 seconds from beginning to end – and the extent of the movement, both indicate the elaborateness of this lower-level action.

During the first 15 minutes of interaction, the women are clearly focused on two different higher-level actions. Anna is engaged in the higher-level action of reading; and Sandra is engaged in the higher-level action of conversing. While each woman is clearly focused on her own higher-level action, they are simultaneously well aware of the other's foregrounded higher-level action (which is also apparent in later conversations).

When utilizing the heuristic notion of the modal density foreground–background continuum for the analysis of Anna's actions, we see that Anna utilizes high modal density in her construction of the higher-level action of reading the magazine. She employs the modes of posture, proxemics (to the magazine), gaze, spoken language, and layout in a fairly intense and complexly interlinked way. Sandra meanwhile employs high modal density in her construction of the higher-level action of conversing in the first image of Plate 6.1. Here, she is leaning back on the bench, her gaze resting on the side of Anna's head, and she intensely employs the mode of spoken language.

While Anna does not respond to Sandra in any communicative mode, she is listening to Sandra's troubles due to the proxemics (to Sandra), the layout, and the audible mode of spoken discourse that she is no doubt hearing. Even though Anna clearly does not focus on Sandra's higher-level action of conversing, she is listening, and therefore paying some attention to it, so that we can say that she is mid-grounding Sandra's higher-level action of conversing.

Similarly, Sandra is listening to Anna's reading of parts of the magazine (which also is apparent in the later conversation, which is not transcribed here). Observable in her employment of the modes of proxemics (to Anna), layout, gaze, and spoken discourse, Sandra is mid-grounding Anna's higher-level action of reading the magazine. Both higher-level actions are mismatched as far as the attention/awareness levels of the participants are concerned, but run smoothly parallel for some time.

Finally, when Anna again points out a certain kind of cheese and starts talking about what she just read, Sandra shifts her topic and tells Anna that the cheese and wine remind her of the times when she went out to dinner with her parents. Here, Sandra's topic shift is triggered by a memory. Right after this topic shift, Sandra employs a *means* of leaning forward in a pronounced way, indicating a shift in foregrounded higher-level action. The peak of this *means* is illustrated in the second image of the second row in Plate 6.1. Of particular interest here is Sandra's shift in topic before she shifts her foregrounded higher-level action. The topic shift from her personal problems to a childhood memory does not indicate a shift in higher-level actions, but is an intermediate step.

Sandra first focuses on her troubles, then Anna points out a certain type of cheese and wine, which triggers Sandra's topic shift. The topic shift is slight – from one personal experience to another, yet it results in Sandra's foregrounding of the cheese and wine in the magazine, which she looks at when she leans forward. So, while the concrete shift in foregrounded higher-level action is indicated through Sandra's use of the *means* of leaning forward in a pronounced manner, the topic shift in her spoken discourse prompts the shift. This indicates that a shift in one communicative mode (and here it is the intense communicative mode of spoken language that Sandra utilizes to construct her higher-level action of conversing) can lead to a shift in higher-level action.

Once Sandra has performed the *means*, she no longer speaks of her personal experiences, but focuses completely on the magazine and Anna's foregrounded higher-level action of reading. Thus, with the completion of the *means* of leaning toward the magazine (and Anna), Sandra shifts her foregrounded higher-level action from conversing to reading. Now, Sandra and Anna are both foregrounding the higher-level action of reading and discussing what they read. The women are now in synchrony concerning the focused higher-level action, while they had been asynchronous in their foregrounded higher-level actions before.

The eyebrow flash

Analyzing real-time examples:	We can determine which pronounced lower-level action is a *means* by viewing the prior and following chains of lower-level actions that a participant performs.
	If an individual has performed chains of lower-level actions (exclusive of the pronounced lower-level action under consideration), and then utilizes the pronounced lower-level action, you may have found a *means*.
	Once you believe you have found such a structuring *means*, you next need to analyze whether the participant performs a shift in higher-level action.

| **Semantic or pragmatic function?** | While *means* certainly always function on a semantic and a pragmatic level in interaction, they sometimes have more of a semantic function for the performer. |

The eyebrow flash is an up–down movement of the eyebrows, which is a beat-type means and consists of a two-movement phase just like other beats.

Sandra and Anna are once more sitting at Anna's kitchen table. It is Saturday morning and all of the children are playing nearby. Anna's husband moves in and out of the room and the dog follows him. Besides the two families (which consist of Sandra and her two children, and Anna, her husband and their three children), the researcher is present.

Anna has been engaged in writing a shopping list for the last 20 minutes, while Sandra has been drawing pictures for Anna's little girl, Katie, who is sitting in her lap. In the following example, Anna indicates a shift in foregrounded higher-level action through an eyebrow flash. I use the active verb *indicate*, because the eyebrow flash is a gesture that Anna performs. However, I do not wish to imply that this action is consciously intended by the performer. In fact, performers as well as other participants are largely unaware of an underlying communicative semantics. Even though the underlying semantics is largely out of the awareness of participants, we all indicate and react to these structuring devices, so that they do have a pragmatic property as well.

The brief multimodal transcript in Plate 6.2 illustrates the eyebrow flash and the higher-level actions that Anna engages in before and after employing the *means*. In this transcript, the arrows help to indicate the speaker and the time of the utterance.

The first image in Plate 6.2 shows Anna sitting close to the table, demonstrating a closed posture, holding a cookbook open with her left hand, and writing a list with her right hand. Sandra is sitting at the table, with Katie in her lap. She is holding a pen in her right hand and has a piece of paper in front of her, yet the two women are again engaged in different focused higher-level actions.

While Anna foregrounds the higher-level action of reading cookbooks and compiling a shopping list, Sandra foregrounds the higher-level action of interacting with several participants in the room. She draws pictures for Katie, shows them to Shawn, and speaks with the researcher and with Anna's husband.

There is much activity going on around Anna, yet she does not focus her attention on any of the ongoing interactions. As shown in the first image of Plate 6.2, Anna employs high modal density, by intensely and complexly utilizing modes like proxemics, posture, gaze, and print. For about 20 minutes, Anna focuses on this higher-level action of writing a

Plate 6.2 Semantic/pragmatic *means*: eyebrow flash.

shopping list, only changing her position slightly whenever she is finished with one cookbook, closing it, and putting it on a pile of other thin cookbooks to her left. She repeats these lower-level actions several times.

At the point illustrated in the second row of images in Plate 6.2, Anna has just closed a cookbook, and starts lifting it as illustrated in the first image. In the second image, she holds the cookbook at the highest point, and, in the third image, she is dropping the book. The next row of images illustrates a close-up of the eyebrow flash that Anna performs while placing this cookbook on the stack of other read books. Here, you see that Anna's eyebrows rise with the lifting of the cookbook. Both the book and the eyebrows simultaneously reach the highest point, as illustrated in the second image in both the second and third rows. However, Anna has lowered her eyebrows before the book has reached the pile of other read cookbooks, which indicates the speed of the eyebrow flash. While Anna performs the eyebrow flash, her husband walks into the room and Sandra starts joking about his hair, which is sticking up in all directions. Once Anna has performed the *means* of the eyebrow flash, she turns around, looks at

124 *Semantic/pragmatic* means

her husband and chimes in with the talk that was going on, as illustrated in the last image of Plate 6.2.

Here, we see that Anna has finished the higher-level action of writing the shopping list. When she places the last book on the stack of cookbooks, Anna indicates a shift from one foregrounded higher-level action to another by utilizing the semantic *means* of an eyebrow flash. In other words, she shifts from the foregrounded higher-level action of writing a shopping list to the higher-level action of conversing with other participants in the room through her use of the eyebrow flash. Once Anna has focused on the higher-level action of conversing, she foregrounds this interaction for quite a while, getting highly involved in joking about her husband's hair – employing high modal density.

In this example, we see that the *means* is regulating Anna's foregrounded higher-level actions. While she was initially focused on writing a shopping list, she switches focus to the conversation once she has performed the *means*, which clearly marks the end of one higher-level action and/or the beginning of the next.

The hand/finger beat

Analyzing real-time examples:	*Means* may not only be visual, but may also be audible or have an audible component.
	Hand/finger beats often are audible and do not have to be *seen* by the participants.
	Social actors perform such *means* for the audible effect when other participants are not utilizing the mode of gaze. Thus, the *means* are used (pragmatically) in order to communicate a shift in focus to another participant.
Semantic or pragmatic function?	Sometimes, the pragmatic function of the *means* takes priority over the semantic function.

The hand/finger beat is an up–down movement of the hand and/or fingers, which is a beat-type *means* and consists of a two-movement phase. However, the hand/finger beat, when structuring the foregrounding of higher-level actions, often does not coincide with spoken utterances.

In the following example, the accountant is answering some questions that his assistant has asked. He is leaning against a desk close to his assistant, and is employing high modal density to construct the higher-level action of conversing, as illustrated in the first image of Plate 6.3.

In the first image, the accountant is standing and leaning against a desk, while his assistant is sitting. They are engaged in focused interaction:

Plate 6.3 Semantic/pragmatic *means*: hand/finger beat.

utilizing the modes of layout, proxemics, posture, gesture, gaze, print, and spoken language to construct this foregrounded higher-level action.

This interaction has been going on for about four minutes, and the accountant has answered the questions that his assistant has asked. After the accountant performs three successive hand beats, as illustrated in the three images in the second row of Plate 6.3, his assistant looks at the form in her hands and says "*well.*"

Here we see that the accountant first lifts his right hand in the first image of the second row, then moves it down, slapping his right leg, while simultaneously lifting his left hand up, as illustrated in the second image of this row. Then he moves his left hand down, slapping his left leg and simultaneously lifting his right hand up, as illustrated in the last image of the second row. He then again moves his right hand down, again

126 *Semantic/pragmatic* means

slapping his right leg (as indicated by the arrow), and, during this last beat, the assistant says "*well.*"

The first image of the third row in Plate 6.3, illustrates that once the accountant has performed the three audible hand beats, he stands up but stalls in his movement, and his assistant says "*then I'll put that amount in.*" The second image shows that the accountant is still looking at his assistant while moving away from her. When he says "*yeah, that's it,*" he is no longer employing high modal density for this higher-level action of conversing with his assistant. The third image shows that he has taken a step back towards his assistant, saying "*alright*" and grabbing the document, saying "*you want me to sign that.*" The last image illustrates that the assistant turns towards her computer, while the accountant is walking to his own office where a person is waiting for him.

Although the accountant has clearly marked a shift (through the hand beats) and is employing less modal density for the interaction with his assistant, he is hesitating. The assistant's sequential reaction to the accountant's indication of a shift in his foregrounded higher-level action was the utterance "*well.*" Schiffrin and others point out that the discourse marker *well* is often used with disagreements, denials, and insufficient answers (Schiffrin, 1987: 116). In this example, the accountant appears to interpret his assistant's use of the discourse marker "*well*" as a possibility of having given an insufficient answer. In return, he stalls in his movements until his assistant says: "*then I'll put that amount in here.*"

Here, we see that the assistant is contradicting the end of the focused interaction that the accountant has initiated through her use of language. Only once it has been verified that she understood his answer correctly, does he take the document and complete his shift in foregrounded higher-level action. This example demonstrates the interactive function of the *means*. When one individual performs a *means* to indicate a shift in their own foregrounded higher-level action, other participants may interfere with such a shift – either delaying it or even aborting it altogether. Often, a shift in foregrounded higher-level action by one participant in interaction directly impacts the foregrounding of a higher-level action of another (or other) participant(s). In other words, if two people are engaged in conversation: both focusing on the same higher-level action, and one participant then shifts their focus, the other participant is forced to also shift their foregrounded higher-level action.

Thus, here the *means* takes on pragmatic priority over a semantic function for the participants who are engaged in mutual foregrounded higher-level action. In other words, the accountant performs audible hand beats in order to communicate his shift in foregrounding of a new higher-level action to his assistant.

Assignment

People shift their foregrounded higher-level actions frequently, and therefore constantly utilize *means*. However, since these semantic/pragmatic *means* are usually performed out of the awareness of the performer and the other participants, it will take some practice to see them.

Videotape a 15-minute interaction, and then watch this interaction closely and take notes of the various higher-level actions that the participants are foregrounding. Mark the times of an approximate shift in higher-level action of any one person on a piece of paper, and then try to find the *means* that indicates the shift. Recall that semantic/pragmatic *means* are employed just before the shift occurs – the actual shift in higher-level action may also be delayed.

Once you have learned to see/hear semantic/pragmatic *means* on a videotape, try to observe people. With a little practice (and a lot of concentration), you will be able to see *means* and realize when a person is about to shift their focused attention to another higher-level action.

7 Modal density foreground–background continuum as a methodological framework

Complex interactions

> **Summary:** The modal density foreground–background continuum explicitly links interaction to consciousness, showing that participants can construct several higher-level actions simultaneously – each of which is sequentially structured.
>
> This framework allows us to qualitatively analyze the interplay of embodied and disembodied communicative modes, and we no longer have to differentiate between face-to-face and mediated interaction.
>
> By qualitatively analyzing the multiple modes that participants employ, we recognize that any mode may take on high intensity and thus take on the hierarchically supreme position, structuring the other modes utilized. On the other hand, no mode has to necessarily be hierarchically superior to other modes within a specific interaction.
>
> Complex multimodal interactions are structured by a "communicative semantics/pragmatics" or *semantic/pragmatic means*. Participants structure their own foregrounding of higher-level actions through the performance of *means*, and simultaneously indicate an upcoming shift in their foregrounded higher-level action to other participants.
>
> *Means* can also be specifically used to influence another participant, indicating to a participant that they are expected to follow a shift in foregrounded higher-level action.

In this chapter, I focus on practical examples of day-to-day interactions, to illustrate how this methodology can lead to some new insights about human interaction. Here I draw on some new examples, but also return to some examples from previous chapters.

Multimodal teaching: music instruction

Multimodal teaching:	A teacher can utilize modes that are usually used interdependently (like gesture and spoken language) as two distinct meaning making systems, when such a distinction is beneficial for teaching/learning.
Utilizing a *means*:	A teacher can "pull" the students' focused attention towards the teacher's newly foregrounded higher-level action by employing a *means*.

Instructing a student to learn a musical instrument is a complex and multimodal process. Both teacher and student(s) employ multiple modes to construct the higher-level action of a music lesson. As soon as a teacher and student(s) are fully engaged in the process, the higher-level action of giving/receiving a music lesson is backgrounded, and several other higher-level actions are foregrounded and mid-grounded.

As explained in Chapter 5, the actual hierarchical level of the higher-level actions performed is not too important to the participants, as they keep multiple actions – no matter which hierarchical level – on some level in their consciousness. Consequently, when a teacher instructs a student how to play the guitar, both participants are aware of this higher-level action throughout the interaction – in the background of their attention/awareness.

The following example illustrates the complexity of a music lesson. The teacher is utilizing multiple modes to facilitate learning, and Peter utilizes multiple modes to acquire a new strumming pattern.

The first image of Plate 7.1 shows the guitar teacher lifting his right hand while he says "*up,*" and the second image of the first row illustrates that he lowers his right hand while he says "*down.*" He performs such chains of lower-level actions 19 times between 7:28.46 and 8:03.35.

However, while the chain of lower-level actions of the hand/arm movement does not change, the chain of the lower-level actions of saying "*up*" and "*down*" is not concurrent with all the movements of the teacher's arm. The teacher utilizes the mode of spoken language, saying "*up*" or "*down,*" to indicate that Peter has to stroke the strings at those times. Whenever the teacher only moves his hand/arm up or down without uttering the co-occurring words, Peter is not supposed to touch the strings, but move his hand up and down to keep the rhythm and ensure that his hand is in the right position when he comes to the next note that requires strumming. During the 19 iterations of hand/arm movements of the teacher, he only utilizes co-occurring utterances, saying *up* or *down* 11 times.

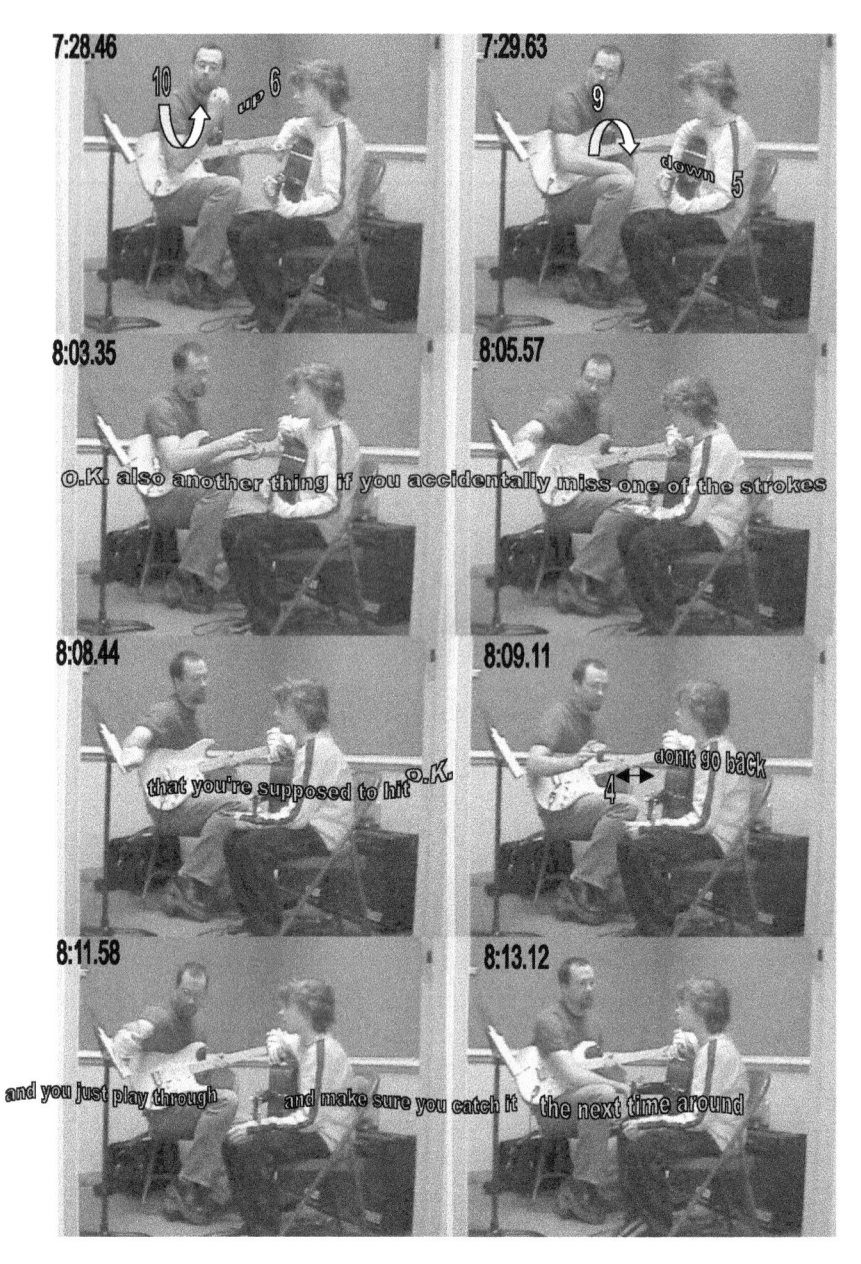

Plate 7.1 Transcript: music instruction.

The hand/arm gestures of the teacher are used iconically to depict the movement of the student's hand/arm or, in other words, the gestures convey – through pictorial content – the correct hand/arm movements that Peter is supposed to employ. Thus, the teacher utilizes these iconic hand/arm gestures to communicate and facilitate the movement, scaffolding to help Peter perform the regular movements that are necessary for the new strumming pattern. Concurrently, the teacher utilizes the mode of spoken language to communicate the voiced part of the strumming pattern to his student, again scaffolding to help the student to perform the new strumming pattern.

Here, the two modes are sometimes used together, and sometimes only the mode of hand/arm gesture is employed. However, during the times when gesture and spoken utterance are employed simultaneously, these two modes actually convey two different concepts. The hand/arm gesture always and only communicates the correct rhythmic movement of the hand/arm to the student, while the spoken utterances always and only communicate the actual strumming of the strings to Peter. Thus we see that the two modes, which sometimes co-occur, are used by the teacher and understood by the student as separate meaning-making resources.

During 17 up/down hand/arm movements, the teacher and his student are in synchrony. They are both utilizing the modes of gaze and print: reading the strumming pattern from a book that is placed on the music stand, as well as the mode of hand/arm movement and music. The teacher's hand/arm movements are prominent, and Peter can follow these movements in his peripheral vision. Once Peter has performed 17 movements, he becomes confused, and he stops playing after performing two more movements, as his teacher keeps making hand movements. For the last two movement phases, Peter and his teacher are no longer in synchrony. While the teacher keeps the rhythm, Peter lags slightly behind in his movements.

As soon as the teacher stops his up/down movements, he performs a *means*; at 8:03.35 the teacher points to Peter with a quick deictic hand movement (as illustrated in the first image of the second row in Plate 7.1) and says "*OK, also another thing.*"

This *means* indicates a shift in higher-level action, from practicing the new strumming pattern with his student to verbal teaching. The guitar teacher utilizes the *means* pragmatically causing his student to refocus on the teacher's newly foregrounded higher-level action. Once the teacher has performed the *means*, he points to the book on the music stand (as illustrated in the second image of the second row in Plate 7.1) and says "*if you accidentally miss one of the strokes.*" Here he starts turning his head towards Peter. The first image in the third row shows that the teacher is now looking at Peter while he continues to speak saying "*that you're supposed to hit.*" Here, Peter is gazing at the teacher's index finger, but, only a second later, Peter has shifted his gaze towards the teacher (as illustrated in the second image of this row). At this point, the teacher performs four quick back-and-forth hand movements that resemble erasing something, as illustrated by the arrow and the number four in the second image in the third row. While the teacher performs this iconic gesture, he says "*don't go back.*" The teacher then points at the pattern in the book (as illustrated in the first image of the last row) saying "*and you just play through.*" While continuing his utterance, saying "*and make sure you catch it the next time around,*" he moves his hand back into a rest position, gazing at Peter (as illustrated in the last image of Plate 7.1).

Multimodal methodology: independence or interdependence of modes

This example demonstrates that even modes that are usually interdependent – here, gesture and language – can be utilized simultaneously, yet independently. The up/down movements of the teacher's right hand/arm and the utterances "*up*" and "*down*" build two distinct chains of lower-level actions: being utilized as two distinct meaning-making resources by the teacher and the student. Between 7:28.46 and 8:03.35, the modes of gesture and spoken language are distinct and of equal value when trying to hierarchize the modes. Each mode is utilized to communicate a separate aspect of the strumming pattern, and both are of equal importance.

Only when we think of communicative modes as heuristically distinct chains of lower-level actions, can we realize when the modes are used as distinct modes and when they are used in a highly interdependent way.

As we saw in the second image of the third row in Plate 7.1, this iconic gesture that the teacher performs is highly dependent upon the utterance "*don't go back.*" This gesture could not be understood properly by the student, without the teacher's use of the mode of spoken language. Therefore, this gesture is dependent upon the mode of spoken language or, in other words, the mode of spoken language is in this instance the superior mode (as the utterance can be understood without the gesture), while the mode of gesture takes on the subordinate role (as the gesture cannot be properly understood without the utterance). Thus, we see that the modal configuration, including the distinctiveness and interdependence as well as the hierarchical structure of modes, can change quickly within an interaction.

Multimodal methodology: **means** *used to influence another participant*

The music lesson example also shows how one participant can influence a shift in foregrounded higher-level action in other participants by utilizing a *means*. In the last chapter I discussed the notion that an individual indicates a shift in foregrounded higher-level action by utilizing some pronounced deictic- or beat-type lower-level action, which I call *means*. Such a shift in foregrounded higher-level action has direct influence on the person(s) that the individual interacts with in focused interaction, as it simultaneously forces them to adjust their foregrounded higher-level action.

The music teacher utilizes the co-construction of focused interaction and the fact that his employment of a *means* has direct impact on his student. He points to Peter in a pronounced deictic hand gesture: indicating that he is shifting the foregrounded higher-level action from practicing to verbal teaching. This deictic means leads Peter to also shift his foregrounded higher-level action from practicing to listening to the verbal teaching. Here, we see that a *means* can foster co-constructed foregrounding of specific higher-level actions. In a teacher–student interaction, you will find many *means* that the teacher utilizes to *pull* the students' focused attention from one higher-level action to the next.

Multimodal teaching: language instruction

A few years ago I conducted an eight-month-long study in a first-grade classroom of a German/English bilingual elementary school. In that study I was mainly interested in the connection between autonomy and intrinsic motivation. Without going deeply into learning theory I would like to revisit the example of classroom discourse from Chapter 3. There, I introduced an example in which the teacher was trying to explain the word "*Graben*" ["moat"] without referring to the English term. The children had learned this word in the last lesson, and the teacher was helping the children to remember it.

Classroom discourse

As you will recall from Chapter 3 (pp. 59–60), Bob is excited that he found "*a guy*". The following excerpt starts at line (16). Here, Joe and Jon chime in, and the teacher acknowledges in line (19) that there really is a guy that she had not focused on before.

(16) *Bob:*   I JUST found a GUY!
(17) *Joe:*   (pointing at own handout) a GUY right HERE.
(18) *Jon:*   (gaze shift to Joe's handout/Joe's finger) that's a guarder
(19) *T:*   (gaze shift to Joe's finger, then Bob) *ja, da IST einer*
        [yes, there IS someone]
(20) *Bob:*   here, right HERE (pointing at own handout)
(21) *Joe:*   right there (pointing at own handout)
(22) *T:*   (gaze to Bob's handout) *GENAU da ist er.* [EXACTLY there he is]
(23)   *mhm und was MACHT der denn da oben?*
        [mhm and what is he DOING up there?]
(24)   *Bob, was MACHT der denn da oben?*
        [Bob, what is he DOING up there?]

(25) Bob: der der [he he]
(26) Jon: oh, what do you call it
(27)   what do you call it
(28)   tower
(29) T: Turm [Tower]
(30)   der steht auf dem Turm? [he is standing on the tower?]
(31) Jon: der steht auf dem Turm [he is standing on the tower]
(32) T: der steht auf dem Turm [he is standing on the tower]
(33) Bob: die Mauer [the wall]
(34) T: mhm.
(35)   steht der auf der Mauer? [is he standing on the wall?]
(36) Bob: der steht auf der Mauer [he is standing on the wall]

In line (17) Joe performs a deictic gesture, exclaiming excitedly "*a guy right here.*" This deictic gesture does not only point, but is also a *means*, which can be surmised from the reactions of Jon and the teacher – who both shift their attention to Joe's focus in line (18) and (19). From here on, the exchange is fast, without perceptible pauses, as the children are excited about the person in the handout. The teacher has refocused her attention from the moat to the person in the handout, and she develops a teaching opportunity by exploring the children's focus of attention. Thus, the teacher shifts from focusing on her own agenda of discussing the moat to the children's agenda of speaking about the person in the handout.

Joe's *means* (his deictic gesture) indicates his own shift in foregrounded higher-level action from speaking about the moat, which he was visibly focused on in line (5), to speaking about the person in the handout in line (17). The fact that the teacher allows Joe's *means* to restructure her foregrounding of higher-level actions, can be seen in line (19), where she gazes at Joe's handout and acknowledges the existence of a person in the same line. Here, we notice that a shift in one person's foregrounded higher-level action can (and sometimes has to) lead to a shift in a participant's higher-level action. Clearly, the teacher could have overruled this shift in focused attention, but she uses this interest as a teaching opportunity. The teacher scaffolds and leads the students to use the target language.

When we follow Joe's lines from the complete excerpt, we see that Joe was engaged in focused interaction with the teacher before the shift:

(5) Joe: ground. (looking at T's pointing finger)
(10) Joe: (gaze shift to Bob, then to Bob's handout)
(17) Joe: (pointing at own handout) a GUY right HERE.
(21) Joe: right there (pointing at own handout)

In line (5) Joe had shared the teacher's foregrounded higher-level action of speaking about the moat. In line (10) he looks at Bob and Bob's handout; in line (17) Joe indicates a shift, which is taken up by Jon and the teacher;

and in line (21) Joe follows up on his previous utterance. Reviewing the complete excerpt once again, we see that Jim, Joe, and Jon show awareness of Bob and his focus on the person in the picture, by shifting their posture and their gaze towards Bob and his handout starting from line (9). When we follow Bob in the excerpt, we see that he starts out focusing on the person in the picture – not paying attention to the teacher at all:

(3) Bob: A GUY.
(8) Bob: a guy (almost inaudible)
(16) Bob: I JUST found a GUY!
(20) Bob: here, right HERE (pointing at own handout)
(25) Bob: der der [he he]
(33) Bob: die Mauer [the wall]
(36) Bob: der steht auf der Mauer [he is standing on the wall]

Bob first announces that he has found "*a guy*" by using emphatic stress in line (3); in line (8) he repeats his utterance almost inaudibly; but in line (16) he again uses emphatic stress to exclaim "*I just found a guy*," emphasizing the words "just" and "guy". At this point, the other children (Jim, Joe, and Jon) all shift their postures and their gaze towards Bob and his handout, showing interest, and Joe then indicates a shift in focus by employing the *means* following Bob's utterance. Bob now also says "*Here, right here*" in line (20), and follows the utterance by pointing at his own handout.

Then the teacher speaks to Bob, and Bob starts by uttering words in the target language. From line (25) to line (36), Bob only employs the target language. Jon, who had not spoken before the shift to the person in the handout, also employs the target language:

(18) Jon: (gaze shift to Joe's handout/Joe's finger) that's a guarder
(26) Jon: oh, what do you call it
(27)   what do you call it
(28)   tower
(31) Jon: der steht auf dem Turm [he is standing on the tower]

Of course, the target language is employed with much scaffolding by the teacher, and Jon only repeats the sentence given to him, but he does employ the target language without being explicitly asked to do so. Similarly, Bob employs the target language. But Bob has a specific interest in this person in the handout, and, when Jon claims that the person is standing on a tower, Bob disagrees in the target language by saying "*Mauer*" ["wall"]. Now the teacher again scaffolds and asks the question "*steht der auf der Mauer?*" ["is he standing on the wall?"] and Bob answers in a grammatically correct sentence, saying "*der steht auf der Mauer*" ["he is standing on the wall"].

136 *Complex interactions*

Multimodal methodology: allowing a means to influence personal focus

In the above example, we find that a teacher can utilize a shift in students' foregrounded higher-level actions as a teaching opportunity. As in other focused interaction, each participant who is engaged in mutual focused higher-level action can be directly influenced by a person's shift in foregrounded higher-level action. This explains why the teacher shifts her focus once Joe has indicated a shift in foregrounded higher-level action, but does not shift her focus when Bob is voicing that he has found a guy.

Bob had been focused upon the person in the image from the outset; however, the teacher did not shift her attention to Bob's focus in the beginning. When we review the first few lines, we see that Jim and Joe shared the teacher's foregrounded higher-level action of speaking about the moat. Thus, Jim and Joe had been co-constructing the teacher's focus, while Bob had not entered into focused interaction with the teacher before this shift in focus occurred. In lines (3) and (8), Bob's focused higher-level action of speaking about the person in the handout was mid-grounded by the other children. Then Joe indicates his shift in foregrounded higher-level action from the teacher's to Bob's focus, and Jon and the teacher react to this shift. By the time that the teacher refocuses, three of her four students in the group show interest in the person in the handout.

While teachers often overrule shifts in their student's foregrounded higher-level actions so that they can follow their own agendas, teachers can also go along with such a shift and develop the students' interest into a teaching opportunity. Instead of pulling the students towards her foregrounded higher-level action of speaking about the moat, the teacher allowed the students to pull her towards their foregrounded higher-level action of speaking about the person in the handout.

Motivation

When the teacher refocuses her foregrounded higher-level action to the person in the handout, she validates Bob's autonomy. Bob had been autonomous from the very beginning, but the teacher had taken no notice of him. She had only refocused once Joe, who had shared her foregrounded higher-level action, had refocused.

Through this shift in foregrounded higher-level action, the teacher is allowing Bob to be excited about the person, and to lead the group to his discovery. The teacher fosters his intrinsic motivation, resulting in Bob speaking in the target language. Jon, who had not been sharing the teacher's focus in the beginning, is also motivated by this shift in foregrounded higher-level action, and speaks in the target language. Joe on the other hand, does not profit from this shift, even though he had initiated it.

Findings like this illustrate that teachers react to students with whom they are engaged in focused interaction, while they do not react to students who are autonomous. Yet it is particularly the autonomous student who profits from fostering their autonomy. As we can see in the example above, Bob takes true interest in his findings and voluntarily speaks in the target language, while Joe does not use the target language once in the excerpt.

While the teacher utilizes a shift in her students' foregrounded higher-level action as a teaching strategy and actually taps into the students' intrinsic motivation, we need to question this truly interactive use of *means* in teaching. The shift does result in fostering intrinsic motivation in Bob; however, it seems that Bob's intrinsic motivation could have been stimulated from the outset, and we may want to start thinking about devising a teaching strategy that facilitates to foster autonomy in students who are not engaged in focused interaction with the teacher.

As van Lier (1996) points out, autonomy is closely tied to motivation and achievement, and language teaching is most effective when the teacher "stimulates intrinsic motivation, so as to take advantage of natural interests, curiosity and emergent rewards" (van Lier, 1996: 112). While many teachers are aware of this, teaching is interactively constructed and teachers are bound by communicative semantics, which facilitates shifting foregrounded higher-level actions with others in focused interaction, but does not facilitate shifting higher-level actions with others who are not engaged in focused interaction. Yet it is particularly those students who are not in focused interaction with the teacher, who are autonomous and who profit most from a shift by the teacher to their foregrounded higher-level action.

Construction of social worlds

Construction of a social world:	Every higher-level action that a social actor engages in constructs the person's social world.
	Higher-level actions that an individual performs simultaneously may run parallel and construct one aspect, or be disparate and construct competing aspects of a person's social world.

In previous chapters, I have given several examples with Sandra and Anna as participants. These examples come from a vast collection of diverse data, which I collected over a year of ethnographic study of these two women and their everyday lives. As we recall, they own a catering business together; Sandra has two children and is currently going through a divorce, while Anna has three children and is married.

In Chapter 1, I discussed the mode of proxemics, showing Anna ironing the family's clothes while watching TV, with Katie playing behind her. There I claimed that Anna and Katie were influencing each other's actions to some extent, due to their *Anwesenheit*. This claim is based on my extensive study of many different data sets, as well as my ethnographic observations.

138 *Complex interactions*

In Chapter 4, I showed how music took on high modal density for Sandra, when the deep male voice sang *"Mama, I wet my bed last night."* Again, the *Anwesenheit* of Sandra's young son shapes her actions to some extent, and her son's actions are in turn shaped by the *Anwesenheit* of his mother. Again, I analyzed this piece through careful triangulation – not solely based on the visual aspects of the setting. Margolis, speaking of historic photographs, rightfully warns that "it is not possible to photograph social relationships" (Margolis, 1999: 34). It is, however, possible to analyze social relationships through careful and extended ethnographic methods, including analysis of video data.

Here I use stills to demonstrate the social worlds that both Anna and Sandra are constructing: analyzed through rigorous triangulation of a vast set of different kinds of data. Since video data capture many visible and audible channels and do not record snapshots – but events – such data lend themselves to the scrutiny of social relationships and social worlds. However, as a note of caution, I would like to add here that one cannot look solely at a photograph and come to a correct analysis of the social relationships among the people in the image. Here, the image is used to depict part of the analysis, and thus is used as a transcriptual tool.

In Chapter 5, I explicated the foreground–background continuum of attention/awareness by looking at an example in which Sandra is simultaneously engaged in six higher-level actions. At this time all five children are present, while the two women are working. Simultaneously, a friend is calling Sandra, and the researcher is present. When we glimpse the women's social world, we find that they are constantly performing several simultaneous higher-level actions: juggling the construction of their families as well as their business and their various friendships.

Shifts in foregrounded higher-level actions are often quick, and often the women's focus gets pulled by a shift that their children perform. For example, we recall the first image in the second row of Plate 4.2, where Sandra and Anna are shopping and Anna's younger son is attracting Anna's focused attention by employing postures as an intense mode. Although the children had been told to stay close to the shopping cart, such requests are difficult for children to follow, and quite often the women have to pay focused attention to their children during a shopping trip.

At least some of the children are almost always present – greatly structuring Sandra's and Anna's days. Here, I would like to show a few other examples, illustrating how family, work, and friendships are relentlessly juggled by both women.

Parallel higher-level actions

The first image in Plate 7.2 shows Sandra pushing a stroller with Anna's daughter, Katie. Sandra is walking through a shopping street to find a store in which to buy a present for a mutual friend of Anna and Sandra.

Plate 7.2 Construction of social worlds.

In the meantime, Anna is at home, working. This instance shows that Sandra and Anna are helping each other out to juggle their many demands.

When focusing on the image, we realize that Sandra constructs the higher-level action of shopping (by walking towards a specific store), and the higher-level action of watching the child (by pushing the stroller). The cityscape structures Sandra's walking path, and the other people and the cars in the street influence her movement pattern, yet Sandra has backgrounded the higher-level action of walking through the city streets. During informal questioning, Sandra surmises that she takes little notice of the signs, the people, or the cars, even though she is aware of all of them to some extent when walking through the city. She further explains that she only wanted to buy that present in a specific store, and that she took Katie along so that Anna could work in peace.

Here Sandra foregrounds the higher-level action of shopping and midgrounds the higher-level action of watching Katie. Yet, the higher-level actions shift every so often. One such example is given in the second image in the first row of Plate 7.2. Here Sandra is standing in the store and cannot decide how much money to spend on the present. She is calling Anna on her cell phone, when Katie points to a picture on a box and exclaims "*Käpten Blaubär*" ["Captain Bluebear"], which is a German comic character. Here Sandra shifts her focused attention to Katie, and says "*oh Käpten Blaubär das ist auch schön*" ["oh Captain Bluebear that is nice too"], before she goes back to calling. Thus, Sandra shifts her foregrounded higher-level action from shopping for a friend, to calling Anna, to interacting with Katie, and back to calling. While Sandra shifts her focus, the other higher-level actions are being pushed back in her attention/awareness continuum, but are all simultaneously present in her consciousness. When she pays focused attention to Katie, she is still well aware of her higher-level action of making a phone call and the higher-level action of shopping for a present.

Divergent higher-level actions

In another instance, Sandra and Anna are shopping for dessert dishes and glasses for an upcoming catering event.

The first image in the second row of Plate 7.2 shows Sandra, Anna, and Katie walking in a store. Anna is pushing the stroller in which Katie had been sitting, and Katie is running beside it. Their four boys are running a little further ahead of them, which is not visible in this image. Sandra and Anna are focused on the higher-level action of shopping for the dishes, and are mid-grounding the higher-level action of watching the five children. The second image of the second row shows Anna, Sandra, and Sandra's older son David at the cash register of a grocery store. The other four children are also present. Here, Anna and Sandra, who have been shopping for one of their catering events, are getting ready to pay. David is helping, while the other children are playing at a small distance from the cash register.

Both Anna and Sandra are foregrounding the higher-level action of compiling the items in groups that will make it easier for them to package the items, transport them, and arrange them in two kitchens. Simultaneously, both mothers are mid-grounding the higher-level action of watching David: asking him to place certain items in specific spots, and are mid- to backgrounding the higher-level action of watching the four children, who are playing at some distance. While the higher-level action of shopping is backgrounded, this higher-level action certainly structures the other higher-level actions that the women perform.

Multimodal methodology: parallel simultaneously constructed higher-level actions

When Sandra shops for a present for a mutual friend of herself and Anna, Sandra constructs one aspect of her social world, which we can term the aspect of friendships, on various levels.

This aspect of Sandra's social world is actively constructed: Sandra shops to buy a present for a friend, she watches the daugher of another friend (Anna), and calls Anna to discuss the present. Here we see that Sandra is actively building an aspect of her social world which not only involves the friends and a friend's child, but also the specific store that is located in the middle of the city that she walks to in order to buy the "right kind" of present. She largely foregrounds the higher-level action of buying the present, thereby constructing the friendship between herself and the friend that the present is for, as well as the friendship between herself and Anna. Simultaneously, Sandra largely mid-grounds the higher-level action of watching Anna's little girl. Through this higher-level action, Sandra again constructs the aspect of the social world that we can call friendship. She has taken Katie along so that Anna can focus on her work. Finally, when Sandra calls Anna from the store to discuss the various prices and possible presents, she again constructs a piece of this aspect of her social world. When we follow Sandra a little longer, we find that she picks up the two younger boys (hers and Anna's) from preschool, and provides all of the children with lunch as soon as the two older boys come home from school. Thus she further constructs her social world that here revolves around friendship.

As demonstrated in the example, Sandra constructs one aspect of her social world: the friendships, by constructing various higher-level actions simultaneously. As her day progresses, she continuously constructs simultaneous higher-level actions that construct this one part of her social world, and the higher-level actions run smoothly parallel to one another.

Multimodal methodology: divergent simultaneously constructed higher-level actions

As illustrated in the second row of Plate 7.2, Sandra and Anna are looking for glasses and buying food for a catering event.

Both women perform actions similar to those that Sandra performs in the previous example. The women largely foreground the higher-level actions of looking for dishes and placing food items on the counter, and mid-ground the higher-level action of watching the children. Simultaneously, the higher-level action of shopping is largely backgrounded. However, this time both Sandra and Anna are struggling to shift their foregrounded higher-level actions when the children demand it. The women often tell the children not to interrupt, and thereby contradict the requested shift in foregrounded higher-level actions. Also, the tone that the women employ is stricter than in many other situations that I have observed. Both Sandra and Anna try to keep their main focus on their work, and try to keep the higher-level action of watching the children in the mid-ground of their attention/awareness.

In these instances, the women perform simultaneous higher-level actions that are disparate as they construct competing aspects of their social worlds. Here, Sandra and Anna are constructing the aspect of their working worlds through buying items for their next catering event, while they are simultaneously constructing the aspect of their family worlds by watching the children. Because the two different aspects of the women's social world are constructed simultaneously, they compete, and you hear the women saying to each other that they do not like to take the children when shopping for their business. In conversations, they also speak about the fact that they do not mind taking the children shopping when they buy food for their families. These examples show that individuals can perform almost the same higher-level actions (shopping and watching the children) on almost the same attention/awareness levels (shopping largely in the foreground; and watching the children largely in the mid-ground) with almost the same participants (adult(s) and the children), and yet the strain for the individual juggling the various higher-level actions may be quite different.

As long as the simultaneous higher-level actions construct one aspect of an individual's social world, these higher-level actions are easily juggled because they run synchronously. In contrast, if an individual constructs different aspects of their social world through the performance of almost the same higher-level actions, the higher-level actions may compete, and it may be more difficult for a person to juggle the various higher-level actions because they run divergently.

Multimedia and interaction

Multimedia and interaction:	People interact with others through their use of phones, computers, and faxes. By writing an email and its being read, one interacts with a person.
Real-time/timescales:	The concept of real-time interaction is stretched when we think about computers.
	We write the email at our own speed (our real-time), and the other person reads it and responds according to their real-time.
	As with "snail mail", there is often a lag between the sent message and the response. When we think about instant messaging, the response time is shortened and comes much closer to what we originally called face-to-face interaction.
	When thinking of interaction as happening on different timescales, we no longer have to differentiate between face-to-face interaction and computer/phone-mediated interactions on the grounds of time.
	Real-time is not one time, but rather is made up of various timescales.

Whalen *et al.* studied the work practices of a sales representative in an office equipment company and found that these practices were "organized through an improvisational choreography of action involving not only the turn-by-turn interchange with customers on the telephone but also the concurrent utilization of a variety of tools and artifacts" (Whalen *et al.*, 2001: i).

Such choreography of action involving diverse tools and artifacts can be found in many office settings. While Whalen *et al.* focus on one person choreographing his actions in accordance with specific telephone calls, let us now return to the accountant's office.

As shown in earlier chapters, the accountant interacts with his assistant in her office, utilizing many modes: including the disembodied mode of print in the form of a document. When we follow the accountant into his office, we see how he interacts with various people simultaneously by utilizing a variety of tools and artifacts.

The transcript in Plate 7.3 precedes and follows the interaction between the accountant and his assistant that I discussed in the last chapter. There, the accountant had utilized the three audible *means* to indicate a shift in his foregrounded higher-level action. We saw that the assistant invoked a delay in his actual shift, but, after a brief exchange, the accountant does complete the shift and walks over to his office.

The first four images in Plate 7.3 illustrate the accountant's work practice before the previously discussed interaction with his assistant, and the next four images illustrate his work practices following the interaction. As mentioned in the last chapter, the accountant has a visitor, with whom he continuously interacts while in his office.

The first two images in Plate 7.3 show the assistant standing in the door of the accountant's office announcing a call, and then the accountant taking the call. The next image in this row shows the accountant conversing with his visitor. The first image of the second row illustrates that the accountant is holding a computer mouse in his right hand and looking at his computer screen. The second image of this row shows that he has turned around slightly, opening up his posture – he is now gazing directly at the visitor and they are engaged in conversation.

Between these four transcribed images and the next images in this plate, the interaction between the accountant and his assistant takes place in her office. As soon as the accountant returns to his office, in which the visitor is still sitting in the same spot, he sits down at his desk and signs the document, as illustrated in the first image of the third row in Plate 7.3. Following the signing of the document, the accountant stands up and is again involved in conversation – gazing at his visitor as illustrated in the second image of the third row in Plate 7.3. Here, the accountant is holding the signed document in his hands, while speaking about a different topic with the visitor.

In the first image of the last row, we see that the assistant has come into the accountant's office, and the accountant is handing her the document. No words are spoken between the accountant and his assistant at

Plate 7.3 Transcript: multimedia and interaction.

this time, and the accountant converses without perceptible pause with his visitor. The last image illustrates that the accountant has taken a seat at his desk again. He is still involved with his visitor and has again taken hold of the computer mouse.

These snapshots of the accountant's work practices show that he is choreographing several personal interactions – the interaction with his assistant, the interaction with the visitor, and the interaction with the client on the phone – while he is at appropriate times utilizing the computer and signing a printed document. This very short, about seven-minute-long, excerpt of one of his days illustrates the quick successions and sometimes overlapping actions that he performs.

All of these choreographed actions take place in real-time. But what are the different scales of real-time here?

Lemke suggests that:

> each act participates in local constructions of meaning on shorter timescales at the same time that it also participates in the systematic networks of interdependent activities that sustain institutions and societies over much larger distances and longer times.
> Lemke, http://www-personal.umich.edu/~jaylemke/
> (accessed 25/02/04)

This historical view of the extent of actions, simultaneously constructing local meaning as well as institutional and social meaning, is important for our understanding of human interaction on a micro and a macro level.

In addition, the notion of time needs to be considered for a multimodal analysis of interaction on different levels. Real-time is not just one concept, but rather is a multitude of concepts that are categorized as one. While some actions fall at one and the same time, so that the accountant, for example, signs the document while the visitor is sitting in his office, or the assistant is picking up the form while the accountant is speaking with the visitor, all of these actions started at a different moment in time. Every action has a different duration and will likely also be completed at a different time.

The concept of a modal density foreground–background continuum can give us insight into the workings of human interaction beyond focused interaction. When we analyze the higher-level actions that the accountant engages in simultaneously, we discover that he is constantly engaged on some level with his assistant (the foreground, mid-ground, or background). His assistant can enter his office when he is engaged in focused higher-level action with the visitor, and the accountant interacts with her, giving her the floor when needed (i.e. when she needs to give him a message) or by simply handing her the document. Simultaneously, he is engaged in interaction with the visitor – at times foregrounding the higher-level action of conversing with the visitor – and mid- or backgrounding this action if other higher-level actions are more important at a certain moment in time. When he speaks on the phone, he gives the client his focused attention and, when reading something on his computer, his attention is briefly focused on the screen. Similarly, when he signs the document his attention is briefly focused on the document.

While there is certainly much simultaneity in higher-level actions, we need to remember that the starting points, the duration, and the completion of the higher-level actions are usually quite different. Also, when, for example, tracing the higher-level actions that involved the document, we will see that the assistant is engaged in a higher-level action: filling out the document, and the accountant is also engaged in a higher-level action: signing the document. These higher-level actions are somewhat overlapping (when the accountant is answering the assistant's questions about the form) and somewhat distinct (when the assistant fills it out and when the accountant signs it).

Depending upon the focus of study, we can heuristically tease out the actions that each participant is performing, and thereby focus on particular social actors, or we can look at the actions that are structured around the document, and thereby focus on the document. However we focus, we can trace the higher-level action on a timeline within the office, and we can consider the historical timeline of the document and also the social and organizational meaning of it. The actions that the accountant and the assistant perform in less than seven minutes concerning this document are only a part of the sequence of actions that evolve around it.

While the higher-level actions that the accountant and the assistant engage in involving the document are fairly short-lived, there are other actions that are occurring simultaneously, which have a much longer duration.

The higher-level action of interacting between accountant and assistant, for example, has been occurring for many years. There is a routine, a pattern, and knowledge between these two social actors that has evolved through a history of encounters. The assistant has asked many questions and the accountant has signed many documents. The assistant has entered the accountant's office many times when he has had visitors, to announce an important call. Thus, while these particular higher-level actions are occurring at this time, both social actors have acquired what Nishida (1958) calls a *historical body*, or an understanding of each other's actions and ways of being, that make the interaction run smoothly.

Just as the accountant and the assistant have developed mental representations and processes of discourse among themselves, they have also developed mental representations and processes about the use of documents. The timelines of the higher-level actions that involve the document and involve the interaction between accountant and assistant are, however, of different durations, different structures, and different types. Yet, one impacts the other.

Thus, the accountant not only choreographs the higher-level actions that involve the turn-by-turn interchanges with his assistant, his visitor, and his client on the phone (by utilizing a variety of tools and artifacts), he also juggles the different timescales that each one of these higher-level actions entails.

Assignment

Carefully look at the example in the accounting firm. Pick one particular instance and draw modal density circles for the higher-level actions that the accountant performs at that moment. Then place the various higher-level actions on a foreground–background continuum. Now look once more at the transcripts (Plates 6.3 and 7.3) and note down the levels of attention/awareness that the accountant places on each higher-level action at each point illustrated.

Videotape an interaction and analyze some of the complexity that you find. Share your video and your analysis.

8 Analyzing multimodal interaction
A postscript

In this book I have outlined a qualitative methodology to analyze multimodal interaction. The reason that I developed this framework was my belief that we can only *truly* understand interaction if we investigate the visual channels of communication as well as the audible channels. Here, I draw on a wide range of examples to illustrate the applicability of the framework and, while it is applicable in all kinds of different situations, we are really only at the very beginning of multimodal interactional analysis. At this point, I outline some of the notions that have been developed, then I describe the affordances and constraints that this framework brings with it and, after that, I outline what the framework cannot do, and where I think we should go from here.

What is interaction?

I started the first chapter with the sentence: "All interactions are multimodal," and I have shown throughout the book that analyzing multimodal interaction requires the investigation of both visual and audio communicative modes. In order to analyze multimodal interaction, we have to analyze how participants employ the array of communicative modes involved.

I have attempted to present a methodological framework that allows us to overcome two major challenges that we encounter when trying to analyze interactions in their multimodal complexity. These challenges are the different *structures* and *materiality* of the various communicative modes. We overcome them by employing the mediated action as our unit of analysis. When viewing communicative modes as structured in sequential lower-level actions which build chains, and when viewing the many different chains of lower-level actions building higher-level actions, we can compose higher-level actions arranged through many different material and structured modes.

There is no mediated action without people. The distinction between face-to-face and mediated interaction has always been fuzzy. Kress and Van Leeuwen note "... by communicating we *interact*, we do something to or for or with people ..." (2001: 115), and when we interact we often utilize a variety of communicative modes to achieve this process of communicating. Communicating *is* interaction if one person conveys a message and another person perceives it. The modes utilized for interacting do not create a communicative moment as an interaction, but rather the process of doing something to or for or with people allows us to understand a communicative moment as an interaction.

This understanding of interaction also is aligned with what Habermas calls a *communicative action*. He notes that:

> The concept of communicative action refers to the interaction of at least two subjects capable of speech and action who establish interpersonal relations (whether by verbal or extra verbal means). The actors seek to reach an understanding about the action situation and their plans of action in order to coordinate their actions by way of agreement. The central concept of interpretation refers in the first instance to negotiating definitions of the situation which admit of consensus.
>
> Habermas (1984: 86)

What does the methodological framework for multimodal interaction allow us to do?

Context

A modal density foreground–background continuum allows us to analyze large aspects of what has traditionally been termed *context* in discourse analysis, by making it possible to analyze (inter)actions beyond language and beyond focused ones.

For an extensive period of time, language has been viewed as the central – if not the only meaning-making – mode of communication. Therefore, *context* was everything that was outside of the verbal. We also viewed the interactions that lay outside of the (verbally) focused interaction as *context*. Much of this focus was due to the tape recorder, which focuses the analyst on the audible mode of spoken language. Similarly, the video camera as a data-collection device has had a great influence on how we view our worlds, and the framework that I presented throughout this book was developed largely because of video data. Video data diffuse the focus on language and illustrate that there is much more going on in any interaction than just language and *context*.

The example of Sandra employing many communicative modes and engaging in six higher-level actions simultaneously, shows this point. There, Sandra does *something to or for or with people* other than the verbal focused interactions. Sandra writes a shopping list *with* Anna; Sandra speaks *with* her friend on the telephone; Sandra plays a game *with* the two older boys; Sandra makes sure that the younger boys are safe, doing something *to* the children (interfering with their actions) when she deems it necessary; Sandra allows the researcher to observe and videotape her, doing something *for* the researcher; and Sandra constructs the meeting *with* Anna. Focusing only on the spoken language that Sandra employs gives at best a distorted picture – as she does not speak to the two elder boys or to the researcher or even the younger children during the excerpt. Likewise, focusing only on the aspects of interaction that Sandra focuses on (her focused interaction of writing a shopping list with Anna, or her focused interaction of speaking with her friend on the phone) at best gives us a distorted picture – as Sandra is simultaneously paying attention to and is aware of four other higher-level actions.

Modal density

Modal density – the intensity or complexity of modes that an individual in interaction employs to construct a higher-level action – allows participants (and also the analyst) to perceive the expressed attention/awareness that the individual places on a specific higher-level action. If modal density is high, the individual focuses on the higher-level action constructed, and if modal density is low, the individual backgrounds the higher-level action, even though they will be somewhat aware of it. Thus, modal density decreases with the decreasing attention/awareness of a social actor – or so it is communicated and perceived in interaction.

Foreground–background continuum

This continuum is a heuristic model that represents the human attention/awareness levels in interaction. This model is by no means thought of as a one-to-one representation. In contrast it is *only* heuristic. Such heuristic visualization of attention/awareness levels allows us to discern many different levels of (inter)action that a person is simultaneously engaged in.

Attention/awareness levels have to be considered in human interaction for two reasons:

1 without differing attention/awareness levels, simultaneous interaction would not be possible; and
2 expressing and perceiving (as displayed through expressing) are both performed at least partially with the mind of the social actor.

When expressing and perceiving, or interacting, people experience, think, and feel something. These notions of experiencing, thinking, and feeling are linked to a person's consciousness or mind. While there does not have to be – *and most likely is not* – a one-to-one account of what a person is actually experiencing, thinking, or feeling and what the person is expressing, it is this *expressing* by one person and *interpreting* by another person that makes interaction possible.

While we do not – and cannot – know what others are experiencing, thinking, or feeling, we can perceive what a person in interaction is expressing; and people in interaction interpret what a person is expressing as a representation of their experiences, thoughts, and feelings. Thus, there are two aspects of interaction: expressing and perceiving. Both aspects of interaction involve social actors' attention/awareness. Attention and awareness is not one single state, but has many different levels, and, as I have outlined in previous chapters, the level of attention/awareness that a social actor *perceivably* places on a specific higher-level action is analyzable by analyzing the modal density that the social actor employs to construct the higher-level action.

Emphasis is placed on *perceivably*, because perceiving is one aspect of interaction. When analyzing interaction, we do not try to understand what a person is actually experiencing, thinking, or feeling, but what the participants are communicating to one another.

Certainly, we can imagine situations in which a person is perceivably paying attention to something or somebody, but in truth is thinking about something very different. However, this person is still communicating to others that they are paying attention. As long as people perceive the person as paying attention through their use of modal density, this is the interactional state that the person is communicating – no matter what is truly going on in their minds.

Means

Means are the devices that help structure a person's and participants' foregrounded higher-level action. These *means* point to the presence of a communicative semantics, and they are indicators that people truly do structure their attention/awareness levels as heuristically proposed in this book. The *means* discussed here are certainly not the only *means* that people in interaction utilize, but these are important ones.

Modal density foreground–background continuum

As our theoretical assumptions and world views are embedded in our methodologies, the methodological framework outlined in this book brings with it affordances and constraints.

Affordances

1   The framework allows us to discern the many communicative modes that social actors utilize in interaction. Here, we do not presume that one mode is superior to others, and we do not assume that specific modes are always inextricably linked.

    When analyzing multimodal interaction, we differentiate as much as possible among the modes, and then analyze how they communicate separate messages or play together to communicate a joint message.

2   The heuristic model allows us to discern the many simultaneously constructed higher-level actions that an individual is engaged in. These simultaneous higher-level actions are then placed on the continuum in relation to one another.

When analyzing multimodal interaction, we differentiate as much as possible among the higher-level actions that a person is engaged in and analyze the attention/awareness level that the person employs (through modal density). Once we have identified the higher-level actions constructed, we can follow the shifts in attention/awareness and also see how one higher-level action impacts another.

Constraints

1   The framework utilizes the notion of communicative modes and, by discerning one mode from another, modes are unavoidably construed as distinct entities. This, however, is incorrect. As I have emphasized before, modes are not bounded units. A mode is a loose concept of a grouping of signs that have acquired meaning in our historical development.

While I have introduced communicative modes that are useful for the analysis of multimodal interaction, we need to realize that modes can be defined quite differently. For example, what I have called the mode of print can also be divided into the mode of images and the written word, or into a range of other equally *correct* communicative modes. *We need to keep an open mind about communicative modes and think of them as loosely bounded units rather than distinct entities.*

2   The heuristic model that I call a modal density foreground–background continuum visualizes simultaneous higher-level actions on various attention/awareness levels, as if the conscious mind were a linear construction.

The graph demonstrates that the higher-level actions in which a participant communicates (i.e. expresses) engagement are discernible through the expressions that lead the other participants (and the analyst) to the perception of how much attention/awareness the person pays to the higher-level action. *We need to keep an open mind about human consciousness and always remember that the graph is only a heuristic model to help us move beyond focused interaction.*

What does the methodological framework for multimodal interactional analysis NOT allow us to do?

This framework does not allow us to perform quantitative analysis, because:

- The concept of modal density only implies a qualitative notion, *not* a quantitative notion. Modes *cannot* be counted.

- The concept of a foreground–background continuum of human attention/awareness is only useful in relational terms. Higher-level actions can be placed on this heuristic continuum in relation to one another, but higher-level actions *cannot* be counted, as they are *not* given units.
- The visual-based transcription that I have proposed in Norris (2002a) and developed further in this book is of a qualitative nature, and does not lend itself to quantitative scrutiny.

The modal density foreground–background continuum does not allow us to make valid claims of a person's consciousness other than what a person A is expressing and person B is perceiving (observable by B's expressions). Both the processes of expressing and perceiving (as counter-expressing) are accomplished through consciousness. But the extent of what we can glean of consciousness is only the small part that is perceptible through expressiveness.

While actual experiences, thoughts, and feelings are usually not discussed, and in most everyday interactions are not even considered, they may be discussed in intimate situations through the employment of the mode of spoken language. Let us examine an interaction between a person A and a person B. Here, A asks B *"What are you experiencing, thinking, or feeling?"* and B answers this question.

In such interaction we find the *expressions* (verbalized by B) of experiences, thoughts or feelings, which can only partially articulate the actual experiences, thoughts, and feelings of B, and the following interpretation by A (of B's *expressions*) as a representation of the "actual" experiences, thoughts, and feelings of B as A understands them. The perception and interpretation by A can be analyzed only by analyzing A's reactions (expressions) to B's account, which in turn is just a fragment of the actual understanding/interpretation of A.

Thus, even when people are truly interested in someone else's conscious experiences, thoughts, and feelings, interaction and interactional analysis still does *not* allow us to enter another person's mind beyond the person's expressions.

Some further thoughts

Where do we go from here? is probably a question that comes to mind at this point and, when looking back at this book and the methodology introduced, perhaps you will find that it opens up the study of interaction to new scrutiny.

In socio- and applied linguistics we may ask ourselves: What is the *true role of* language in interaction and how can this so thoroughly developed and well understood system of representation shed light on the other modes that are interactionally employed?

In education we may want to think about the multiple ways of communicating meaning. *Which mode* is more useful than others to engage students in the learning process? And we may want to ask: When is it necessary for a student to pay *focused interactional attention* in order to learn, and when is learning better served if a student pays less interactional attention? As Chalmers points out, learning is largely a psychological property and, as I have argued in this book, interactional attention is largely a phenomenal quality.

In sociology, we may want to explore how relationships are formed through higher-level actions and build a person's social world(s). The degree of attention a person pays to the construction of particular relationships may provide insight into the person's place in society.

In anthropology – a field that I have explored little in this book (only looking at two cultures: German and American, and two languages: German and English that I feel I have native *interaction competence* in), we may want to study the interactional differences in the different cultures and explore questions like: Which semantic/pragmatic *means* are preferred in a specific culture (or are there semantic/pragmatic *means* that are preferred in a specific culture)?

In *interactional child development* (note that we can no longer speak of language development alone) we want to ask questions like: When do children acquire the ability to function interactionally on *different levels of attention/awareness*? McNeill (1992) points out that children do not acquire beats before the age of five, and that beats are not abundant until children reach the age of 11. Since beats also function as communicative semantics and aid the social actor to structure consciousness, McNeill's findings about beats appear to correspond with my preliminary findings that young children only function on one level of attention/awareness and slowly acquire the ability to function on several levels of attention/awareness with increasing age.

Finally, in psychology, we may want to link this piece of the phenomenal concept of mind to a much broader understanding of consciousness, cognition, and mind.

What is next?

I originally developed the methodological framework for multimodal interactional analysis because I had set out to study the everyday identity construction of Sandra and Anna. During my research I found that the two women constructed their identity fragments through a multiplicity of communicative modes on various levels simultaneously. While I could "see" that such simultaneous identity construction was going on, and while I "knew" that the women utilized much more than just the mode of spoken language, I could not scientifically explain the multiplicity and simultaneity of modes used and identity fragments constructed. Thus, I devised the methodological framework. Once I had formulated the framework, I set out to study many different interactions, using the framework as my explanatory tool to test the validity of it.

In this book I have explicated the methodological framework and I have given a variety of examples that show the breadth and applicability. Now that this book is written, I am returning to my initial question of identity construction.

Sandra and Anna not only construct their social worlds, as explicated in the last chapter, they continuously construct their identities. Mead asserts that:

> The self is not something that exists first and then enters into relationship with others, but it is, so to speak, an eddy in the social current and so still a part of that current.
>
> Mead (1974: 182)

As I discussed in the last chapter, Sandra and Anna construct their social worlds through the construction of relationships. Concurrently, they construct their identities through relationships, and just as the relationships are built through actions in the world, the identities are built through actions in the world. Mead (1974: 379) states "We are what we are through our relationship to others," and our relationship to others is constructed through a multiplicity of modes and true actions that we undertake in the world. But I will end here, as a comprehensive discussion of multimodal identity construction will take up another book.

References

In the first section below I have summarized some notes on the main sources that I have used in writing this book. I provide some general comments in order to avoid excessive footnotes and citation. While I have ordered the notes by chapter and topic, I would like to point out that much of the literature has influenced my thinking in a general way. The second section includes the actual citations in the book as well as the ones discussed here.

Further reading and notes

Chapter 1

The most central theoretical notions that I build on in this book come from three major directions of thinking.

Mediated discourse analysis/nexus analysis

First and foremost I build on Ron Scollon's works of mediated discourse and nexus analysis (1998, 2001a, 2001b), where he develops a theory of human action that is organized by the three principles of social action, communication, and history.

Multimodality

I also employ many notions developed by Kress and Van Leeuwen, but build here mainly on Kress *et al.* (2001) and also Kress and Van Leeuwen (2001), where they demonstrate in different contexts that language can no longer be thought of as the primary mode of communication, and that other semiotics have to be taken into account when analyzing communication.

Interactional sociolinguistics

The works by Goffman (1959, 1961, 1963, 1974, 1981); Gumperz (1981, 1982), Tannen (1979, 1984, 1989a, 1989b), and Tannen and Wallat (1993) which comprise some major works in the field of interactional sociolinguistics, have had great influence on my thinking and writing of this book.

Mind/consciousness

My thinking about mind was greatly influenced by the following scholars: Bateson (1972) argues that we do not have access to our intentions through our conscious mind; Searle (2001) describes many connections between mind, language, and society; Chalmer (1996) discusses the conscious mind; Chafe (1980, 1987, 1992, 1994) writes about consciousness, the information flow and language units; Wertsch (1991, 1985a, 1985b, 1985c) emphasizes the inherent cultural, historical, and institutional context to mental functioning; Bruner (1986) discusses the mind–world connection; Vygotsky (1978) gives insight into higher psychological processes, and defines consciousness as "the objectively observable *organization* of behavior that is imposed on humans through participation in sociocultural practices" (Wertsch 1985c: 187); Mead (1974) discusses the genesis of the self and the nature of mind with a special interest in language; Bakhtin (1981) elucidates the notion of voice involving "the speaking consciousness" (Holquist and Emerson, 1981). On a general philosophy of mind and reason, see Hegel (1988) and Kant (1973 [1787]); and also Wittgenstein (1998).

Context

Duranti and Goodwin (1992), Goodwin and Goodwin (1992), Kendon (1992), as well as van Dijk (1977, 1980) and his current thinking (http://www.discourse-in-society.org/teun.html; accessed 22/02/04) have influenced my thinking about context.

Interaction

Pike (1967) delineates a theory that incorporates language and behavior. J. Habermas (1999) elucidates how the cognitive–instrumental, the moral–practical, and the aesthetic–expressive all play a role in communicative action.

Ruesch and Bateson (1968 [1951]) and Ruesch and Kees (1956) were probably the first to undertake a multimodal study. I base much of my thinking – practical and methodological – on their works.

Frozen action

See Norris (2002b, 2003b); see notes for Chapter 5, below, as well.

Chapter 2

Communicative modes

In this section, I base the development of my thinking about mediated action on Scollon (1998, 2001a, 2001b), who extensively discusses the notion of action; and on Wertsch (1998), who developed the mediated action as the action that a social actor takes with or through a mediational means or cultural tool. Wertsch also discusses the question of materiality, which greatly helped me to develop my thinking about the different materiality of communicative modes.

158 References

In Norris (2002a, 2002b, 2004), I discuss my own notions of the concepts of lower- and higher-level actions, and develop the notion of frozen actions in detail.

From Kress and Van Leeuwen (2001), I take the notion of the communicative mode as a loosely bounded unit with rules and regularities attached to it.

See Peirce (1958) on signs and semiotics; Barthes (1967) on elements of semiology; and Eco (1972) about semiotics.

See Saussure (1959) on general linguistics; Sapir (1921) about language and communication; Whorf (1956 (1940)) on language, thought, and reality; Levinson (1983) on pragmatics; and Mey (2001), also on pragmatics, but especially Part III on macropragmatics. See Ciccourel (1980) on some philosophical and empirical issues of language and social interaction. Erickson and Schultz (1982) speak in detail about interviews, and Fasold (1990) on the sociolinguistics of language.

See Goodwin (1979), Goodwin and Heritage (1990), Jefferson (1974), Sacks (1973, 1974) and Sacks *et al.* (1974), as well as Schegloff (1972a, 1972b, 1977, 1979a, 1979b, 1980, 1981), and Schegloff and Sacks (1973) about conversation analysis and the sequentiality of talk. See Grice (1957, 1968, 1975, 1981, 1989) on word, sentence, and meaning; also on logic and conversation. See Halliday (1973, 1974, 1985, 1998) on a functional perspective and language as a social semiotic. See Hymes (1961, 1966, 1972a, 1972b, 1973, 1974a, 1974b, 1974c, 1974d) on sociolinguistics and the ethnography of communication; Milroy (1987) on observing and analyzing natural language; Searle (1969) on speech acts; Kendon (1974, 1977) on behavior in social interaction; Silverstein and Urban (1996) on the natural history of discourse; and Boars (1916) on language.

Schiffrin (1977) discusses opening encounters; Schiffrin (1985) elucidates some constraints on discourse options; and Schiffrin (1986) discusses turn-initial variation. See Schiffrin (1987) for an analysis of discourse markers; Schiffrin (1988a, 1988b, 1990) on conversation analysis and sociolinguistic approaches to discourse; and see Schiffrin (1994) for a comprehensive summary of the many different concepts and approaches to discourse. See Tannen (1984, 1989a, 1989b) on conversational style, repetition, and overlap and interruptions; Scollon (1998, 2001) on language as action; Erickson (1976, 1982, 1990) on topical cohesion and gatekeeping encounters; Brown and Levinson (1987) on politeness; Merritt (1976) on questions in service encounters; and Clark and Murphy (1982) on audience design.

Wodak (1989, 1995, 1996, 2001) elucidates language, power, and ideology, critical discourse analysis, and also some disorders of discourse. Fairclough (1985, 1989, 2001) discusses critical discourse analysis and language and power. Fairclough and Wodak (1997) give an overview of critical discourse analysis. Foucault (1993) writes about the order of discourse. Garfinkel (1952, 1967, 1972, 1974) writes about the perception of the other and routine everyday activities. Ehlich (1972, 1993, 1994) discusses speech act theory and discourse analysis. See Wittgenstein (1998), Descartes (1984), Giddens (1979), Habermas (1984), and Heims (1977) generally on language, philosophy, and social theory.

On proxemics I have relied foremost on Hall (1959, 1966). Scollon (2001) on habitus and intention; Scollon and Scollon (2003) also discuss proxemics.

Dittman (1987) has been valuable for my thinking about posture. See also, Kendon (1972, 1974, 1990) and Scheflen (1964, 1974) on posture; and Birdwhistell (1970) on kinesics.

McNeill's (1992) work: *Hand and Mind*, illustrating the connection between language and gesture, has guided me in my thinking about the connectedness of modes. See also Efron (1941), Goodwin (1986), and Streek (1988) on gesture. All of the classifications of gestures come from McNeill and Kendon. See Kendon (1972, 1980, 1981, 1982, 1987, 1994, 1997) on the delineation of gesture. On pointing gestures, see also Haviland (1993, 2000); see Ekman and Friesen (1969) on nonverbal behavior and Schiffrin (1981) on handshakes.

The classifications of head movements come from Altorfer *et al.* (1992, 1998, 2000): Jossen *et al.* (2000); Kaserman *et al.* (2000).

On gaze, Argyle and Dean (1965), Argyle and Cook (1976), Exline and Fehr (1982), Kendon (1967, 1978), and Goodwin (1980, 1994, 1995).

See Van Leeuwen (1999) and Unger-Hamilton *et al.* (1979) on music, and Scollon (1982) on rhythmic organization of talk.

See Kress and Van Leeuwen (1998, 2001) on print, images, and layout. See de Saint-Georges and Norris (1999, 2000), de Saint-Georges (2000), Johnston (2000), Norris (2000), Scollon and Scollon (2000, 2003), and Zavala (2000) on signs and language in the material world, and layout; Jewitt and Oyama (2001) on visual meaning; T. Habermas (1999) on objects and layout.

On interconnection of modes see: Streek (1988, 1993, 1994, 1996), Goodwin (1996, 2000, 2001), Kress and Van Leeuwen (1998, 2001), Van Leeuwen and Jewitt (2001), Kress *et al.* (2001), Scollon and Scollon (2003), and Norris (2002b, 2003a, 2003b). On facial expression, see Frielund *et al.* (1987).

Chapter 3

See Gail Jefferson (in Sacks *et al.*, 1974), Du Bois (1991), Du Bois *et al.* (1992, 1993), Tannen (1984), Ochs (1979), Scollon (1979); Dittmar (2002), and Norris (2002b) on transcription.

Chapter 4

I arrived at the concept of modal density through my studies in inorganic chemistry, where the density of elements is of great importance to an element's behavior. For discussions and an illustration of the density of water, see, for example, Christen (1980).

The analogy of the density of chemical compounds to the density of modes is couched in the following terms: chemical compounds are made up of various elements, as in the case of water, which is made up of oxygen and hydrogen. Of course, it takes many water molecules to make up a drop of water.

Similarly, a higher-level action is made up of various lower-level actions, as in the case of a conversation – which is made up of spoken language, posture, proxemics, gesture, and gaze, for example. Of course, it takes many utterances, postural and gaze shifts, gestures, and so on, to build a conversation. Note also that lower-level actions draw on various modes as systems of representation, and there is no lower-level action without a mode and no mode without a lower-level action.

On modal density, see Norris (2002b; 2003b).

Chapter 5

On attention, see Wickens (1984, 1989), who proposes that there are multiple resource pools for processing stages and modalities; also see Schmidt (2001) on attention and learning, and Jones (2004) on attention.

160 References

On foreground, mid-ground, and background see Weis and Belton (1985), Schafer (1977), Van Leeuwen (1999), and Norris (2002b, 2003b).

The notion of a modal density foreground–background continuum is solely of a heuristic nature. Using an analogy from chemistry, the density of water decreases slowly with increasing temperature. The highest density for water is at 4° C, which means that the molecular structure is tightest at this point. With increasing temperature, the molecular structure becomes looser. When we look at a graph that displays water's decreasing density with increasing temperature (Christen, 1980: 468), we see that the y-axis represents the density, and the x-axis represents the temperature. The curve indicates a decrease in density with increasing temperature, which is always the same for (clean) water.

I have devised a similar type of graph that I call a *modal density foreground–background continuum*. The y-axis represents increasing modal density, and the x-axis represents the decrease in attention/awareness of a social actor. The curve that heuristically indicates the fact that modal density decreases in degree as a social actor's attention/awareness decreases, does not change in this heuristic graph (by analogy with the density of water, which also does not change).

Frozen actions

I mentioned in the text that the notion of frozen action is comparable to the notion of water. In frozen form, water is solid. There, I said that a frozen (higher-level) action is entailed in an object. Please note that ice has a much lower density than (fluid) water. Without wanting to carry the analogy with water too far, however, a frozen (higher-level) action in this analogy *does not* entail high modal density.

Chapter 6

On attention, see Kahneman (1973), who explains that one of the main characteristics of attention is capacity; and LaBerge (1995), who speaks of preparatory attention, which includes accuracy in perceptual judgment, categorization, and speed in performing actions.

On semantics and pragmatics, as they are pertinent to language use, see Austin (1962), Bolinger (1965); Brown and Levinson (1978), Clarke (1973), Fauconnier (1975), Finnegan (1999), Fillmore (1968, 1977, 1982, 1985), Grice (1957, 1968, 1975, 1981, 1989), Jackendoff (1972, 1983), G. Lakoff (1965, 1972, 1986, 1987), R. Lakoff (1972) Levinson (1983, 1987), Luhman (1998), Ochs (1979), Searle (1969), Slobin (1973), Sperber and Wilson (1986), Sweetser (1990), Winograd (1972), and Wilson (1975).

See Kendon and Ferber (1973), Goffman (1974), and Kendon (1992) on disattended tracks. See Ekman and Friesen (1969) on regulators within conversation.

See Baars (1988) and Raskin (2000) on focused attention.

See Krahmer *et al.* (2002) on eyebrows and focus; Ekman (1979) on emotional and conversational signals; and Condon and Ogston (1967) on segmentation of behavior.

On beats, see Dray and McNeill (1990); McNeill (1992); and Norris (2002b, 2002c).

On deixis, see Fillmore (1982); McNeill (1992); and Norris (2002a, 2002b).

Chapter 7

Generally, for this chapter, see Brathes (1967, 1977); Bruner (1986, 1990); Kress and Van Leeuwen (1998, 2001); Kress et al (2001); Lemke (1998, 2000a, 2000b, 2000c, 2002); and van Lier (1988).

On motivation, see Butzkamm (1980); Cohen and Manion (1985); Crookes and Schmidt (1991); Csikszentmihalyi (1985); Deci (1971); Deci and Ryan (1985, 1992); Deci *et al.* (1991); Fischer (1978); Keller (1983); Montessori (1965); Piaget (1976, 1978); Smith (1974); Trudge (1990); van Lier (1995); Vygotsky (1986 (1962)).

See de Saint-Georges (2002, 2003); Johnston (2002, 2004); and Whalen *et al.* (2001) on work in an office setting and the interaction between social actors when documents and computers are involved; and Engström and Middleton (1998) on cognition and communication at work.

See van Dijk (http://www.discourse-in-society.org/teun.html) about context and mental structures.

See Nishida (1958); Bourdieu (1977, 1988, 1990) on habitus.

On time, see Lemke (2000, 2003) and http://academic.broklyn.cuny.edu/education/jlemke (accessed 22/02/04); Sklar (1977).

Chapter 8

See Mead (1974) on the self; and Norris (2000, 2001, 2002c, 2002d, 2002e, 2003) on identity construction.

References cited

Altorfer, A., Goldstein J., Miklowitz, D.J., and Nuechterlein, K.H. (1992) "Stress-indicative patterns of non-verbal behavior: their role in family interactions," *British Journal of Psychiatry*, 161 (suppl. 18): 103–113.

Altorfer, A., Kermann M.L., and Hirsbrunner, H. (1998) "Arousal and communication: the relationship between nonverbal, behavior, and physiological indices of the stress response," *Journal of Psychophysiology*, 12: 40–59.

Altorfer, A., Jossen, S., Würmle, O., Käsermann, M., Foppa, K., and Zimmermann, H. (2000) "Measurement and meaning of head movements in everyday face-to-face communicative interaction," *Behaviour Research Methods, Instruments & Computers*, 32 (1): 17–32.

Argyle, M. and Cook, M. (1976) *Gaze and Mutual Gaze*, Cambridge: Cambridge University Press.

Argyle, M. and Dean, J. (1965) "Eye-contact, distance and affiliation," *Sociometry*, 28: 289–304.

Austin, J.L. (1962) *How To Do Things with Words*, Oxford: Oxford University Press.

Baars, B.J. (1998) *A Cognitive Theory of Consciousness*, Cambridge: Cambridge University Press.

Bakhtin, M.M. (1981) *The Dialogic Imagination*, Austin, TX: University of Texas Press.

Barthes, R. (1967) *The Elements of Semiology*, London: Cape.

Barthes, R. (1977) *Image-Music-Text*, Glasgow: Fontana.

Bateson, G. (1972) *Steps to an Ecology of Mind*, New York: Ballantine.

Birdwhistell, R.L. (1970) *Kinesics and Context*, Philadelphia, PA: University of Pennsylvania Press.

Boars, F. (1916) *The Mind of Primitive Man*, New York: Macmillan.
Bolinger, D. (1965) "The automization of meaning," *Language*, 41: 555–573.
Bourdieu, P. (1977) *Outline of a Theory of Practice*, Cambridge: Cambridge University Press.
Bourdieu, P. (1990) *The Logic of Practice*, Stanford, CA: Stanford University Press.
Bourdieu, P. (1998) *Practical Reason: on the Theory of Action*. Stanford, CA: Stanford University Press.
Brown, P. and Levinson, S.C. (1978) "Politeness: some universals in language usage," in E. Goody (ed.) *Questions and Politeness*. Cambridge: Cambridge University Press.
Brown, P. and Levinson, S.C. (1987) *Politeness*, Cambridge: Cambridge University Press.
Bruner, J. (1986) *Actual Minds, Possible Worlds*, Cambridge, MA: Harvard University Press.
Bruner, J. (1990) *Acts of Meaning*, Cambridge, MA: Harvard University Press.
Butzkamm, W. (1980) "Verbal play and pattern practice," in S. Felix (ed.) *Second Language Development: Trends and Issues*, Tübingen, Germany: Günther Narr, pp. 233–248.
Chafe, W. (1980) "The development of consciousness in the production of a narrative," in W. Chafe (ed.) *The Pear Stories: Cognitive, Culture and Linguistic Aspects of Narrative Production*, Norwood, NJ: Ablex Press, pp. 9–50.
Chafe, W. (1987) "Cognitive constraints on information flow," in R. Tomlin (ed.) *Coherence and Grounding in Discourse*, Amsterdam: John Benjamin Press.
Chafe, W. (1992) "Prosodic and functional units of language," in J. Edwards and M. Lampert (eds) *Talking Data: Transcription and Coding in Discourse Research*, Hillsdale, NJ: Lawrence Erlbaum Associates.
Chafe, W. (1994) *Discourse, Consciousness, and Time: the Flow and Displacement of Conscious Experience in Speaking and Writing*, Chicago: University of Chicago Press.
Chalmers, D.J. (1996) *The Conscious Mind: in Search of a Fundamental Theory*, Oxford: Oxford University Press.
Chaplin, J.P. (1985) *Dictionary of Psychology*, New York: Laurel.
Christen, H.R. (1980) *Grundlagen der allgemeinen und anorganischen Chemie*, Frankfurt am Main: Sauerländer.
Ciccourel, A. (1980) "Language and social interaction: philosophical and empirical issues," in D. Zimmerman and C. West (eds) *Language and Social Interaction*, Special Issue of Sociological Inquiry, 50 (3/4): 1–30.
Clark, H. (1973) "Space, time, semantics, and the child," in T. Moore (ed.) *Cognitive Development and the Acquisition of Language*, New York: Academic Press, pp. 27–63.
Clark, H. and Murphy, G. (1982) "Audience design in meaning and reference," in J. LeNy and W. Kintsch (eds) *Language and Comprehension*, Amsterdam: North Holland Publishing Company.
Cohen, L. and Manion, L. (1985) *Research Methods in Education*, London: Croom Helm.
Condon, W.S. and Ogston, W.D. (1967) "A segmentation of behavior," *Journal of Psychiatric Research*, 5: 221–235.
Crookes, G. and Schmidt, R. (1991) "Motivation: reopening the research agenda," *Language Learning*, 41: 469–512.
Csikszentmihalyi, M. (1985) "Emergent motivation and the evolution of the self," in D.A. Kleiber and M.L. Maehr (eds) *Motivation and Adulthood: Advances in Motivation and Achievement*, vol. 4, Greenwich, CN: LAI Press, pp. 93–120.

Deci, E.L. (1971) "Effects of externally motivated rewards on intrinsic motivation," *Journal of Personality and Social Psychology*, 18: 105–115.
Deci, E.L. and Ryan, R.M. (1985) *Intrinsic Motivation and Self-determination in Human Behavior*, New York: Plenum Press.
Deci, E.L. and Ryan, R.M. (1992) "The initiation and regulation of intrinsically motivated learning and achievement," in A.K. Boggiano and T.S. Pittman (eds) *Achievement and Motivation: a Social–Developmental Perspective*. Cambridge: Cambridge University Press.
Deci, E.L., Vallerand, R.J., Pelletier, L.G., and Ryan, R.M. (1991) "Motivation and education: the self-determination perspective," *Educational Psychologist*, 26: (3/4): 325–346.
de Saint-Georges, I. (2000) "Discussing images: pictures reception and appropriation in focus groups." Paper presented at the Georgetown University Round Table on Languages and Linguistics, Washington, DC, May 4–6.
de Saint-Georges, I. (2003) "Anticipatory discourse: producing futures of action in a vocational program for long term unemployed," Ph.D. Dissertation, Georgetown University: UMI.
de Saint-Georges, I. and Norris, S. (1999) "Literate design and European identity: visual practices of an imagined community." Paper presented at the International Visual Sociology Association Annual Conference, Antwerp, July 14–18.
de Saint-Georges, I. and Norris, S. (2000) "Nationality and the European Union: competing identities in the visual design of four European cities," *Visual Sociology*, 15: 65–78.
Descartes, R. (1984) *The Philosophical Writings of Descartes*, trans. by J. Cottingham, R. Stoothoff, and D. Murdoch, Cambridge: Cambridge University Press.
Dittman, A.T. (1987) "The Role of Body Movement in Communication," in A.W. Siegman and Stanley Feldstein (eds) *Nonverbal Behavior and Communication*, New Jersey: Lawrence Erlbaum Associates.
Dittmar, N. (2002) *Transcription: Ein Leitfaden mit Aufaben für Studenten, Forscher und Laien*, Opladen, Germany: Leske and Budrich.
Dray, N.L. and McNeill, D. (1990) "Gestures during discourse: the contextual structuring of thought," in S.L. Tsohatzidis (ed.) *Meaning and Prototypes: Studies in Linguistic Categorization*, London and New York: Routledge, pp. 466–488.
Du Bois, J.W. (1991) "Transcription design principles for spoken discourse research," *Pragmatics*, 1(1): 71–106.
DuBois, J.W., Cumming, S., Schuetze-Coburn, S., and Paolino, D. (1992) "Discourse transcription," *Santa Barbara Papers in Linguistics*, vol. 4, Santa Barbara, CA: UCSB Press.
Du Bois, J.W., Schuetze-Coburn, S., Cumming, S., and Paolino, D. (1993) "Outline of discourse transcription," in J.A. Edwards and M.D. Lampert (eds) *Talking Data*, pp. 45–90.
Duranti, A. and Goodwin C. (eds) (1992) *Rethinking Context: Language as an Interactive Phenomenon*. Cambridge: Cambridge University Press.
Eco, U. (1972) *Einführung in die Semiotic*, Munich: UTB.
Efron, D. (1941) *Gesture and Environment*, New York: King's Crown Press.
Ehlich, K. (1972) "Thesen zur Sprechakttheorie," in D. Wunderlich (ed.) *Linguistische Pragmatik*, Frankfurt: Athenäum, pp. 122–126.
Ehlich, K. (1993) "Diskursanalyse," in H. Glück, *Metzler-Lexikon Sprache*, Stuttgart: Metzler, pp. 145–146.
Ehlich, K. (1994) (ed.) *Diskursanalyse in Europa*, Frankfurt: Lang.

Ekman, P. (1979) "About brows: emotional and conversational signals," in M. von Cranach, K. Foppa, W. Lepenies, and D. Ploog (eds) *Human Ethology*, Cambridge: Cambridge University Press.

Ekman, P. and Friesen, W.V. (1969) "The repertoire of nonverbal behavior: categories, origins, usage, and coding," *Semiotica*, 1: 49–98.

Engström, Y. and Middleton, D. (1998) *Cognition and Communication at Work*, Cambridge: Cambridge University Press.

Erickson, F. (1976) "Gatekeeping encounters: a social selection process," in P. Reeves Sanday (ed.) *Anthropology and the Public Interest: Fieldwork and Theory*, New York: Academic Press, pp. 111–145.

Erickson, F. (1982) "Money tree, lasagna bush, salt and pepper: social construction of topical cohesion in a conversation among Italian-Americans," in D. Tannen (ed.) *Analyzing Discourse: Text and Talk*, Georgetown University Round Table on Languages and Linguistics, Washington, DC: Georgetown University Press, pp. 43–70.

Erickson, F. (1990) "The social construction of discourse coherence in a family dinner table conversation," *Conversational Organization and Its Development*, B. Dorval (ed.) Norwood, NJ: Ablex, pp. 207–238.

Erickson, F. and Shultz, J. (1982) *The Counselor as Gatekeeper: Social Interactions in Interviews*, New York: Academic Press.

Exline, R. and Fehr, B.J. (1982) "The assessment of gaze and mutual gaze," in K.R. Scherer and P. Ekman (eds) *Handbook of Methods in Nonverbal Behavior Research*, Cambridge: Cambridge University Press.

Fairclough, N. (1985) "Critical and descriptive goals in discourse analysis," *Journal of Pragmatics*, 9: 739–763.

Fairclough, N. (1989) *Language and Power*, London: Longman.

Fairclough, N. (2001) "Critical discourse analysis as a method in social scientific research," in R. Wodak and M. Meyer (eds) *Methods in Critical Discourse Analysis*, London: Sage, pp. 121–138.

Fairclough, N. and Wodak, R. (1997) *Critical Discourse Analysis. An Overview*, in T. van Dijk (ed.) *Discourse as Social Interaction*, London: Sage.

Fasold, R. (1990) *Sociolinguistics of Language*, Oxford: Blackwell.

Fauconnier, G. (1975) "Pragmatic scales and logic structures," *Linguistic Inquiry*, 6: 353–375.

Fillmore, C.J. (1968) "The case for case," in E. Bach and R.T. Harms (eds) *Universals in Linguistic Theory*, New York: Holt, Rinehart and Winston.

Fillmore, C.J. (1977) "Topics in lexical semantics," in R.W. Cole (ed.) *Current Issues in Linguistic Theory*, Bloomington, Il: Indiana University Press, pp. 76–138.

Fillmore, C.J. (1982) "Towards a descriptive framework for spatial deixis," in R.J. Jarvella and W. Klein (eds) *Speech, Place, and Action: Studies in Deixis and Related Topics*, Chichester and New York: Wiley, pp. 31–59.

Fillmore, C.J. (1985) "Frames and the semantic of understanding," *Quaderni di Semantics*, 6: 222–254.

Finegan, E. (1999) *Language: Its Structure and Use*, Orlando, FL: Harcourt Brace.

Finnegan, R. (2002) *Communicating: the Multiple Modes of Human Interconnection*, London: Routledge.

Fischer, D.D. (1978) "The effects of personal control, competence, and extrinsic reward systems on intrinsic motivation," *Organizational Behavior and Human Performance*, 21: 273–288.

Foucault, M. (1993) *Die Ordnung des Diskurses*, Frankfurt: Fischer.

Frielund, A.J., Ekman, P. and Oster H. (1987) "Facial expression of emotion," in A.W. Siegman and S. Feldstein (eds), *Nonverbal Behavior and Communication*, New Jersey: Lawrence Erlbaum Associates.

Garfinkel, H. (1952) "The perception of the other: a study in social order," Ph.D. Dissertation, Harvard University.

Garfinkel, H. (1967) *Studies in Ethnomethodology*, Englewood Cliffs, NJ: Prentice-Hall.

Garfinkel, H. (1974) "On the origins of the term 'ethnomethodology'," in R. Turner (ed.) *Ethnomethodology*, Harmondsworth: Penguin, pp. 15–17.

Giddens, A. (1979) *Central Problems in Social Theory: Action, Structure, and Contradiction in Social Analysis*, Berkeley and Los Angeles, CA: University of California Press.

Goffman, E. (1959) *The Presentation of Self in Everyday Life*, New York: Doubleday.

Goffman, E. (1961) *Asylum*, New York: Anchor Press.

Goffman, E. (1963) *Behavior in Public Places*, New York: Free Press of Glencoe.

Goffman, E. (1974) *Frame Analysis*, New York: Harper & Row.

Goffman, E. (1981) *Forms of Talk*, Philadelphia, PA: University of Pennsylvania Press.

Goodwin, C. (1979) *Conversation and Organization*, New York: Academic Press.

Goodwin, C. (1980) "Restarts, pauses, and the achievement of mutual gaze at turn-beginning," *Sociological Inquiry*, 50 (3–4): 272–302.

Goodwin, C. (1981) *Conversational Organization: Interaction between Speakers and Hearers*, New York: Academic Press.

Goodwin, C. (1986) "Gestures as a resource for the organization of mutual orientation," *Semiotica*, 62: 29–49.

Goodwin, C. (1994) "Professional vision," *American Anthropologist*, 96 (3): 606–633.

Goodwin, C. (1995) "Seeing in depth," *Social Studies of Sciences*, 25: 237–274.

Goodwin, C. (1996) "Practices of color classification," *Ninchi Kagaku Cognitive Studies: Bulletin of the Japanese Cognitive Science Society*, 3 (2): 62–82.

Goodwin, C. (2000) "Action and embodiment within situated human interaction," *Journal of Pragmatics*, 32 (10): 1489–1522.

Goodwin, C. (2001) "Practices of seeing visual analysis: an ethnomethodological approach," in T.V. Leeuwen and C. Jewitt (eds) *Handbook of Visual Analysis*, London: Sage.

Goodwin, C. and Goodwin, M.H. (1992) "Assessment and the construction of context," in A. Duranti and C. Goodwin (eds) *Rethinking Context: Language as an Interactive Phenomenon*, Cambridge: Cambridge University Press.

Goodwin, C. and Heritage, J. (1990) "Conversation analysis," *Annual Review of Anthropology*, 19: 283–307.

Grice, H.P. (1957) "Meaning," *Philosophical Review*, 67: 377–388.

Grice, H.P. (1968) "Utterer's meaning, sentence-meaning, and word-meaning," *Foundations of Language*, 4: 1–18.

Grice, H.P. (1975) "Logic and conversation," in P. Cole and J. Morgan (eds) *Speech Acts (Syntax and Semantics, Volume 3)*, New York: Academic Press, pp. 41–58.

Grice, H.P. (1981) "Further notes on logic and conversation," in P. Cole (ed.) *Radical Pragmatics (Syntax and Semantics, Volume 9)*, New York: Academic Press, pp. 113–128.

Grice, H.P. (1989) *Studies in the Way of Words*, Cambridge: Cambridge University Press.

Gumperz, J. (1981) "The linguistic bases of communicative competence," in D. Tannen (ed.) *Analyzing Discourse: Text and Talk*, Georgetown University Round

Table on Languages and Linguistics, Washington, DC: Georgetown University Press, pp. 323–334.
Gumperz, J. (1982) *Discourse Strategies,* Cambridge: Cambridge University Press.
Habermas, J. (1984) *The Theory of Communicative Action,* vol. 1, *Reason and the Rationalization of Society,* trans. by T. McCarthy, Boston, MA: Beacon Press.
Habermas, J. (1999) *Moralbewusstsein und kommunikatives Handeln,* Frankfurt am Main: Suhrkamp
Habermas, T. (1999) *Geliebte Objekte: Symbole und Instrumente der Identitätsbildung,* Frankfurt am Main: Suhrkamp.
Hall, E.T. (1959) *The Silent Language,* Garden City, New York: Doubleday.
Hall, E.T. (1966) *The Hidden Dimension,* New York: Doubleday.
Halliday, M.A.K. (1973) *Explorations in the Functions of Language,* London: Edward Arnold.
Halliday, M.A.K. (1974) "The place of 'functional sentence perspective' in the systems of linguistic description," in F. Danes (ed.) *Papers on Functional Sentence Perspective,* The Hague: Mouton.
Halliday, M.A.K. (1978) *Language as a Social Semiotic,* London: Edward Arnold.
Halliday, M.A.K. (1985) *An Introduction to Functional Grammar,* London: Edward Arnold.
Haviland, J. (1993) "Anchoring, iconicity, and orientation in Guugu Yimidhirr pointing gestures," *Journal of Linguistic Anthropology,* 3 (1): 3–45.
Haviland, J. (2000) "Pointing, gesture spaces, and mental maps," in D. McNeill (ed.) *Language and Gesture: Window into Thought and Action,* Cambridge: Cambridge University Press, pp. 13–46.
Hegel, G.W.F. (1988) *Phänomenologie des Geistes,* Hamburg: Felix Meiner Verlag.
Heims, S.P. (1977) "Gregory Bateson and mathematicians: From interdisciplinary interaction to social functions," *Journal of the History of the Behavioral Sciences,* 13: 141–159.
Holquist, M. and Emerson, C. (1981) Glossary for *The Dialogic Imagination: Four Essays by M. M. Bakhtin* in M. Holquist (ed.), trans. by M. Holquist and C. Emerson, Austin, TX: University of Texas Press.
Hymes, D. (1961) "Functions of speech: the evolutionary approach," in F. Gruber (ed.) *Anthropology and Education,* Philadelphia, PA: University of Pennsylvania Press, pp. 55–83.
Hymes, D. (1966) "Two types of linguistic relativity (with examples from Amerindian ethnography)," in W. Bright (ed.) *Sociolinguistics, Proceedings of the UCLA Sociolinguistic Conference* (1964) Janua Linguarum, Series Major, No. 20, The Hague: Mouton, pp. 144–167.
Hymes, D. (1972a) "Toward ethnographies of communication: the analysis of communicative events," in P. Giglioli (ed.) *Language and Social Context,* Harmondsworth: Penguin, pp. 21–43 (excerpts from Hymes, D. (1966) "Introduction: toward ethnographies of communication," *American Anthropologist,* 66 (6): 12–25).
Hymes, D. (1972b) "Models of the interaction of language and social life," in J. Gumperz and D. Hymes (eds) *Directions in Sociolinguistics: the Ethnography of Communication,* New York: Holt, Rinehart and Winston, pp. 35–71.
Hymes, D. (1973) "Speech and language: on the origins and foundations of inequality in speaking," *Daedalus,* Summer: 59–86.
Hymes, D. (1974a) "Toward ethnographies of communication," in *Foundations in Sociolinguistics: An Ethnographic Approach,* Philadelphia, PA: University of Pennsylvania Press, pp. 3–28.

Hymes, D. (1974b) *Foundations in Sociolinguistics: an Ethnographic Approach*, Philadelphia, PA: University of Pennsylvania Press.
Hymes, D. (1974c) "Linguistic theory and functions in speech," in *Foundations in Sociolinguistics: an Ethnographic Approach*, Philadelphia, PA: University of Pennsylvania Press, pp. 145–178.
Hymes, D. (1974d) "Linguistics as sociolinguistics," in *Foundations in Sociolinguistics: an Ethnographic Approach*, Philadelphia, PA: University of Pennsylvania Press.
Jackendoff, R. (1972) *Semantic Interpretation in Generative Grammar*, Cambridge, MA: MIT Press.
Jackendoff, R. (1983) *Semantics and Cognition*, Cambridge, MA: MIT Press.
Jefferson, G. (1974) "Error correction and interactional resources," *Language in Society*, 3: 181–199.
Jewitt, C. and Oyama, R. (2001) "Visual meaning: a social semiotic approach," in T. Van Leeuwen and C. Jewitt (eds) *Handbook of Visual Analysis*," London: Sage, pp. 134–156.
Johnston, A. (2000) "Signs of recovery?: Reading politics and economics in the street signs of Beirut." Paper presented at the Georgetown University Round Table on Languages and Linguistics, Washington, DC, May 4–6.
Johnston, A. (2004) "Files, forms and fonts: mediational means and identity negotiation in immigration interviews" in P. Levine and S. Scollen (eds) *Discourse and Technology: Multimodal Discourse Analysis*, Georgetown University Round Table on Languages and Linguistics, Washington, DC: Georgetown University Press, pp. 116–127.
Johnston, A. (2003) "A mediated discourse analysis of immigration gatekeeping interviews," Ph.D. Dissertation, Georgetown University: UMI.
Jones, R. (2004) "The problem of context in computer mediated communication," in P. LeVine and R. Scollon (eds) *Discourse and Technology: Multimodal Discourse Analysis*, Georgetown University Round Table on Languages and Linguistics, Washington, DC: Georgetown University Press, pp. 20–33.
Jossen, S., Käsermann, M., Altorfer, A., Foppa, K., Zimmermann, H., and Hirshbrunner, H. (2000) "The study of emotional processes in communication: II. Peripheral blood flow as an indicator of emotionalization," *Behaviour Research Methods, Instruments and Computers*, 32 (1): 47–55.
Kahneman, D. (1973) *Attention and Effort*, Englewood Cliffs, NJ: Prentice Hall.
Kant, I. (1973 [1787]) *Immanuel Kant's Critique of Pure Reason*, trans. by N.K. Smith, London: Macmillan Press, pp. 20–33
Käsermann, M., Altdorfer, A., Foppa, K., Jossen, S., and Zimmermann, H. (2000) "The study of emotional processes in communication: I. Measuring emotionalization in everyday face-to-face communicative interaction," *Behaviour Research Methods, Instruments & Computers*, 32 (1): 33–46.
Keller, J.M. (1983) "Motivational Design of Instruction," in D. Reigeluth (ed.) *Instructional Design Theories and Models*, Hillsdale, NJ: L. Erlbaum, pp. 386–433.
Kendon, A. (1967) "Some functions of gaze-direction in social interaction," *Acta Psychologica*, 26: 22–63.
Kendon, A. (1972) "Some relationships between body motion and speech: an analysis of an example," in A.W. Siegman and B. Pope (eds) *Studies in Dyadic Communication*, New York: Pergamon Press.
Kendon, A. (1974) "Movement coordination in social interaction: some examples described," in S. Weitz (ed.) *Nonverbal Communication*, New York: Oxford University Press, pp. 150–168.

Kendon, A. (1977) *Studies in the Behavior of Social Interaction*, Bloomington, IL: Indiana University Press.

Kendon, A. (1978) "Looking in conversation and the regulation of turns at talk: a comment on the papers of G. Beattie and D.R. Rutter *et al.*," *British Journal of Social and Clinical Psychology*, 17: 23–24.

Kendon, A. (1980) "Gesticulation and speech: two aspects of the process of utterance," in M.R. Key (ed.) *Nonverbal Communication and Language*, The Hague: Mouton.

Kendon, A. (1981) "Geography of Gesture," *Semiotica*, 37: 129–63.

Kendon, A. (1982) "A study of gesture. Some observations on its history," *Semiotic Inquiry*, 2, 45–62.

Kendon, A. (1990) *Conducting Interaction: Patterns of Behaviour in Focused Encounters*, Cambridge: Cambridge University Press.

Kendon, A. (1992) "The negotiation of context in face-to-face interaction," in A. Duranti and C. Goodwin (eds) *Rethinking Context: Language as an Interactive Phenomenon*, Cambridge: Cambridge University Press.

Kendon, A. (1994) "Introduction to the special issue: gesture and understanding in social interaction," *Research in Language and Social Interaction*, 27 (3): 171–174.

Kendon, A. (1997) "Gesture," *Annual Review of Anthropology*, 26: 109–128.

Kendon, A. and Ferber, A. (1973) "A description of some human greetings," in R.P. Michael and J.H. Crook (eds) *Comparative Ecology and Behavior of Primates*, London: Academic Press, pp. 591–668.

Krahmer, E., Ruttkay, Z., Swerts, M., and Wesselink, W. (2002) "Pitch, eyebrows and the perception of focus," unpublished manuscript.

Kress, G. and Van Leeuwen, T. (1998) *Reading Images: the Grammar of Visual Design*, London: Routledge.

Kress, G. and Van Leeuwen, T. (2001) *Multimodal Discourse: the Modes and Media of Contemporary Communication*, London: Edward Arnold.

Kress, G., Jewitt, C., Ogborn, J., and Tsatsarelis, C. (2001) *Multimodal Teaching and Learning: the Rhetorics of the Science Classroom*, London: Continuum.

LaBerge, D. (1995) *Attentional Processing: The Brain's Art of Mindfulness*, Cambridge, MA: Harvard University Press.

Lakoff, G. (1965) "On the nature of syntactic irregularity," *Report NSF-16*, The Computation Laboratory of Harvard University.

Lakoff, G. (1972) "Hedges: a study in meaning criteria and the logic of fuzzy concepts," in P.M. Peranteau, J.N. Levi, and G.C. Phares (eds) *Papers from the Eighth Regional Meeting of the Chicago Linguistics Society*. Chicago. Reprinted in *Journal of Philosophical Logic*, 2 (1973): 458–508.

Lakoff, G. (1986) "Frame-semantic control of the coordinate structure constraint," *CLS*, 22: 152–167.

Lakoff, G. (1987) *Women, Fire, and Dangerous Things: What Categories Reveal About the Mind*, Chicago: University of Chicago Press.

Lakoff, R.T. (1972) "Language in context," *Language*, 48: 907–927.

Lemke, J. (1998) "Multiplying meaning: visual and verbal semiotics in scientific text," in J. Martin and R. Veel (eds) *Reading Science*, Routledge: London.

Lemke, J. (2000) "Introduction: language and other semiotic systems in education," *Linguistics and Education*, 10 (3): 307–334.

Lemke, J. (2000a) "Across the scales of time: artifacts, activities, and meanings in ecosocial systems," *Mind, Culture, and Activity*, 7 (4): 273–290.

References

Lemke, J. (2000b) "Opening up closure: semiotics across scales," in J.L.R. Chandler and G. Van de Vijver (eds) *Closure: Emergent Organizations and Their Dynamics*, Annals of the New York Academy of Sciences, vol. 901, pp. 100–111.

Lemke, J. (2002) "Travels in hypermodality," *Visual Communication*, 1 (3): 299–325.

Lemke, J. http://www.personal.umich.edu/~jaylemke/ (accessed 25/02/04).

Levinson, S. (1983) *Pragmatics*, Cambridge: Cambridge University Press.

Levinson, S. (1987) "Minimization and conversational inference," in M. Papi and J. Vershueren (eds) *The Pragmatic Perspective*, Amsterdam: John Benjamins Press, pp. 61–129.

Luhmann, N. (1998) *Gesellschaftsstruktur und Semantik*, Frankfurt am Main: Suhrkamp.

McNeill, G.H. (1992) *Hand and Mind: What Gestures Reveal About Thought*, Chicago: University of Chicago Press.

Margolis, E. (1999) "Class pictures: representation of race, gender and ability in a century of school photography," *Visual Sociology*, 14: 7–38.

Mead, G.H. (1974) *Mind, Self, and Society from the Standpoint of a Social Behaviorist*, Chicago: University of Chicago Press.

Merritt, M. (1976) "On questions (in service encounters)," *Language in Society*, 5: 315–357.

Mey, J.L. (2001) *Pragmatics: an Introduction*, Oxford: Blackwell Publishers.

Milroy, L. (1987) *Observing and Analyzing Natural Language*, Oxford: Blackwell Publishers.

Montessori, M. (1965) *Spontaneous Activity in Education*, New York: Shocken.

Morris, C.H. (1938) *Foundation of the Theory of Signs*, Chicago: University of Chicago Press.

Nishida, K. (1958) *Intelligibility and Philosophy of Nothingness*, Tokyo: Maruzen.

Norris, S. (2000) "Visual semiotics: a reflection of sociopolitical currents in Germany." Paper presented at the Georgetown University Round Table on Languages and Linguistics, Washington, DC, May 4–6.

Norris, S. (2001) "Implications of visual research for discourse analysis: the notion of context." Paper presented at the Annual Meeting of the Internatiuonal Visual Sociology Association, Minneapolis, MN, July 11–15.

Norris, S. (2002a) "The implications of visual research for discourse analysis: transcription beyond language," *Visual Communication*, 1(1): 93–117.

Norris, S. (2002b) "A theoretical framework for multimodal discourse analysis presented via the analysis of identity construction of two women living in Germany," Ph.D. Dissertation, Georgetown University: UMI.

Norris, S. (2002c) "Embodied means as higher-level discourse structure." Paper presented at the First Annual Meeting of the International Society of Gesture Studies, Austin, TX, June 5–8.

Norris, S. (2002d) "The orchestration of identities through multiple modes." Paper presented in the Colloquium "Modalities of Access" at the Sociolinguistic Symposium 14, Ghent, Belgium, April 4–6.

Norris, S. (2002e) "Nationality and the social bond. One woman two national identities." Paper presented at the annual meeting of the International Visual Sociology Association, Santorini, Greece, July 14–18.

Norris, S. (2003a) "A photoseries: the construction of a European identity through symbols," *Contexts Magazine*, 2 (2): 26–32.

Norris, S. (2004) "Multimodal discourse analysis: a conceptual framework," in P. Levine and R. Scollon (eds) *Discourse and Technology: Multimodal Discourse Analysis*, Georgetown University Round Table on Languages and Linguistics, Washington, DC: Georgetown University Press, pp. 101–115.

References

Ochs, E. (1979) "Transcription as theory," in E. Ochs and B.B. Schieffelin (eds) *Developmental Pragmatics*, New York: Academic Press.

Peirce, C.S. (1955) "Logic as semiotic: the theory of signs," in J. Buchler (ed.) *Philosophical Writings of Peirce*, New York: Dover Publications, pp. 98–119.

Piaget, J. (1976) *The Grasp of Consciousness: Action and Concept in the Young Child*, Cambridge, MA: Harvard University Press.

Piaget, J. (1978) *Success and Understanding*, Cambridge, MA: Harvard University Press.

Pike, K.L. (1967) *Language in Relation to a Unified Theory of the Structure of Human Behavior*, The Hague: Mouton.

Raskin, J. (2000) *The Human Interface: New Directions for Designing Interactive Systems*, New York: W.W. Norton.

Ruesch, J. and Bateson, G. (1951) *Communication*, New York: W.W. Norton.

Ruesch, J. and Kees, W. (1956) *Nonverbal Communication: Notes on the Visual Perception of Human Relations*, Berkeley, CA: University of California Press.

Sacks, H. (1973) "On some puns with some imitations," in R.W. Shuy (ed.) *Sociolinguistics: Current Trends and Prospects*, 23rd Annual Round Table on Languages and Linguistics, Washington, DC: Georgetown University Press, pp. 135–144.

Sacks, H. (1974) "An analysis of the course of a joke's telling in conversation," in R. Bauman and J. Sherzer (eds) *Explorations in the Ethnography of Speaking*, Cambridge: Cambridge University Press, pp. 337–353.

Sacks, H., Schegloff, E., and Jefferson, G. (1974) "A simplest systematics for the organization of turn-taking for conversation," *Language*, 50: 696–735.

Sapir, E. (1921) *Language*, New York: Harcourt, Brace, and World.

Sapir, E. (1933) "Communication," *Encyclopedia of the Social Sciences*, 4: 78–81.

Saussure, F. de (1959 [1915]) *Course in General Linguistics*, C. Bally and A. Sechehaye (eds); trans. W. Baskin, New York: Philosophical Library.

Schafer, R.M. (1977) *The Soundscape: Our Sonic Environment and the Tuning of the World*, Rochester, VT: Destiny Books.

Scheflen, A.E. (1964) "The significance of posture in communication systems," *Psychiatry*, 27: 316–331.

Scheflen, A.E. (1974) *How Behaviour Means*, Garden City, NY: Doubleday.

Schegloff, E. (1972a) "Sequencing in conversational openings," in J. Gumperz and D. Hymes (eds) *Directions in Sociolinguistics*, New York: Holt, Rinehart and Winston, pp. 346–380.

Schegloff, E. (1972b) "Notes on a conversational practice: formulating place," in D. Sundow (ed.) *Studies in Social Interaction*, New York: Free Press, pp. 75–119.

Schegloff, E. (1979a) "The relevance of repair to syntax for conversation," in T. Givon (ed.) *Syntax and Semantics, 12: Discourse and Syntax*, New York: Academic Press, pp. 261–288.

Schegloff, E. (1979b) "Identification and recognition in telephone conversation openings," in G. Psathas (ed.) *Everyday Language: Studies in Ethnomethodology*, New York: Irvington, pp. 23–78.

Schegloff, E. (1980) "Preliminaries to preliminaries," in D. Zimmerman and C. West (eds) *Language and Social Interaction*, Special Issue of *Sociological Inquiry*, 50 (3/4): 104–152.

Schegloff, E. (1981) "Discourse as an interactional achievement: some uses of 'uh huh' and other things that come between sentences," in D. Tannen (ed.) *Analyzing Discourse: Text and Talk*, Georgetown University Round Table on Languages and Linguistics, Washington, DC: Georgetown University Press, pp. 71–93.

Schegloff, E. and Sacks, H. (1973) Opening up closings, *Semiotica*, 7 (3/4): 289–327.
Schegloff, E., Jefferson, G., and Sacks, H. (1977) "The preference for self-correction in the organization of repair in conversation," *Language*, 53: 361–382.
Schiffrin, D. (1977) "Opening encounters," *American Sociological Review*, 42 (4): 671–691.
Schiffrin, D. (1981) "Handwork as ceremony: the case of the handshake," in A. Kendon (ed.) *Nonverbal Communication, Interaction and Gesture*, The Hague: Mouton, pp. 237–250.
Schiffrin, D. (1985) "Multiple constraints on discourse options: a quantitative analysis of causal sequences," *Discourse Processes*, 8 (3): 281–303.
Schiffrin, D. (1986) "Turn-initial variation: structure and function in conversation," in D. Sankoff (ed.) *Diversity and Diachrony*, Philadelphia, PA: John Benjamins Press, pp. 367–380.
Schiffrin, D. (1987) *Discourse Markers*, Cambridge: Cambridge University Press.
Schiffrin, D. (1988a) "Conversation analysis," in F. Newmeyer (ed.) *Linguistics: the Cambridge Survey*, Cambridge: Cambridge University Press, pp. 251–276.
Schiffrin, D. (1988b) "Sociolinguistic approaches to discourse. Topic and reference in narrative," in K. Ferrera *et al.* (eds) *Linguistic Contact and Variation*, Austin, TX: University of Texas Press, pp. 1–28.
Schiffrin, D. (1990) "Conversational analysis," *Annual Review of Applied Linguistics*, 11: 3–19.
Schiffrin, D. (1994) *Approaches to Discourse*, Oxford: Blackwell Publishers.
Schmidt, R. (2001) "Attention," in P. Robinson (ed.) *Cognition and Second Language Instruction*, Cambridge University: Cambridge University Press.
Scollon, R. (1979) "A real early stage: an unzipped condensation of a dissertation on child language," in: E. Ochs and B.B. Schieffelin (eds) *Developmental Pragmatics*, New York: Academic Press, pp. 215–227.
Scollon, R. (1982) "The rhythmic integration of ordinary talk," in D. Tannen (ed.) *Analyzing Discourse: Text and Talk*, Georgetown University Round Table on Languages and Linguistics 1981, Washington, DC: Georgetown University Press, pp. 335–349.
Scollon, R. (1998) *Mediated Discourse as Social Interaction*, London: Longman.
Scollon, R. (2001a) "Action and text: toward an integrated understanding of the place of text in social (inter)action," in R. Wodak and M. Meyer (eds) *Methods in Critical Discourse Analysis*, London: Sage.
Scollon, R. (2001b) *Mediated Discourse: the Nexus of Practice*, London: Routledge.
Scollon, R. and Scollon, S.W. (2003) *Discourses in Place: Language in the Material World*, London: Routledge.
Scollon, S. (2001) "Habitus, conciousness, agency and the problems of intention: how we carry and are carried by political discourses," *Folia Linguistica*, XXXV/1–2: 97–129.
Scollon, S. and Scollon, R. (2000) "Indescription and the politics of literate design." Paper presented at the Georgetown University Round Table on Languages and Linguistics, Washington, DC, May 4–6.
Searle, J. (1969) *Speech Acts*, Cambridge: Cambridge University Press.
Searle, J. (2001) *Geist, Sprache und Gesellschaft*, Frankfurt am Main: Suhrkamp.
Silverstein, M. and Urban, G. (1996) "The natural history of discourse", in M. Silverstein and G. Urban (eds) *Natural Histories of Discourse*, Chicago: University of Chicago Press, pp. 1–17.

Sklar, L. (1977) *Space, Time, and Spacetime*, Berkeley, CA: University of California Press.
Slobin, D. I. (1973) "Cognitive prerequisites for the development of grammar", in C.A. Ferguson and D.I. Slobin (eds) *Studies of Child Language Development*, New York: Holt, Rinehart and Winston, pp. 175–276.
Smith, W.E. (1974) "The effects of social and monetary rewards on intrinsic motivation," Ph.D. Dissertation, Cornell University.
Sperber, D. and Wilson, D. (1986) *Relevance: Communication and Cognition*, Cambridge, MA: Harvard University Press.
Streek, J. (1988) "The significance of gesture: how it is established," *IPRA Papers in Pragmatics*, 2 (1): 60–83.
Streek, J. (1993) "Gesture as communication I: its coordination with gaze and speech," *Communication Monographs*, 60 (4): 275–299.
Streek, J. (1994) "Gesture as communication II: the audience as co-author," *Research on Language and Social Interaction*, 27 (3): 223–238.
Streek, J. (1996) "How to do things with things," *Human Studies*, 19: 365–384.
Sweetser, E.E. (1990) *From Etymology to Pragmatics*, Cambridge: Cambridge University Press.
Tannen, D. (1979) "What's in a frame? Surface evidence of underlying expectations," in R. Freedle (ed.) *New Directions in Discourse Processing*, Norwood, NJ: Ablex Publishing, pp. 137–181.
Tannen, D. (1984) *Conversational Style: Analyzing Talk Among Friends*. Norwood, NJ: Ablex.
Tannen, D. (1989a) *Talking Voices: Repetition, Dialogue, and Imagery in Conversational Discourse*, Cambridge: Cambridge University Press.
Tannen, D. (1989b) "Interpreting interruption in conversation." Papers from the 25th Annual Regional Meeting of the Chicago Linguistics Society, Chicago, pp. 266–287.
Tannen, D. and Wallat, C. (1993) "Interactive frames and knowledge schemas in interaction: examples from a medical examination/interview," in D. Tannen (ed.) *Framing in Discourse*, New York and Oxford: Oxford University Press, pp. 57–76.
Trudge, J. (1990) "Vygotsky, the zone of proximal development, and peer collaboration: implications for classroom practice", in L.C. Moll (ed.) *Vygotsky and Education: Instructional Implications and Applications of Sociohistorical Psychology*, Cambridge: Cambridge University Press, pp. 155–172.
Unger-Hamilton, C., Fairbairn, N., and Walters, D. (1979) *Die Musik: Menschen, Instrumente und Ereignisse in Bildern und Dokumenten*, Munich: Christian Verlag.
van Dijk, T. (1977) *Text and Context: Explorations in the Semantics and Pragmatics of Discourse*, London: Longman.
van Dijk, T. (1980) *Textwissenschaft: Eine interdisziplinäre Einführung*, Munich: DTV.
van Dijk, T. http://www.discourse-in-society.org/teun.html (accessed 22/02/04).
Van Leeuwen, T. (1999) *Speech, Music, Sound*, London: Macmillan Press.
Van Leeuwen, T. and Jewitt, C. (2001) *Handbook of Visual Analysis*, London: Sage.
van Lier, L. (1988) *The Classroom and the Language Learner*, London: Longman.
van Lier, L. (1995) "Some features of a theory of practice," *TESOL Journal*, 4 (1): 6–10.
van Lier, L. (1996) *Interaction in the Language Curriculum: Awareness, Autonomy and Authenticity*, London: Longman.
Vygotsky, L.S. (1978) *Mind in Society: the Development of Higher Psychological Processes*, ed. M. Cole, V. John-Steiner, S. Scribner, and E. Souberman, Cambridge, MA: Harvard University Press.

Vygotsky, L.S. (1986 [1962]) *Thought and Language* (new edition A. Kozulin), Cambridge, MA: MIT.
Weis, E. and Belton, J. (eds) (1985) *Film Sound – Theory and Practice*, New York: Columbia University Press.
Wertsch, J.V. (ed.) (1981) *The Concept of Activity in Soviet Psychology*, Armonk, NY: M.E. Sharpe.
Wertsch, J.V. (ed.) (1985a) *Culture, Communication and Cognition: Vygotskian Perspectives*, New York: Cambridge University Press.
Wertsch, J.V. (ed.) (1985b) *Introduction to Culture, Communication, and Cognition: Vygotskian Perspectives*, New York: Cambridge University Press.
Wertsch, J.V. (ed.) (1985c) *Vygotsky and the Social Formation of Mind*, Cambridge, MA: Harvard University Press.
Wertsch, J.V. (1998) *Voices of the Mind: a Sociocultural Approach to Mediated Action*, Cambridge, MA: Harvard University Press.
Whalen, J., Whalen, M., and Hendersson, K. (2001) "Toward a naturalistic sociology of work: improvisational choreography in a teleservice job," unpublished manuscript.
Whorf, B.L. (1956 [1940]) "Science and linguistics," in J.B. Carroll (ed.) *Language, Thought, and Reality*, Cambridge, MA: MIT Press, pp. 207–219.
Wickens, C. (1984) "Processing resources in attention," in R. Parasuraman and D.R. Davis (eds) *Varieties of Attention*, New York: Academic Press, pp. 63–102.
Wickens, C. (1989) "Attention and skilled performance," in D. Holding (ed.) *Human Skills*, New York: Academic Press, pp. 71–105.
Wilson, D. (1975) *Presuppositions and Non-Truth-Conditional Semantics*, New York: Academic Press.
Winograd, T. (1972) *Understanding Natural Language*, New York: Academic Press.
Wittgenstein, L. (1998) *Abhandlung Tractatus logico-philosophicus*, Frankfurt am Main: Suhrkamp.
Wodak, R. (1989) *Language, Power and Ideology*, Amsterdam: Benjamins.
Wodak, R. (1995) "Critical linguistics and critical discourse analysis," in J. Verschueren, J.-O. Östman, and J. Blommaert (eds) *Handbook of Pragmatics: Manual*, Amsterdam: Benjamins, pp. 204–210.
Wodak, R. (1996) *Disorders of Discourse*, London: Longman.
Wodak, R. (2001) "What CDA is about – a summary of its history, important concepts and its developments," in R. Wodak and M. Meyer (eds) *Methods in Critical Discourse Analysis*, London: Sage, pp. 1–13.
Zavala, V. (2000) "Public images of literacy in Andahugylas." Paper presented at the Georgetown University Round Table on Languages and Linguistics, Washington, DC, May 4–6.

Index

actions: communicative 149; defined 11, 13; divergent higher-level 140; divergent simultaneous higher-level 141–2; frozen 11, 13–14, 15, 46; higher-level 11, 15, 21, 26, 81, 99–100, 101–6; lower-level 11; mediation 113; modes and 81–2; parallel higher-level 138–40; parallel simultaneous higher-level 140–1; six simultaneous higher-level 101–6, 138, 149
affordances 151–2
Altorfer, A.: "Measurement and meaning of head movements" 33
anthropology 154
Anwesenheit 21, 22, 107, 137, 138
arm movements *see* gesture
attention/awareness 3–7, 91–4, 138, 150; background 97–8; levels 5, 92, 95–111, 154; foreground 97–8; foreground–background continuum 98–101; methodological framework 98–101; mid-ground 97

background 97
beats 114–15, 154
body position *see* posture

Chafe, W.: *Discourse, Consciousness, and Time* 16
Chalmers, D. J.: *Conscious Mind* 3, 5–6, 154
Chaplin, J. P.: *Dictionary of Psychology* 5
classroom discourse 133–5
color 12, 109

communicative modes 11–57; defined 11; embodied/disembodied 51–6; heuristic units 11–12; hierarchical structures 52–6; interaction and 12–13; interconnection of 51–7; meaning 52; meaning potential 52; unit of analysis 13–15; *see also* gaze; gesture; head movement; language, spoken; layout; music; posture; print; proxemics
communicative pragmatics 112–27
communicative semantics 112–27
complexity *see* modal complexity
computers 142–7; *see also* email *and* Internet
constraints 152
context 149–50
conversation 1, 4, 14, 37, 46–8, 87–8, 92–3, 120–1; and interview 21; telephone and face-to-face 113
culture 25, 37, 48

data: collection 62; log 62–3; video 63–4, 149
deixis 115
density *see* modal density
discourse analysis 58–60
disembodied modes 65; defined x–xi
distance *see* proxemics
Dittman, A. T.: "Role of body movement" 24
dress 12, 92, 109
drinking 14
duality of mind 3

eating 14
email 142
embodied modes 65; defined x–xi
ethics 61
eyebrow flash 121–4

face-to-face interaction 112, 113
facial expression 12, 60
Fairbairn, N.: *Die Musik* 42
faxes 142–7
feelings 3–4, 5
fieldnotes 62
Finnegan, R.: *Communicating* 113
Foppa, K.: "Measurement and meaning of head movements" 33
foreground 97
foreground–background continuum 97–8, 138, 150–1, 153; methodological framework 98–101; modal density 99, 100, 109–10, 128, 145, 149
furniture 3, 13

gaze 2–3, 11–12, 13, 27, 32, 36–41, 46, 48, 53, 55–6, 60, 65, 83, 90, 92, 107, 109; conventions 72; structure 37, 38; transcription 72–3
gesture 2, 11–12, 13, 14, 28–32, 46, 48, 60, 65, 90, 92, 93, 109, 132; beat 28, 29–30; conventions 69; deictic 28, 29–30, 32, 34, 56; gesture phrase 30–2; iconic 28, 29–30, 132; materiality 3; metaphoric 28, 29–30; spoken language and 29–30; telephone 52–3; transcription 69–71
Goffman, E.: *Forms of Talk* 22
Goodwin, C.: *Conversational Organization* 37, 38, 64, 72

Habermas, J.: *Theory of Communicative Action* 149
Hall, E. T.: *Hidden Dimension* 19, 20, 23
hand movements *see* gesture
head movement 2, 11–12, 32–6, 52, 53, 56, 90, 92, 93, 109; complex 32; conventions 72; deictic 32, 33, 34, 36, 117–18; directional shifts 32; gaze shifts 32; head beats 32; postural shifts 32; simple 32; transcription 72

Hendersson, K.: "Toward a naturalistic sociology of work" 143
heuristic units 11–12
hierarchical structures 52–6
historical body 146

images 1–2, 44–9, 138
independence of modes 132
intensity *see* modal intensity
intentionality 4
interaction competence 154
interactional awareness *see* attention/awareness
interactional child development 154
interactional meaning 1–2
interactional perception 92–3
interactional sociolinguistics 10
interactions: complex 128–47; defined 4, 147–9; multimedia and 142–7
interconnection among modes 51–7, 83
interdependence of modes 51–7, 132
Internet 1
interviews: conversation and 21
intonation unit 15, 16

Jefferson, G.: "Error correction" 66
Jewitt, C.: *Multimodal Teaching and Learning* 2, 81
Jossen, S.: "Measurement and meaning of head movements" 33

Käsermann, M.: "Measurement and meaning of head movements" 33
Kendon, A.: "Gesticulation and speech" 30; "Some functions of gaze-direction" 37, 38, 72; "Some relationships between body motion and speech" 30
Kress, G.: *Multimodal Discourse* 65, 148; *Multimodal Teaching and Learning* 2, 81
Kress, G. and Van Leeuwen, T.: *Multimodal Discourse: the Modes and Media of Contemporary Communication* 11, 48, 148, 156, 158, 159, 161

language, spoken 1, 2, 11–12, 13, 14, 15–19, 52, 53, 56, 58–60, 65, 83–4, 90, 109, 132; conventions 66; gesture and 29–30; intonation unit 15, 16;

materiality 3; pitch 83; punctuation 66; telephone 52–3, 67–8; transcription 66–8
language teaching 133–7
language, written 1, 12; *see also* print
layout 13, 49–51, 65, 90, 109; conventions 75; high intensity 84–6; materiality 3; transcription 75
leaning towards an object/participant, deictic 118–21
Lemke, J. L. 145
linguistics 58–60

McNeill, G. H.: *Hand and Mind* 28, 30, 154
Margolis, E.: "Class pictures" 138
materiality 2–3, 148
Mead, G. H.: *Mind, Self, and Society* 155
meaning 52; interactional 1–2; potential 52
means 112–27, 128, 143, 151; beat-type 113; deictic-type 113; function of 116–17, 124; influencing others 132–3, 136; pragmatic 112–27, 154; semantic 112–27, 154; utilizing 129
mediated action *see* actions
mediated discourse analysis 10
methodological framework: function 149–51, 152–3; modal density foreground–background continuum 128–47
mid-ground 97
modal complexity 79, 87–9, 89–91, 150
modal density 79–94, 150; circles 106–9; foreground–background continuum 109–11, 128–47, 151–2; perception and 91–4
modal intensity 79, 83–7, 89–91, 150; high 79, 83, 86–7; low 79; medium 79
modes: actions and 81–2; disembodied/embodied 13; phenomenal mind and 82–3
motivation 136–7
multimedia: interaction and 142–7
multimodal interaction *see* interactions
multimodal interactional analysis 112–13

multimodality 10
multimodal transcription *see* transcription
music 41–4, 45; conventions 74; embodied/disembodied 41–2, 43–4, 45, 74, 90; high intensity 84–6; teaching 129–33; transcription 74

native interaction intuition 25
nexus analysis 10
Nishida, K.: *Intelligibility and Philosophy of Nothingness* 146
Norris, S.: "Implications of visual research" 153

object handling 12, 107, 109
Ogborn, J.: *Multimodal Teaching and Learning* 2, 81

perceptions 3–4, 5
phenomenal mind, the 3, 4, 5, 6, 82, 93–4, 115; means 112–27; modes and 82–3
pitch 83
posture 2, 11–12, 24–8, 46, 48, 52, 54–5, 56, 60, 65, 83, 90, 92, 109; conventions 68; high intensity 86–7; open and closed 24–5, 26–7; transcription 68–9
pragmatics *see* communicative pragmatics *and* means
print 13, 44–9, 88, 90, 109; conventions 74–5; embodied/disembodied 44, 45–6, 74, 143; high intensity 86–7; materiality 3; transcription 74–5
proxemics 11–12, 19–24, 48, 54, 56, 90, 92, 109, 137; conventions 68; transcription 68

questions 16; open-ended 21; questioning the obvious 80; research 58

reading 120–1
representation 11–12, 12–13, 14, 20

semantics *see* communicative semantics *and* means
semiotics 11

setting *see* layout
social world: constructing 137–42
socialization 20, 25
space *see* proxemics
speech *see* language, spoken
structure 2–3, 148

Tannen, D.: *Conversational Style* 15, 66
teaching, multimodal 129–37
telephone 26–7, 52, 67–8, 113, 142–7; attention/awareness 103; final transcript 76–7, 78, 80–1; gaze 73, 82–3; gesture 70–1; head movement 73; posture 69, 70; proxemics 69, 70
television 1, 22
text 44–9; *see also* print
thought 3–4, 5
timescales 142
touch 107
transcription 58–78; and analysis 60; beyond language 58–60; complete 75–8, 78, 80–1; conventions 59; gaze 72–3; gesture 69–71; head movement 72; higher-level actions 99–100, 101–6; layout 75; multimodal 61, 100; music 74; posture 68–9; print 74–5; proxemics 68; simultaneous higher-level actions 99; spoken language 66–8, 100; step-by-step 65–78; video data 61–5
Tsatsarelis, C.: *Multimodal Teaching and Learning* 2, 81

Unger-Hamilton, C.: *Die Musik* 42

Van Leeuwen, T.: *Multimodal Discourse* 65, 148; *Speech, Music, Sound* 15
van Lier, L.: *Interaction in the Language Curriculum* 137
video data 53, 61–5, 100, 138, 149

Walters, D.: *Die Musik* 42
weight of a mode 79
Whalen, J. and M.: "Toward a naturalistic sociology of work" 143
"with" 21, 22
Würmle, O.: "Measurement and meaning of head movements" 33

Zimmermann, H.: "Measurement and meaning of head movements" 33

Related titles from Routledge

Discourses in Place

Language in the material world

Ron Scollon and Suzie Wong Scollon

'Written with directness and charm, and an abundance of persuasive examples, this book locates meaning not just in language but in the richness and complexity of the lived world... its insights will start a generation of new thinking, and research. It marks a turning point in linguistics and semiotics alike.'

Gunther Kress,
Institute of Education, University of London, UK

Discourses in Place develops the first systematic analysis of the ways we interpret language as it is materially placed in the world.

It argues that we can only interpret the meaning of public texts like road signs, notices and brand logos by considering the social and physical world that surrounds them. Drawing on a wide range of real examples, from signs in the Chinese mountains to urban centres in Austria, France, North America and Hong Kong, this textbook equips students with the methodology and models they need to undertake their own research in 'geosemiotics', and is essential reading for anyone with an interest in language and the ways in which we communicate.

ISBN 0–415–29048–1 (hbk)
ISBN 0–415–29049–X (pbk)

Available at all good bookshops
For ordering and further information please visit:
www.routledge.com

Related titles from Routledge

Communicating
The multiple modes of human interconnection

Ruth Finnegan

'This book is a wonderful celebration of the immensely creative and diverse methods that humans have invented to connect and make sense together. After reading it, one will find most other accounts of communication narrow and dull.'

Jurgen Streeck,
The University of Texas at Austin, USA

Communicating uncovers the amazing array of sounds, sights, smells, gestures, looks, movements, touches and material objects which humans use so creatively to interconnect both nearby and across space and time.

Focusing on embodied and material processes, and on practice rather than text, this comparative analysis counters the cognitive and word-centred emphases of many current accounts of communication.

An essential trans-disciplinary overview for researchers and advanced students in anthropology, communication and cultural studies, this authoritative but accessible book will also fascinate anyone with an interest in the remarkable ways in which we communicate.

ISBN 0–415–24117–0 (hbk)
ISBN 0–415–24118–9 (pbk)

Available at all good bookshops
For ordering and further information please visit:
www.routledge.com

eBooks – at www.eBookstore.tandf.co.uk

A library at your fingertips!

eBooks are electronic versions of printed books. You can store them on your PC/laptop or browse them online.

They have advantages for anyone needing rapid access to a wide variety of published, copyright information.

eBooks can help your research by enabling you to bookmark chapters, annotate text and use instant searches to find specific words or phrases. Several eBook files would fit on even a small laptop or PDA.

NEW: Save money by eSubscribing: cheap, online access to any eBook for as long as you need it.

Annual subscription packages

We now offer special low-cost bulk subscriptions to packages of eBooks in certain subject areas. These are available to libraries or to individuals.

For more information please contact webmaster.ebooks@tandf.co.uk

We're continually developing the eBook concept, so keep up to date by visiting the website.

www.eBookstore.tandf.co.uk

Milton Keynes UK
Ingram Content Group UK Ltd.
UKHW020025091024
449458UK00005B/13